Social Psychology in Sport and Exercise

Social Psychology in Sport and Exercise

Linking Theory to Practice

Ann-Marie Knowles

*Lecturer in Physical Activity for Health,
University of Strathclyde, UK*

Vaithehy Shanmugam

*Lecturer in Sport and Exercise Psychology,
University of Central Lancashire, UK*

and

Ross Lorimer

*Lecturer in Sport, Social Psychology and
Coaching Pedagogy,
Abertay University, UK*

 macmillan education   palgrave

First published 2015 by
PALGRAVE

Palgrave in the UK is an imprint of Macmillan Publishers Limited, registered in England, company number 785998, of 4 Crinan Street, London, N1 9XW.

Palgrave in the US is a division of St Martin's Press LLC, 175 Fifth Avenue, New York, NY 10010.

Palgrave is a global imprint of the above companies and is represented throughout the world.

Palgrave® and Macmillan® are registered trademarks in the United States, the United Kingdom, Europe and other countries.

ISBN: 978–1–137–30628–9

This book is printed on paper suitable for recycling and made from fully managed and sustained forest sources. Logging, pulping and manufacturing processes are expected to conform to the environmental regulations of the country of origin.

A catalogue record for this book is available from the British Library.

A catalog record for this book is available from the Library of Congress.

Printed in China

Contents

List of Illustrations   viii

Preface   ix

Acknowledgements   xi

Publisher's Acknowledgements   xiii

1   The Coach   1
    1.1   Learning objectives   1
    1.2   Introduction to the context   1
    1.3   The coach–athlete relationship   3
    1.4   Interpersonal communication   7
    1.5   Relationship conflict   10
    1.6   Managing an effective and successful relationship   12
    1.7   Summary   17
    1.8   Case study   17
    1.9   Further study and recommended reading   20

2   Teammates   21
    2.1   Learning objectives   21
    2.2   Introduction to the context   21
    2.3   Peer-oriented motivational climate: an overview of
          theory and indicative research   23
    2.4   Team cohesion: a conceptual framework   26
    2.5   Intragroup conflict: definitions and conceptualisations   33
    2.6   Summary   39
    2.7   Case study   39
    2.8   Further study and recommended reading   42

3   Competition   44
    3.1   Learning objectives   44
    3.2   Introduction to the context   44
    3.3   How individuals judge their own success   46
    3.4   How we perceive opponents   52
    3.5   Intergroup conflict   56
    3.6   Dark side of competition   59
    3.7   Summary   60
    3.8   Case study   61
    3.9   Further study and recommended reading   63

4   Audience and Spectators   64
    4.1   Learning objectives   64
    4.2   Introduction to the context   64

	4.3	The effects of the presence of others on personal effort: a review of early theoretical processes	65
	4.4	Home advantage	68
	4.5	Choking under pressure	75
	4.6	Summary	80
	4.7	Case study	80
	4.8	Further study and recommended reading	83

5 The Family and Significant Others — 84
- 5.1 Learning objectives — 84
- 5.2 Introduction to the context — 84
- 5.3 Promoting athletic involvement: the role of parents — 86
- 5.4 The changing role of parental involvement in athletes' sport participation — 93
- 5.5 Significance of siblings in shaping athletes' sporting experiences — 96
- 5.6 Significance of romantic and marital partners — 97
- 5.7 Optimising athletes' sporting experiences by cultivating their social relationships — 98
- 5.8 Summary — 100
- 5.9 Case study — 100
- 5.10 Further study and recommended reading — 104

6 Schools — 105
- 6.1 Learning objectives — 105
- 6.2 Introduction to the context — 105
- 6.3 The role of PE teachers — 107
- 6.4 The role of peers — 113
- 6.5 The role of parents — 119
- 6.6 Summary — 121
- 6.7 Case study — 122
- 6.8 Further study and recommended reading — 124

7 Workplaces — 126
- 7.1 Learning objectives — 126
- 7.2 Introduction to the context — 126
- 7.3 The role of the employer — 129
- 7.4 The role of the employee — 133
- 7.5 Effectiveness of workplace interventions on psychosocial factors and physical activity — 136
- 7.6 Practical applications for workplace physical activity programmes — 139
- 7.7 Summary — 143
- 7.8 Case study — 143
- 7.9 Further study and recommended reading — 146

8 Gyms and Leisure Centres — 147
- 8.1 Learning objectives — 147
- 8.2 Introduction to the context — 147
- 8.3 The role of the exercise leader — 149
- 8.4 Self-presentational issues in a gym setting — 154
- 8.5 Group cohesion and social processes in an exercise class setting — 160
- 8.6 Exercise leaders and group cohesion — 163
- 8.7 Summary — 165

	8.8	Case study	165
	8.9	Further study and recommended reading	167
9	**Primary Health Care**		**169**
	9.1	Learning objectives	169
	9.2	Introduction to the context	169
	9.3	Role of health care professionals in physical activity behaviour change	172
	9.4	Impact of the consultation style on physical activity behaviour change	174
	9.5	Exercise referral schemes and physical activity behaviour change	181
	9.6	Summary	187
	9.7	Case study	188
	9.8	Further study and recommended reading	190
10	**The Outdoors**		**191**
	10.1	Learning objectives	191
	10.2	Introduction to the context	191
	10.3	Proposed mechanisms underlying the green space effect	193
	10.4	Outdoor activities and psychosocial development	194
	10.5	The green space effect of exercise on psychosocial well-being	196
	10.6	The green space effect in action	204
	10.7	Summary	206
	10.8	Case study	206
	10.9	Further study and recommended reading	208

References   209

Index   236

List of Illustrations

Figures

1.1	An illustration of Jowett's 3+1 Cs Model of the Coach–Athlete Relationship	4
1.2	Mediated communication	10
3.1	An illustration of Weiner's attribution theory	47
3.2	An illustration of Gist and Mitchell's theory: the relationship of attributions, self-efficacy, and performance	50
3.3	An illustration of Funder's realistic accuracy model	55
6.1	Proposed conceptualisation of Harter's (1978) competence motivation theory in relation to physical activity behaviour	117
7.1	Essential elements of goal-setting theory and the high-performance cycle	132
8.1	Conceptual framework used as a basis for the implementation of a team-building program in fitness classes	166
9.1	A continuum of self-determination in terms of different types of motivation	176
10.1a	Dose-response data for the effect of exposure duration in green exercise on self-esteem	203
10.1b	Dose-response data for the effect of exposure duration in green exercise on total mood disturbance	203

Tables

6.1	Using Ames's TARGET framework to develop a task or performance climate in PE	113
7.1	Motivational readiness questionnaire	145

Preface

Situational variables can exert powerful influences on human behaviour,
more so than we recognise or acknowledge.

– Zimbardo

Social psychology is defined as the study of human behaviour in a social context; in the realms of sport and exercise, social interactions occur on a regular basis. Over the past decade, there has been a substantial increase in the study of sport and exercise from a psychosocial perspective in both applied and research domains. The Olympic Games held in London (2012) and the Commonwealth Games in Glasgow (2014) are examples of the growing interest in and importance of elite sporting performance in the United Kingdom and beyond. Moreover, the financial revenue and publicity that elite sport generates through sponsorship, television deals, and social media further increases consumer interest in elite athletes and their performances. Consequently, understanding the psychosocial processes affecting athletes, coaches, teammates, and spectators is critical in determining optimal performance.

Outside the realm of elite sport, the importance of participating in regular physical activity remains at the forefront of the political and economic agenda. Understanding the psychosocial processes that influence behaviour change in exercise contexts has become a salient research area. It is of particular importance for health care professionals aiming to address the sharp rise in such lifestyle-related disorders as obesity, cardiovascular disease, and type II diabetes.

This book is aimed at a diverse audience: athletes, coaches, sport psychologists, parents, exercise psychologists, teachers, physical activity practitioners, health care professionals, workplace managers, and urban planners. Developed to fill a gap in the market encompassing social psychology and sport and exercise literature, the book addresses the psychosocial processes that occur in key sport and exercise contexts. Using relevant theory and research, these concepts focus on understanding and changing behaviour of athletes and exercisers. We hope the concepts help practitioners understand not only the 'what' of the social psychology of sport and exercise contexts but, more importantly, the 'how', in order to optimise behaviour change for performance and adherence in sport and long-term exercise. The book should also be a valuable resource for undergraduate and postgraduate students involved in social psychology, sport psychology, sport and exercise science, and physical activity and health-related courses.

To guide the reader through the content readily, all chapters have a similar format, and each finishes with an applied case study that links theory to practice. The first five chapters focus on social psychology in sport contexts. Chapter 1 examines the context of the training environment and the pivotal role of the coach in the development of athletes. Chapter 2 examines the significance of peers and teammates in sport and their contribution to athletic performance. Chapter 3 considers the role of competition and opponents in the quality of athletes' experiences and performance. Chapter 4 examines the significance of the audience and spectators and their influence on athletic performance. Chapter 5 focuses on the function of family and significant others and their role in shaping athletes' sporting experience.

The second half of the book shifts focus to social psychology in exercise contexts. Chapter 6 examines the social context of schools and their importance in shaping physical activity behaviour in children and young adults. Chapter 7 considers the social and organisational context of the workplace and its potential influence on the physical activity behaviour of employees. Chapter 8 examines the social context of gyms and leisure centres and their importance in relation to volitional exercise enjoyment and long-term adherence. Chapter 9 focuses on the social context of the primary health care setting and its importance for individuals who have been advised to exercise by a health care professional but whose motivational readiness for exercise is often limited. Chapter 10 examines the social context of exercising outdoors, its role in developing social networks, and its restorative effects on physical and mental health and well-being.

A final note to readers: whilst we have 'contextualised' the chapters for sport and exercise, the psychosocial processes, theories, and concepts discussed in each are often applicable from one chapter to the next and should be so regarded. Gaining a holistic understanding of the social psychology of sport and exercise is paramount; it will enable researchers and practitioners to further everyone's knowledge of elite sport performance and long-term exercise behaviour.

Acknowledgements

Knowledge is, in the end, based on acknowledgements, and so, unsurprisingly, there are a number of personal acknowledgements I wish to make. Those that know me will smile wryly as I start by paying tribute to the great J. B. Fletcher for her help in getting this book across the finishing line! Sincere thanks also go to my colleagues and academic peers, who continue to influence my development as a lecturer, researcher, and practitioner and whose ideas and published work have contributed significantly to this book. Thanks also to Isabel and Paul at Palgrave Education for their patience, support, and guidance during my first attempt at writing a book. Thanks to my friends and family for their unwavering support in everything I do. Finally, a special thanks to Cagey Gibson for the detailed and honest feedback on the chapters. Every single day you encourage and challenge me in everything I do yet you always believe in me. For you, there is a light that never goes out (The Smiths, 1986).

Ann-Marie Knowles

You never walk alone on the journey of life. Just where and how do you start to thank those people who have supported you along the way, held your hand and walked with you rather than race ahead of you, and paved the way for you? Over the years, I have had, and worked with, many wonderful colleagues, mentors, and peers who have influenced my continual development not only as a researcher, a practitioner, or a lecturer but also as a person. Apart from the effort of the authors involved, the completion of this book depended largely on the work of many esteemed academics. I take this opportunity to express my sincere gratitude to them for their ideas, their insight, and their knowledge, as this book essentially has been defined by their contribution. Thanks to the team at Palgrave Education for their ever-present encouragement, guidance, and support throughout this whole process. A special thanks to my family and friends for their unconditional support and encouragement, not just over the past year but throughout my life. Thank you to Luke especially, who read, reread (and re-reread) many versions of these chapters. Finally, I thank Kanna, my brother, for all that he has done for me, for the person he is and the person he inspires me to be.

Vaithehy Shanmugam

I first extend thanks to Paul at Palgrave Education, for first approaching and convincing me that this would be a good opportunity, and to Paul and Isabel for their patience during the writing process. Secondly, I thank my colleagues at Abertay for their advice and encouragement. Finally, a thank you to my family and especially my friends, who have both supported and tolerated me as I worked on this project.

Ross Lorimer

Publisher's Acknowledgements

The publisher and the authors thank the organisations and people listed below for permission to reproduce material from their publications:

American Psychological Association, for permission to reproduce Figure 7.1, Essential elements of goal-setting theory and the high-performance cycle. From Locke, E. A. and Latham, G. P. (2002). Building a practically useful theory of goal setting and task motivation: a 35-year odyssey. *American Psychologist*, 57(9), 705–717.

American Psychological Association, for permission to reproduce Table 7.1, Motivational readiness questionnaire. From Marcus, B., Rossi, J. S., Selby, V. C., Niaura, R. S., and Abrams, D. B. (1992). The stages and processes of exercise adoption and maintenance in a workplace sample. *Health Psychology*, 11, 386–395.

Human Kinetics, for permission to reproduce Figure 8.1, Conceptual framework used as a basis for the implementation of a team-building program in fitness classes. From Carron, V. and Spink, K. S. (1993). Team building in an exercise setting. *Sport Psychologist*, 7(1), 8–18.

Routledge, for permission to reproduce and adapt Figure 9.1, A continuum of self-determination in terms of different types of motivation. From Biddle, S. J. and Mutrie, N. (2008). *Psychology of Physical Activity: Determinants, Well-Being and Interventions*, 2nd edn, figure 4.3, 86.

American Chemical Society, for permission to reproduce Figure 10.1a, Dose response data for the effect of exposure duration in green exercise on self-esteem, and Figure 10.1b, Dose response data for the effect of exposure duration in green exercise on total mood disturbance. From Barton, J. and Pretty, J. (2010). What is the best dose of nature and green exercise for improving mental health? A multi-study analysis, *Environmental Science and Technology*, 44(10), 3947–3955. Copyright © (2014), American Chemical Society.

1   The Coach

1.1   Learning objectives

The purpose of this chapter is to examine the context of the training environment and the coach's role in the development of athletes. It focuses on the importance of coaches forming a supportive relationship with athletes in order to create a positive environment, increase retention, and provide competitive success. The key learning objectives are:

- to consider the nature of the relationship that is formed between the coach and the athlete by defining the quality of that relationship using the 3 + 1 Cs Model of Coach–Athlete Relationships;
- to examine interpersonal communication and the key role it can play in enhancing coach–athlete interaction;
- to investigate how conflict can be a constructive influence for coaches and athletes via the Competence-Based Model of Interpersonal Conflict;
- to discuss the potential strategies given by the COMPASS model for management of an optimal coach–athlete relationship in regard to the quality of the coach's and athlete's experiences and competitive success;
- to look at how relationship-maintenance strategies can be used by a coach, athlete, or psychologist to intervene in a poor quality training environment and repair an ineffective coach–athlete relationship.

1.2   Introduction to the context

For every moment of competition that athletes are involved in, they will have participated in multiple hours of training. Hence, athletes spend their time predominately involved in training for their sport and preparation for competition. Research has suggested that it can take over 10,000 hours of quality training for an athlete to compete effectively at an elite level, and these 10,000 hours are usually accumulated over a minimum of 10 years (Ericsson and Charness 1994). This means that elite athletes will typically spend an average of three hours per day over a 10-year period training for their sport. Much of this time will be spent under the guidance of a sports coach. That is, athletes spend a substantial amount of time with a coach on a daily basis; thus, the coach is potentially an important social influence in the athlete's life.

However, it is not only elite athletes who spend a large proportion of their time with their coach in the training environment. In the UK over 25% of adults involved in any form of sport report that they have worked with a coach in the previous 12 months. As frequency of participation increases, so does frequency of contact with a coach: 84% of surveyed adults in the UK who participated in sports in a given week had received coaching (MORI 2011).

Coaches play a central function in the management and direction of the training environment and hence the development of the performance and effectiveness of athletes. Coaches are responsible for directing their athletes' development – physically, technically, and psychologically – through the application of their knowledge, experience, and expertise (Lyle 2007). This development primarily unfolds in training, during periods of practicing the requisite skills required by the athlete; the manner in which coaches and athletes interact can have a profound impact upon the effectiveness of these training sessions (Jowett and Poczwardowski 2007). Coaches and athletes must work closely together in the training environment and have a high degree of interaction with each other. Coaches and athletes must therefore rely upon each other to fulfil their goals, and this is expressed in the athlete's need to develop competence, the coach's need to develop the athlete, and the need for them both to be able to translate their interactions into positive outcomes, such as performance success (Antonini Philippe and Seiler 2006).

The performance success of athletes is typically measured by an athlete's achievements during competition. When successful, the athlete and the coach, in particular, are commended, and their roles acknowledged and praised. Equally, when an athlete is unsuccessful, it is often the coach that receives a large portion of the blame and responsibility. There is therefore an important emphasis placed during training sessions on enhancing performance. However, as a result of a mutual dependence and long hours spent together, it is not unusual for coaches and athletes to form strong associations and develop a close relationship over time (Jowett and Poczwardowski 2007). Therefore, while the majority of coaches and athletes focus to some extent on performance enhancement, emphasis must also be placed on the personal and social development of athletes through involvement in training with their coach. Jowett (2005) has stated that the relationship between a coach and an athlete can be conceptualised by the element of success and effectiveness. While success is related to skill development and competition results, effectiveness focuses on personal satisfaction and the development of a rewarding relationship. The coach therefore has a fostering role to play, one that emphasises personal growth and development, that nurtures the trust, mutual care, and respect implicit in a personal relationship that potentially provides a key source of social support for athletes in both the training and competitive environments.

1.3   The coach–athlete relationship

A relationship is a form of social exchange. It has been suggested that individuals form relationships based on the benefits these partnerships can offer (Kelley et al. 1983). This means that individuals such as coaches and athletes form relationships based upon the mutual tangible and intangible rewards that association brings. As these relationships can both enhance and hinder the personal development of an individual, they develop as part of a cost-benefit analysis: the coach and the athlete are content with the relationship when the positive outcomes, such as satisfaction and performance or competitive success, outweigh such negative outcomes as conflict, distress, and lack of progression. However, a relationship is more than the pursuit of individual reward. Berscheid, Snyder, and Omoto (1989) have stated that many of the positive outcomes of a relationship are at least partially joint-generated. This means that the desired outcome can come about only through interaction of the two members of the relationship. For example, an athlete's abilities will not improve unless the athlete puts in the required effort and is also instructed by the coach in the correct technique. Hence, a relationship describes both the interdependence of two individuals who interact to achieve common goals and the level of understanding between them. This means that the relationship between a coach and an athlete can serve as the social vehicle for the often long road to performance success, with positive relationships enhancing this experience and negative relationships prolonging or disrupting progression and personal development.

While relationships have been studied for as long as social psychology has been a recognised field, it is only since the start of the 21st century that sport psychology has seen the development of conceptual models to describe the nature and quality of the coach–athlete relationship. This relationship is broadly defined as the interdependence of a coach and athlete's affect, behaviour, and cognitions, the aim being to develop effective personal growth and performance success in sport (Jowett 2005). This means that the nature and quality of the coach–athlete relationship are determined by how a coach's and athlete's emotions, actions, and thoughts interrelate and so are likely to change over time as part of a dynamic social environment. While several models have been proposed, the most prominent and widely applied is the 3 + 1 Cs Model (see Figure 1.1), which provides an operational definition whereby the coach–athlete interdependence and the nature and quality of their relationship is described through four constructs: Closeness, Complementarity, Commitment, and Co-orientation (Jowett 2007). The first three encapsulate only those elements of affect, behaviour, and cognition that have been identified as having direct relevance to the coach–athlete relationship; the final construct, co-orientation, represents

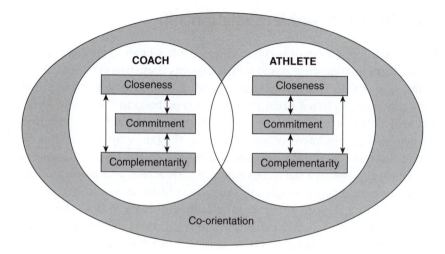

Figure 1.1   *An illustration of Jowett's 3+1 Cs Model of the Coach–Athlete Relationship*

the degree of concurrence between coach's and athlete's views and interpersonal perspectives (Jowett and Cockerill 2003).

1.3.1   Closeness

The construct of closeness encapsulates the affective qualities of the coach-athlete relationship. It describes how the coach and athlete perceive the emotional elements of their partnership and daily interaction, including positive mutual feelings and emotional intimacy (Jowett 2005). The concept of closeness suggests the presence of interpersonal liking between two individuals as well as a level of mutual trust. Liking has been shown to be strongly associated with open, candid communication, and evidence suggests that high levels of trust between two individuals can foster sincere and open disclosure between them (Argyle 1994). In the training environment, upfront and forthright communication is essential to preventing secretive or dangerous behaviour, such as an athlete hiding an injury or being unwilling to attempt certain training drills. It also allows the coach and the athlete to voice reciprocal and corresponding needs and helps prevent interpersonal conflict. Another important facet of closeness is mutual respect, an acceptance or feeling that the other individual in the relationship has something to offer, such as knowledge or positive actions, and is worthy of acknowledgement because of this (Douge 1999). Mutual respect is essential in any relationship and particularly so in the context of the training environment. For example, respect facilitates the transfer of knowledge and skill between coach and athlete. If an athlete does not feel that the coach has anything to offer, the athlete will be unwilling to give much consideration to the coach's advice or guidance and thereby limit his or her progress. Feelings of closeness in a relationship can also bring higher levels of personal satisfaction with daily interactions (Yoshida 1972). The development of athletic performance is a long-term and ongoing process, either for development of increased performance or retention of individuals within a sport. The more that individuals are content with how they are treated, the more they are likely both to remain together and to remain within their sport.

1.3.2 Complementarity

The construct of complementarity is concerned with the behavioural qualities of the coach–athlete relationship. It describes how the coach and athlete perceive their cooperative interactions, such as mutual effort or responsiveness, during training and the type of interaction that the coach and the athlete perceive as cooperative and useful (Jowett 2005). The concept of complementarity suggests the ability of each individual in a relationship to feel comfortable with the other and accept the contribution of the partner in the relationship. Cooperative interactions are divided into two categories: corresponding and reciprocating (Kiesler 1997). A corresponding behaviour involves an action that draws the opposite but complementary action from the other person; for example, where the coach exhibits a dominant behaviour (such as directing the training session) and the athlete responds by exhibiting a submissive behaviour (such as taking direction). A reciprocal behaviour involves an action that draws the same action from the other person; for example, if the coach is friendly towards the athlete, this should also attract friendly behaviour from the athlete. Complementarity, then, is primarily concerned with individuals' readiness to do their best and respond to the needs and behaviour of the other, which in turn encourages the other to respond in kind. If a coach–athlete relationship is to be complementary, the coach and athlete should display similar levels of readiness and responsiveness during training (Jowett 2002). This responsiveness facilitates the ease with which the coach and athlete can work together and coordinate their efforts in training. Partners who feel that their needs are not being listened or responded to are likely to become dissatisfied; this can create a negative training environment and may even lead to the dissolution of the coach–athlete relationship and the athlete discontinuing participation in the sport (Jowett and Meek 2000). Coaches who try to enforce particular styles of coaching or who don't adapt to individual athletes often create conflict; an athlete who dislikes direct authority would need to be handled using increased levels of peer-to-peer discussion rather than simply being told what to do.

1.3.3 Commitment

The construct of commitment encapsulates the cognitive qualities of the coach–athlete relationship. It expresses how the coach and the athlete perceive the long-term direction of their relationship, their place within it, and their dedication to it (Jowett and Ntoumanis 2004). The concept of commitment suggests an intention to maintain the coach–athlete relationship over time and a high level of positive expectations for that relationship and its related outcomes. As already noted, the progression of an athlete to high levels of performance is a long-term development (Ericsson and Charness 1994); as such, it requires time and perseverance from both the athlete and the coach. If an athlete is to progress within a sport, it is vital that the coach and athlete have similar views of the direction and goals of their relationship and an appropriate level of commitment to see these goals through to completion. Two potential conflicts exist within commitment. The first is incompatible views; for example, the coach may wish the athlete to progress to a higher level, while the athlete may see the sport as a hobby. The second is inappropriate levels of commitment relative to desired outcomes; for example, the coach and athlete may wish to progress to national level but train only once a week. In neither situation is the relationship likely to be effective or successful. Commitment is also strongly connected to complementarity and closeness. Rusbult (1983) proposed that commitment to a relationship is based upon a positive cost analysis (i.e., high rewards and low costs). In a relationship low in closeness, where coach and athlete lack trust, liking, and respect, there is likely to be a negative cost analysis and hence a lower level of investment. Additionally, it has been suggested that commitment is linked to a greater predisposition towards the use of accommodating behaviours, such as ability to compromise and negotiate, and hence is a fundamental factor in the success and effectiveness of a relationship (Rusbult et al. 1991).

1.3.4   Co-orientation

The construct of co-orientation encapsulates interchange and concurrence of closeness, commitment, and complementarity in the coach–athlete relationship. It describes how the coach and the athlete perceive themselves and each other (Jowett 2005). The concept of co-orientation suggests a degree of common ground between coach and athlete and an alignment of interpersonal perspectives. Duck (1994) postulates that relationship members are motivated to achieve and sustain a level of similarity; this similarity, either real or perceived, connects the two people, forming a foundation for their relationship by validating their views and opinions. Similarity in attitudes and the ability to understand and make accurate judgements are thought to increase individuals' trust and appreciation for each other, to confirm their intention to continue a relationship, and to assist them in responding and reacting appropriately to each other's behaviours. In sport it has been suggested that differences in viewpoints might indicate a potential conflict or power struggle within the coach–athlete relationship (Jowett 2003). Since individuals rarely have identical viewpoints and opinions, understanding and accurately perceiving others' viewpoints can help individuals identify and resolve these issues before they lead to negative conflict experiences (Acitelli, Kenny, and Weiner 2001). Hence, the quality and effectiveness of the interaction of coach and athlete may not simply be a factor of how much time or opportunity they have to interact but rather of the degree to which individuals understand each other and can therefore react appropriately.

Specifically, within the 3 + 1 Cs model, the construct of co-orientation refers to two interpersonal perspectives: direct perspective and metaperspective (Jowett 2009). Direct perspective refers to coach's and athlete's self-perceptions of closeness, complementarity, and commitment. For example, 'I like and appreciate my coach.' Metaperspective refers to coach's and athlete's perceptions of the partner's self-view about closeness, complementarity, and commitment. For example, 'I think my coach likes and appreciates me.' Essentially it is an inference about another's opinions and beliefs regarding the coach–athlete relationship. The two perspectives can be assessed for both coach and athlete; the combination provides three new constructs: similarity, assumed similarity, and empathy. Similarity is how well the coach's and athlete's direct perspectives match. For example, do they like each other, are they equally committed to the athlete's development, do they both put forth the same effort in training sessions? Assumed similarity is the congruence of an individual's direct perspective and metaperspective. For example, if an athlete trusts the coach, does the athlete also believe the coach reciprocates that trust? Finally, empathy is the congruence between either coach's or athlete's metaperspective and the other's direct perspective. For example, if an athlete believes the coach trusts her, does the coach actually trust her, or is the athlete's inference inaccurate? In combination these three constructs describe how co-oriented the coach and the athlete are in how they perceive and accurately understand each other; it is therefore an indicator of the quality of their relationship. Understanding how coach and athlete perceive their relationship is vital to understanding the relationship's quality. Knowledge of co-orientation then is essential for coach and athlete in the management of their relationship, and it can provide valuable information to sport psychologists working with those individuals.

1.4 Interpersonal communication

A key factor related to the quality of the coach–athlete relationship and the promotion of mutual understanding is the concept of communication. Communication is both a complex and an inescapable part of any social environment. Typically defined as any exchange of information between individuals (Dainton and Zelley 2011), the term 'communication' can cover both verbal (e.g., a coach giving instructions or advice) and non-verbal communication (e.g., body language of an athlete who is being given feedback). In the training environment, particularly between coach and athlete, 'communication' more specifically refers to a meaningful exchange between two or more individuals in which one intends to affect the response of another. An example would be a coach giving positive encouragement in order to elicit extra effort from the athlete. As such, communication is tied to the interdependence of coach and athlete and is the primary means by which each influences the other's emotions, thoughts, and actions.

Communication can be thought of as containing two distinct elements (DeVito 1986). The first is content. When individuals communicate they are often most focused on the information they are trying to convey – such as a coach giving teaching points or advice to an athlete. As the content element is the primary means by which a coach transmits technical and tactical skills to an athlete, it is essential in developing competence and improving performance (Poczwardowski, Barott, and Henschen 2002). This makes the content of any communication essential in creating a successful coach–athlete relationship. The second element is relation. Often overlooked or poorly managed, the relational element is the way in which individuals pass information between them. For example, the same teaching points can be communicated by a coach in a positive, friendly manner or in a negative, stern tone. How we communicate information is often more important than the information itself, and it can profoundly influence how others respond to that communication (Montgomery 1988). Thus, the relational element of communication is the primary means by which coach and athlete build rapport and develop mutual respect and appreciation. This makes the relational element of any communication essential to creating an effective coach–athlete relationship. Therefore, both coaches and athletes need to be aware of how they communicate as well as what they are trying to communicate.

The content element of communication is typically either verbal actions (e.g., giving instructions) or conscious non-verbal actions (e.g., physically demonstrating a skill). The relational element of communication is more frequently the transmission of information using unconscious non-verbal actions such as body language, eye contact, and facial expressions, though it may also include tone of voice. Individuals typically exert less conscious control over the relational element. This can be particularly problematic, as research suggests that nearly 70% of all perceived communication is non-verbal (Burke 2005). Coaches and athletes need to consider how they are communicating, how what they communicate may be interpreted by their partner, and what affect it may have on the success and effectiveness of their relationship. Sagar and Jowett (2012) have shown that an athlete's emotions correspond to the perception of a coach's feedback. This is particularly the case when a coach gives feedback on poor competitive results.

Where a coach is perceived as reacting negatively, an athlete demonstrates dissatisfaction with the relationship and shows a decline in motivation and performance. Where a coach is perceived as reacting more positively, an athlete instead demonstrates increased satisfaction and improved motivation and performance. It is therefore important for coaches to consciously promote a constructive training environment. To do this they first need to be aware of the influence their communication has on the athlete and ensure that their communication is, as much as possible, framed in a positive manner.

Effective communication between coach and athlete can be said to occur when the desired response results from an individual's correct interpretation of shared information, with no unintentional consequences (DeVito 1994). An example of this would be a coach providing feedback with the intent of motivating the athlete to correct his technique. If the athlete misinterprets the communication – perhaps because the coach unintentionally shares information through uncontrolled negative body language (e.g., folded arms or an aggressive posture) – the communication has been ineffective. However, should the athlete take on board the constructive comments and continue to put effort into improving his technique, then the communication has been effective.

In order for coach and athlete to maximise the effectiveness of their communication, they must consider how they communicate and how this communication may be interpreted by their partner. When a coach and an athlete communicate, they encode the message in language (e.g., choice of words, metaphors, jargon); it is transmitted via a medium (most commonly speech but sometimes another channel, such as email or text) and is then decoded and interpreted by the partner. This is known as mediated communication (DeVito 1994). Coach and athlete must first consider what it is they want to communicate – the core idea or the response they wish to elicit. They must then take care to choose how they encode the message. This means carefully selecting words that the person being communicated with will understand. For example, when a coach wishes to motivate an athlete, the desired response is the same regardless of the athlete being communicated with. However, the way in which the coach words that communication will differ widely depending on the age and background of the athlete. When communicating with a child, a coach may use positive, encouraging, friendly language. With an older and more experienced athlete, the coach may focus on constructive feedback regarding technique. It is also important that coach and athlete take care to carefully decode any communication to avoid misinterpreting the message and jumping to conclusions. In a team meeting after training, an athlete may yawn or seem distracted when talking with the coach. The coach could interpret this to mean the athlete is uninterested or bored and is indicating a lack of respect or appreciation

Figure 1.2   *Mediated communication*

for the coach's feedback. However, it could also simply indicate the training session has been long and tiring for the athlete (see Figure 1.2).

It has been suggested that communication is the glue that binds the coach–athlete relationship (Jowett and Poczwardowski 2007). The quantity of communication, the content of communication, and how that communication is framed can either bring coach and athlete together or push them apart. It is through communication that coach and athlete share goals and expectations and establish roles. Without communication coach and athlete could not interact or share inner worlds. Communication therefore is essential in maintaining the quality of a coach–athlete relationship and, through it, achieving desired outcomes, such as competitive success.

1.5   Relationship conflict

Conflict is an unavoidable consequence of social relationships. Relationship conflict occurs when two interdependent people disagree. Disagreements can focus on incompatible goals, personal values, and which course of action to take; they typically occur most frequently in high-pressure situations with highly valued outcomes, such as the coach–athlete relationship (Rahim 2002). An outdated view of conflict is that it is always destructive. It has been suggested that conflict can cause tension and antagonism between individuals and that in turn they have a negative impact on the individuals' relationship, productivity and satisfaction (Rahim 2002). While this is one possible outcome, conflict can also be constructive, and individuals often learn the most from what are perceived as negative experiences. Conflict provides the opportunity for different views and perspectives to be voiced, and research has shown that individuals make better decisions when confronted with a variety of different options and opinions (see, e.g., Schwenk 1990). Additionally, in the absence of conflict individuals are more likely to continue on the same course of action unaware of any potential inefficiencies or potentially more productive alternatives (Schulz-Hardt, Jochims, and Frey 2002). Conflict can also stimulate personal growth and the effectiveness of a relationship. Individuals must learn to balance different views and understand each other's perspectives, developing creativity and a readiness to respond in different ways (Rahim 2002).

To understand how conflict can have both positive and negative effects on coaches and athletes, it is important to refine how conflict is defined.

It has been suggested that conflict can be divided into multiple categories. While terminology varies, typically researchers divide conflict into two categories: task and personal (e.g., Jehn and Mannix 2001). 'Task conflict' refers to disagreements about a particular task and to differences in viewpoints and opinions about how to deal with it. 'Personal conflict' refers to individuals' disagreements about each other and their relationships and so arises from interpersonal incompatibilities. Task conflict can be facilitative, as it encourages individuals to discuss different options and to consider a task in more detail, which in turn results in a greater understanding of the task. As such it can encourage coaches and athletes to develop new approaches and to optimise their training and preparation. However, in everyday tasks that already have a well-developed and effective approach, task conflict can still be destructive by interfering with these well-practised routines (Rahim 2002). In contrast, personal conflict is not thought to be facilitative under any circumstances. Instead personal conflict disrupts the training and competition environments by focusing the coach's and athlete's efforts on personal disagreements rather than on training and competing. Thus it can decrease trust, loyalty, and respect and reduce the desire to work effectively together, which in turn decrease satisfaction and performance (Rahim 2002).

1.5.1   Effective conflict

The potentially positive benefits of task conflict are thought to be based upon the careful control and management of that conflict. While task conflict can facilitate new ideas and directions, these benefits can quickly disappear when individuals perceive the conflict to become more intense, competitive or aggressive. The competence with which a conflict is handled, then, can directly influence the outcome of that disagreement. The competence-based model of interpersonal conflict (Canary, Stafford, and Semic 2002) provides a theoretical framework for how conflict can be potentially managed. Conflict episodes first stem from the perception of incompatible goals or direction. These conflicts can have both a positive and negative impact on intrapersonal outcomes (e.g., personal satisfaction or performance) and relational outcomes (e.g., relationship quality and interpersonal satisfaction). However, the impact of conflict episodes is mediated by episodic assessments and conflict management strategies. 'Episodic assessments' refer to individual evaluations of the competence of communication during that conflict and the individual's satisfaction with that interpersonal communication. This means that during a conflict, coach and athlete make conscious and unconscious judgements about how the conflict is unfolding and how happy each is with the partner's interaction. For example, a coach might be telling an athlete she is being dropped from a squad. If the athlete perceives that the coach is understanding, has good reason for acting, and explains how the athlete may regain her position, then she will be more likely to respond constructively. Conversely, if the coach simply tells the athlete she is dropped and does not listen to her concerns, then the athlete is likely to respond negatively. Conflict management strategies include any actions individuals take to improve the outcome of episodic assessments. As will be discussed, management strategies can include increased discussion and openness and an increased effort to work together effectively. As the impact of conflict episodes on intrapersonal and relational outcomes are mediated by episodic assessments and conflict management strategies, it is difficult to predict a conflict's outcome. It can vary greatly depending on how coaches and athletes perceive and judge each other and on their cognitive maturity and past experiences with each other and with other coaches and athletes. Thus, coaches and athletes should strive hard to improve the competency with which they communicate during conflicts and the positivity of their judgements of each other.

1.6 Managing an effective and successful relationship

It has been suggested that all individuals seek out relationships that are both stable and long lasting. This is particularly desirable in coach–athlete relationships, where long-term commitment is needed if athletes are to complete their journey from beginner to expert or if long-term retention of individuals in sport is to be encouraged. The 3 + 1 Cs conceptualisation of the coach–athlete relationship incorporates this concept in the construct of commitment, which expresses a coach's and an athlete's intention to remain together and their belief in the long-term direction of the relationship. However, research has shown that a large amount of time and effort must be invested in any relationship and that individuals must actively work at maintaining a relationship to prevent a decline in its quality, which would lead to a decrease in its effectiveness and success (Canary, Stafford, and Semic 2002).

'Maintenance strategies' are defined as an individual's approach to sustaining a relationship in a particular state (Dindia and Canary 1993). Additionally they indicate an active effort to improve, not just maintain, the relationship's perceived quality. Individuals involved in sport can therefore use these maintenance strategies to (i) prevent any decline in the quality of their relationship, (ii) develop the relationship further, and/or (iii) repair the relationship if it has experienced a period of decline or interpersonal conflict (Rhind and Jowett 2011). The specific use of maintenance strategies in everyday relationships has been linked with improvement in levels of closeness (increased trust; Stafford, Dainton, and Hass 2000), complementarity (decreased power struggles; Canary and Stafford 1992), and commitment (Canary and Stafford 1992). However, the bulk of this research (and applied guidelines resulting from it) has focused on relationships involving parents, friends, or romantic partners. Yet the coach–athlete relationship is distinctly different from these partnerships. As this sport-specific relationship between coach and athlete forms in a range of specific contexts (e.g., sport-type, sport-culture, competitive level) and under specific pressures (e.g., funding, performance expectations, performance outcomes), it is important that any set of maintenance strategies applied in this setting be specific to the coach–athlete relationship. Rhind and Jowett (2010) have suggested that all forms of relationship maintenance can be encompassed by seven broad categories, the names of which form the acronym COMPASS: conflict management, openness, motivation, positivity, advice, support, social networks. This framework provides the most widely accepted guidelines for both coaches and athletes – and for psychologists working in sport.

1.6.1   Conflict management

Conflict management can be subdivided into proactive management and reactive management and often includes elements of other relationship maintenance strategies. Proactive management incorporates actions that are designed to avoid conflict occurrence. These include any action that clarifies the expectations of coach and athlete and establishes the consequences for either party's failing to meet these expectations. These strategies are particularly relevant to the coach–athlete relationship, which in general has a greater emphasis on specific outcomes and long-term planning (Gould et al. 2007). Examples of this type of strategy include preseason meetings and establishing of ground rules and mutual goal setting. Reactive management incorporates actions that are designed to ease conflict after it occurs. It covers actions that increase cooperation between coach and athlete during a conflict and facilitate its resolution (Canary and Zelley 2000). This type of strategy includes formalised discussion of an ongoing conflict, the setting of goals to resolve it, and the establishment of consequences should the goals not be met. For example, athletes who are continually late to training may agree to improve their timeliness, with the warning that they will be dropped from the squad if they do not improve.

1.6.2   Openness

Openness relates to how coach and athlete approach communication, primarily in how they choose to disclose their emotions and in the ability to recognise how the partner is feeling. It includes three sets of strategies for improving this aspect of the relationship: non-sport communication, approachability, and awareness. Non-sport communication strategies are about ensuring that time is set aside to discuss issues that are not directly related to training or competition. Topics outside the sporting environment–such as family life, work stresses, and personal issues–can help create a closer bond between two individuals (Stafford and Canary 1991). Additionally, as these may provide a coach valuable insight about the athlete's behaviour, they may help prevent a conflict developing. For example, if an athlete is putting in less effort during training, it may be due to stress from family life; knowing this, the coach can moderate his or her reactions. Approachability strategies are about establishing an environment where coach and athlete feel comfortable talking about anything and so are closely related to non-sport communication. They include assurances about confidentiality and safe communication, so individuals do not feel they will be judged or evaluated (Stafford and Canary 1991). They may include setting aside time outside training where athletes can meet with the coach one on one or may form part of proactive management strategies that establish ground rules and boundaries. Finally, awareness is about making accurate inferences about another's thoughts and feelings. Such accuracy is dependent on a coach and athlete having the motivation to attempt to understand one another and sufficient information on which to base the inference (Funder 1995). Awareness thus is closely related to the other two openness strategies, each of which can act as a major source of information.

1.6.3   Motivation

Motivational strategies revolve around the willingness of coach and athlete to work with each other or the attempt of each to motivate the other to work in cooperation. Rhind and Jowett (2010) highlight an overlap between being motivated to work together to maintain the quality of the relationship and being motivated to enhance performance. However, given that both outcomes are likely to be associated with intrapersonal and interpersonal satisfaction, there seems little need to try and separate them. Motivational strategies can be broken into four categories: effort, demonstrating ability, motivation of others, and enjoyment. Effort reflects the striving during training to demonstrate willingness to work with each other; for example, turning up early or trying your best at all times. This is closely associated with the second category, demonstrating ability, where an individual attempts to show the capability of making the relationship successful. This could include putting in extra effort, demonstrating passion or enthusiasm, or working to improve the relationship through discussion. The third category, motivation of others, is about creating an environment where your partner wants to work with you by, for example, giving encouragement and praise, discussing what coach and athlete have to offer each other, and committing to long-term goals. The final category, enjoyment, is related to the creation of this positive environment. It is about attempting to make any interaction as enjoyable as possible. But it is important to ensure that in doing so a coach or athlete does not distract from the purpose of training (such a distraction would be allowing an athlete just to play games rather than train). These strategies are about positive friendly interactions; they pace training so as to balance enjoyment and skill progression.

1.6.4   Positivity

Strategies based on positivity focus on individual's behaviours, adapting them to suit the coach or the athlete's preferences while at the same time treating individuals fairly according to their individual circumstances. Research on these strategies in other relationship types has focused on solely acting cheerfully and attempting to be encouraging around your partner (Stafford and Canary 1991). However, the coach–athlete relationship has a variety of goals, not just an effective relationship. Thus, positivity must be tempered by other factors (Rhind and Jowett 2010). These strategies have to be broken down into three categories: adaptability, consideration of external pressures, and fairness. Adaptability is about changing behaviours to suit the partner's needs and preferences. For example, a coach might alter her coaching style by making it less autocratic and more democratic. In terms of relationship quality, it could also mean a coach being more lenient in specific circumstances or altering training routines when necessary. Adaptability is also linked to consideration of external pressures. This means that the coach or athlete is adapting to the other's preferences due to knowledge of additional factors. An example would be a coach reducing training loads because a student athlete had exams in the near future. Finally, the category fairness is about balancing the considerations and needs of the athlete and not favouring any one individual. Overall, positivity is about dealing with events in an upbeat manner and customising one's approach to the individual. Coaches and athletes need to ensure they are aware of events in each other's lives and act in a way that ensures the events do not negatively affect their relationship.

1.6.5   Advice

Advice strategies are about giving opinions on sport-specific issues encountered by the coach or the athlete and about rewarding appropriate actions with positive feedback. Whereas previous relationship-maintenance strategies address specific interactions related to training and improvements in sport performance, the role of advice is central, indeed vital, to the coach-athlete relationship (Smith and Smoll 1990). That relationship's effectiveness and success are intrinsically linked, and by enhancing an athlete's success, the relationship quality between athlete and coach can also be maintained or improved. Advice strategies fall into three categories: sport communication, reward feedback, and constructive feedback. Sport communication is based upon frank discussion of issues or problems that directly impact training or competitive performance. This includes discussion of fitness, skills, and tactics and so encapsulates the normal day-to-day business of the coaching process. Reward feedback is about recognising effort and successful behaviours and offering praise. It is not about simply being positive or rewarding all actions, only about rewarding actions that have been identified as desirable and at an appropriate level. Constructive feedback is about giving honest opinions and advice about training and performance and about framing this advice in such a way that it furthers the athlete's performance rather than focus on criticising it and so potentially hinder progression. For example, a coach might point out what an athlete has done wrong and give positive correction rather than simply say that the athlete performed poorly.

1.6.6   Support

Support strategies fall into three categories: assurance, sport-specific support, and personal support. All three concern the need of coach and athlete to demonstrate commitment to each other and to the relationship. Research into other relationship types has consistently demonstrated the need for individuals to demonstrate their support in order to maintain a relationship's quality (Stafford and Canary 1991). However, the coach–athlete relationship, with its focus on measurable outcomes as well as relationship quality, requires support of both sport-related and non-sport issues. Assurance strategies focus solely on demonstrating that a coach or an athlete is committed to the relationship. This means that they are strongly associated with the motivational strategies, effort, and demonstrative abilities discussed previously. Sport-specific support strategies focus on providing necessary care and support after poor performances; for example, providing reassurance, encouragement, or constructive feedback. Sport-specific support overlaps with other strategies, such as advice, but is specific in that it refers to how coach and athlete interact following a lack of competitive success. Personal support strategies focus on providing care and support regarding negative events outside the training and competition environment. This again means there is an overlap with other strategies, particularly openness, but with a focus on negative outcomes.

1.6.7   Social networks

Strategies regarding social networks are focused on the coach and the athlete spending time with each other, potentially along with other team members. The key to these strategies is that the time should be spent outside the sport context and is in addition to any time spent together training or competing. Divided into two dimensions, social networks include socialising and shared networks. Socialising is simply the coach and the athlete finding time to interact outside the sport environment. Spending time together has been shown to improve relationship quality (Stafford and Canary 1991), but more importantly it may also provide a vehicle for other relationship-maintenance strategies. It can provide an environment in which coach and athlete are more open, demonstrate commitment to each other, and de-emphasise the competitive or success element of their relationship by instead focusing on enjoyable, effective personal interaction. The shared network dimension – which relates to the nature of the socialising and emphasises the need to spend time with mutual friends or acquaintances such as fellow team members – may include celebrating competition outcomes or team-building exercises. While shared social networks can de-emphasise the importance of the competitive or success element of relationships, they may also impact related factors, such as team cohesion (Jowett and Chaundy 2004).

1.7 Summary

Coaches play an important role in the social processes of the training environment of athletes. The coach is often the key socialising agent in the behavioural change of an athlete and as such is crucial in the athlete's long-term development and retention in sport and in the athlete's intrapersonal and interpersonal satisfaction, which can be a natural consequence of involvement in sport. The primary vehicle of these social processes is the coach-athlete relationship, the quality of which encompasses the affect, behaviours, and cognitions of coach and athlete, as well as how they perceive each other. As such relationships periodically experience episodes of conflict, they require careful application of relationship-maintenance strategies to repair and enhance them. The case study discusses specific strategies that a coach (or a psychologist working with the coach and the athlete) could use to create an optimal coaching environment for both training and competition.

1.8 Case study

1.8.1 Setting the scene

Gail is a 16-year-old gymnast who has recently secured a place on the national squad. Prior to this, she worked with a coach in her home town for 11 years. They formed a close bond of trust, and Gail won several major regional competitions. Since she has been appointed to the national squad, Gail has had to travel a sizable distance each week to train at the national performance centre with Jill, her new head coach. Jill is 52 years old and has over 30 years of coaching experience, including having coached several successful Olympic medallists. While the first few weeks of training went reasonably well, recently Gail and Jill have experienced conflict and other negative relational issues in their athletic relationship. Gail has said, 'I'm dedicated, I put in the hours. I've been doing this sport my entire life and I have a lot to offer!' Jill, however, feels that 'Gail, while a potentially talented gymnast, is wilful and expects all of my time to be focused on her; she isn't the only girl on the squad.' These conflicts are causing disruption at the national performance centre and impacting the training of both Gail and her fellow gymnasts. If the conflict is not resolved soon, Gail might lose her place on the national squad, and her international career could end before it even started.

How can the coach and the athlete get their conflict under control before going on to repair and re-establish their relationship?

1.8.2   Assessing the situation

The key socialising agent in this situation is likely to be the coach. While the athlete plays a central role, the coach, who is likely to be the older and more knowledgeable of the two, will have had more experience managing coach–athlete relationships. In this situation the coach needs to acknowledge her primary role in managing the coaching process. Jill must recognise that Gail is both a successful athlete and a young girl and that these two identities must be balanced. This conflict would primarily be managed through open and frank discussion between the two individuals. However, it seems that this conflict has progressed too far to be managed solely by the individuals involved. At higher levels of competition there is a greater chance that a sport psychologist will be involved to assist in providing a wider range of information and to facilitate reparations between coach and athlete. In this case the sport psychologist can draw upon two well-established instruments to help assess the situation.

The Coach–Athlete Relationship Questionnaire (CART-Q; Jowett and Ntoumanis 2004) is used to assess the quality of a coach–athlete relationship as conceptualised by the 3 + 1 Cs model. The CART-Q is unique in that in comes in four forms: two each for the coach and the athlete, one for their direct perspective, and one for their metaperspective. This allows them not only to assess how each perceives their relationship but also to assess the similarity and accuracy of their perceptions. The Coach–Athlete Relationship Maintenance Questionnaire (CARM-Q; Rhind and Jowett 2012) is used to assess how frequently a coach and an athlete are using the seven relationship-maintenance strategies conceptualised in the COMPASS model. In the case of Jill and Gail, it is likely that their problem arises from an inaccuracy in their perceptions of each other. Gail is committed to working with Jill and obviously feels that she is trying her best for the coach and the rest of the squad. However, as Jill perceives Gail to be acting in a non-complementary way, she questions Gail's commitment. Their disagreements have probably resulted in decreased levels of trust, liking, and respect in both Gail and Jill. It seems unlikely that either Gail or Jill is using any relationship-management strategies; they have let their relationship deteriorate to a critical level.

1.8.3   Important role of key socialising agents in behaviour change

In this situation, the coach and the sport psychologist both have an important role in resolving the conflict. Potentially the main facilitator will be the sport psychologist, who will act as a mediator. She will first have to ensure that Jill and Gail agree to work with her and then establish a time separate from training when all three can sit down to discuss the problem. It is important for the sport psychologist to remain neutral and not take sides. Additionally, her main role is to ensure that the discussion remains focused on task resolution and does not deteriorate into a personal conflict. To do this, there will need to be ground rules for the discussion to ensure that Jill and Gail contribute equally to the conversation. While the sport psychologist will play an important role, Jill and Gail must learn to work together without the future intervention of a third party. In light of her critical position, the sport psychologist must establish an action plan and follow-up procedures for Jill and Gail to follow. Additionally, Jill and Gail will need to learn appropriate relationship-maintenance strategies to ensure the future effectiveness and success of their relationship. Given Gail's youth, a greater proportion of the responsibility for this may fall upon Jill.

1.8.4   Specific strategies for key socialising agents

The following suggested strategies could be used by coaches and athletes to ensure effectiveness and successful experience in both training and competitions.

- Accept that disagreements will happen and that not everyone sees things the same way. Avoid ascribing blame; realise that conflict can be constructive as well as destructive.
- Develop an understanding of the seven main relationship-maintenance strategies and an awareness of how they can be successfully used. For example, conflict management and openness strategies are likely to be useful, but Jill and Gail are unlikely to be able to socialise or share similar social networks due to the substantial age difference and the fact that Gail lives a significant distance from where she trains.
- Understand and respect any gap in age, culture, or experience. Realise that both individuals will see things in different ways. It is important to appreciate that although opinions will differ, both individuals have potentially important contributions to make to the partnership.
- Discuss conflicts sooner rather than later. Issues left unresolved are likely to create a negative training experience; the longer they are left undiscussed, the more they will grow.
- Always take conflict seriously and give appropriate time and effort to each other's concerns. Always act with empathy and genuine concern.

- Create a safe time and place for discussion that will not disrupt training for either you or other coaches and athletes.
- Mentally rehearse what you want to say prior to confronting the other individual about a problem. Try to ensure your point is made objectively and does not become a personal conflict.
- If unsure about an issue, ask questions to clarify the situation. Attempt to understand the situation as far as possible; do not leap to conclusions.
- Look for common ground and agreement where possible.

1.9   Further study and recommended reading

The following literature is recommended for further reading on key concepts addressed in this chapter.

- Rhind, D., and Jowett, S. (2011). Working with coach-athlete relationships: Their quality and maintenance. In S. Mellalieu and S. Hanton (eds), *Professional Practice in Sport Psychology: A Review*. London: Routledge.
- Jowett, S., and Poczwardowski, A. (2007). Understanding the coach-athlete relationship. In S. Jowett and D. Lavallee (eds), *Social Psychology in Sport* (3–14). Champaign, IL: Human Kinetics.

Additionally, reading of the following relevant documents is recommended; they address areas that are essential in understanding the coaching environment.

- Lorimer, R., and Jowett, S. (2013). Empathic understanding and accuracy in the coach-athlete relationship. In J. Denison, W. Gilbert, and P. Potrac (eds), *The Routledge Handbook of Sports Coaching*. London: Routledge.
- Jowett, S., and Timson-Katchis, M. (2005). Social networks in the sport context: The influence of parents on the coach-athlete relationship. *Sport Psychologist*, 19, 267–287.

2   Teammates

2.1   Learning objectives

The purpose of this chapter is to examine the significance of peers and teammates within the context of the sporting realm and their role in shaping athletes' sporting experiences. The key learning objectives are:

- to understand the importance of peers and teammates within the context of sport;
- to examine the theoretical frameworks that outline the contribution of peers and teammates on athletic performance and well-being;
- to consider the empirical evidence which illustrates the critical role of peers and teammates on athletic performance and well-being;
- to discuss the strategies that athletes, support staff, and sport organisations can use to enhance unity, belongingness, and acceptance within teams.

2.2   Introduction to the context

The athletic community is a social environment which provides frequent and varied opportunities for social interactions with significant others (Jowett 2007). While athletes form many significant and interdependent relationships, attention has been largely limited to the effect and role of coaches in shaping athletes' experiences. However, there is increasing empirical evidence implicating the importance of teammates and peers in shaping the quality of athletes' sporting experiences across every stage of the developmental sporting trajectory (e.g., Keegan et al. 2009, 2014; Keegan et al. 2010). Athletes spend a significant amount of time with their teammates. Unlike athletes' relationship with coaches, whereby coaches have power over athletes, peers and teammates are in the same position as the athlete with whom they practice and compete with or against; thus they are of equivalent social standing and power (see Smith, 2007). They also provide each other with a sense of belonging and offer interpersonal relationship experiences based on intimacy and validation of self-worth (Riley and Smith 2011). Teammates act as a source of advice and support and as an external reference point by which to judge self-progression and performance, but they can also be a source of conflict and friction and promote social pressure, competition, and rivalry. Although conflict is mainly seen as an issue for team sports (e.g., rugby), wherein performance is the result of a collective effort, athletes in individual sports are often part of a squad that trains as a unit and whose performance may be measured by the members' pooled scores (e.g., in gymnastics). This makes teammates a major feature of the training and competition environment.

Not only are peers and teammates important in sport, sport is considered critical to the development of peer relationships (Smith 2007). Specifically, sport encourages athletes to interact with similar others, to engage in cooperative activity, and to pursue outcomes in an exciting and engaging setting. Sport, being a context wherein athletes are exposed to varied and diverse perspectives, cultures, and viewpoints, is salient in shaping athletes' social and moral development through such as virtues as fairness, team loyalty, persistence, and teamwork (Ommundsen et al. 2005). Moreover, via sporting interactions with peers and teammates, athletes develop skills, attitudes, and behaviours that influence both their athletic and personal development (Rubin, Bukowski, and Parker 1998).

Traditionally, the study of peer and teammate experiences within sport has been explored through the broad categories of peer acceptance and peer friendship (see Smith 2007). Accordingly, support for the presence and influence of these constructs has been favourable, with higher peer acceptance and friendship quality associated with a greater sense of self-worth, positive affect, sport enjoyment, commitment, and intrinsic motivation (Smith 2007). However, peer and teammate relationships should be considered distinct from peer friendships. Peer friendships consist of a close dyadic relationship, while peer and teammate relationships are characterised by more generic interactions between those of similar standing (Ntoumanis, Vazou, and Duda 2007).

This chapter outlines the impact of peers and teammates on athletic performance and athlete well-being. For the chapter's purpose, peers and teammates are defined as 'individuals of equal standing, whether this is a function of age, rank or class' (Smith 2007, 42). The chapter draws upon a number of theoretical frameworks which underpin group dynamics, including peer-created motivational climate, team cohesion, and intragroup conflict, to understand the facilitative and debilitative effects of peers and teammates, as well as to review the accompanying evidence underpinning these conceptual frameworks. Finally, an emphasis is placed on practical implications and/or solutions for athletes (and for those undertaking intervention/support work with them) to enhance the quality of team functioning.

2.3   Peer-oriented motivational climate: an overview of theory and indicative research

The examination of the influence exerted by peers on motivation and behaviours in youth sport has been directed by the social cognitive framework of Achievement Goal Theory (AGT; Ames 1992; Nicholls 1989). AGT proposes that individuals strive to demonstrate competence while simultaneously avoiding demonstrating incompetence. Competence is evaluated in two ways, the result being two distinct dispositional achievement orientations: task orientation and ego orientation. Task orientation manifests perceptions of competence; largely self-referenced, it is evaluated in terms of personal development and exercising maximum effort toward the task at hand. Ego orientation manifests perceptions of competence; normatively referenced, it is focused on outperforming others, demonstrating superiority to others, and exerting minimal effort to achieve performance success (see Nicholls 1989; Vazou, Ntoumanis, and Duda 2005). Specifically, task-orientated individuals feel more competent if they improve their skill, learn something new, or master a task, while ego-orientated individuals feel more competent if they demonstrate success and superiority to others (van de Pol, Kavussanu, and Ring 2012). Accordingly, a large body of evidence has demonstrated that task orientation is more closely associated than ego orientation with such positive outcomes as increased enjoyment and satisfaction, commitment to practice and skill development, moral functioning, and reduced anxiety (e.g., Bortoli, Bertollo, and Robazaa 2009; Kavussanu and Roberts 2001; Roberts and Ommundsen 1996; Smith, Smoll, and Cummings 2007).

AGT theorists further postulate that the motivational climate fostered by parents, coaches, teachers, and similar significant others plays a critical role in shaping the achievement behaviours of young athletes. Specifically, Ames (1992) considered the achievement behaviours of young athletes to be products of the interplay between athletes' dispositional goal orientations and the situational motivational climate created by significant others. Motivational climates reflect individuals' perceptions of the structures and expectations that induce the development of a particular dispositional goal orientation (see Ntoumanis et al. 2007). Two variations of motivational climate have been put forward: task-involving/mastery and ego-involving/performance (Ames 1992). A task-involving motivational climate promotes and recognises individual improvement and effort and rewards task mastery. An ego-involving motivational climate places an emphasis on normative ability and encourages social comparison between members. Adult-created task-involving motivational climates (e.g., those of coaches and parents) have been linked to more positive affective, cognitive, and behavioural outcomes than ego-involving motivational climates (see Duda and Balaguer 2007; White 2007).

Given the predominant focus on the impact of adult-created motivational climate, Vazou and colleagues conducted a series of studies to understand the nature, structure, and dimensions of peer-induced motivational climates in youth sport (e.g., Ntoumanis and Vazou 2005; Vazou et al. 2005, 2006). In-depth interviews, first conducted with 30 athletes competing in both individual and team sports about their perception and experiences of motivational climates in youth sport (Vazou et al. 2005), illustrated a total of 11 dimensions of peer-induced motivational climate. Specifically, the mechanisms through which peer-induced motivational climates were related to improvement ('encouraging and providing feedback for improvement to teammates'), equal treatment ('believing that everyone has an important role on the team and treating teammates in a non-preferential way'), relatedness support ('fostering the feeling of being part of a group and creating a friendly atmosphere on the team'), cooperation ('helping each other and working together in order to learn new skills'), effort ('emphasising the importance of exerting effort and trying one's hardest'), intrateam competition ('promoting interindividual competition and comparison'), intrateam conflict ('exhibiting negative and unsupportive behaviours that are not directly related to competing with others'), normative ability ('emphasising normative ability and interacting only with the most competent teammates'), autonomy support ('perceiving that peers allow each other input in decision making and freedom in the way they play or perceiving that their peers act in a controlling manner'), mistakes ('worrying about how peers might react if athletes make mistakes; giving positive and negative reactions following athletes' mistakes'), and evaluation of competence ('using normative or self-referenced criteria to evaluate athletes' competence'; Ntoumanis et al. 2007, 148).

Extending this, Vazou et al. (2006) examined the effects of peer-created and coach-created motivational climate on such affective and behavioural motivational indices as physical self-esteem, enjoyment, competitive state anxiety, and sport commitment among young athletes. In relation to physical self-esteem, task-involving peer climate was found to be the exclusive predictor, with athletes who perceived their peers to encourage personal improvement, effort, and task mastery reporting higher perception of self-worth. Similarly, task-involving peer climate was also associated with increased enjoyment and sport commitment, implying that a motivational climate focused on promoting task-related cues enhances not only young athletes' enjoyment but also their desire to continue participating in sport. However, peer-created climate (e.g., task or ego) was not related to competitive state anxiety. Rather, ego-involving coaching climate was predictive of heightened anxiety in young athletes. Gender and age differences in athletes' perceptions of peer-induced motivational climates were also noted by the authors. Specifically, compared to male athletes, female athletes perceived their coaching environment to be characterised by greater levels of task-involving motivational climate. Older athletes reported greater intrateam conflict than younger athletes, while younger athletes reported greater levels of intrateam competition/ability than their older counterparts.

2.3.1 Peer-oriented motivational climate: recent developments in research

Since the publication of these seminal studies, a body of research has further examined the factors that affect and are affected by peer-induced motivational climates. For example, Vazou (2010) examined the factors that predict perceptions of peer-orientated and coach-orientated motivational climate among young athletes. She found that group factors such as team success and the coach's gender influenced athletes' perception of peer-induced motivational climate. Specifically, team success was found to positively predict peer-induced task-involving motivational climate and negatively predict ego-involving motivational climate. Female coaches were noted as promoting more peer task-involving motivational cues than male coaches. In addition, individual factors such as goal orientation, gender, and age were also found to predict variations in peer-induced motivational climate. In particular, athletes high in task orientation reported high peer task-involving motivational climate, while athletes high in ego orientation reported high peer ego-involving motivational climate. Moreover, athletes' perception of peer ego-involving motivational climate was also found to be dependent on the levels of ego orientation exhibited by athletes. Specifically, the perceptions of athletes reporting high or low levels of ego orientation differed from those of athletes reporting moderate levels of ego orientation. As in the initial findings of Vazou and colleagues (2006), gender and age differences were also noted in this study, with boys and older athletes perceiving higher peer ego-involving motivational climate than girls and younger athletes. Factors such as the coach's age, team size, number of years coaching the team, and number of years competing with the team were not found to distinguish between athletes' perceptions of peer-induced motivational climates.

On the other hand, athletes' gender and length of sport participation has been found to influence athletes' perceptions of peer-created motivational climate (e.g., Jõesaar and Hein 2011; Smith, Gustafsson, and Hassmén 2010). For instance, Smith and colleagues noted that male athletes report greater perceptions of an ego-involving peer-created motivational climate than female athletes. Specifically, male athletes reported higher levels of social comparison and interindividual competition, as well as negative and unsupportive behaviours, than female athletes, while female athletes reported higher levels of effort between team members. In another study, Jõesaar and Hein found athletes' perception of peer-created motivational climate to vary across years of sport participation. The authors noted that athletes with one to three years of sport participation reported greater ego-involving peer-motivational climate, in terms of interteam conflict, than athletes with less than one and more than three years of training. Athletes with more than three years of sport participation reported greater task-involving peer-motivational climate, in terms of greater effort, than those athletes with less than one year of sport participation.

The factors affected by peer-induced motivational climates include motivation, effort, vitality, good sporting behaviours, athlete burnout, and persistence with sport (e.g., Jõesaar and Hein 2011; Jõesaar, Hein, and Hagger 2011, 2012; Le Bars, Gernion, and Ninot 2009; Ntoumanis, Taylor, and Thøgerson-Ntoumanis 2012). For example, Ntoumanis and colleagues reported that athletes' perceptions of task- and ego-involving peer- and coach-motivational climate were associated with pro-social and antisocial attitudes, burnout, vitality, levels of effort, and intentions to return to team the following season. Specifically, task-involving peer-motivational climate was associated with greater pro-social attitudes in sport, higher respect for convention, reduced levels of burnout, greater levels of vitality, and higher ratings of effort. Ego-involving peer-motivational climate, on the other hand, was associated with greater antisocial attitudes in sport, increased levels of burnout, and reduced vitality and ratings of effort. Likewise, Jõesaar and colleagues (2011) reported that athletes who persisted in sport reported greater perceptions of task-involving peer-motivational climate, psychological needs satisfaction, and intrinsic motivation than dropout athletes. In particular, task-involving peer-motivational climate indirectly predicted athletes' intrinsic motivation and persistence in sport 12 months later through athletes' perceived needs satisfaction (relatedness, competence, and autonomy). This suggests that athletes who perceived a greater task-involving peer-motivational climate reported greater desire to engage in their sport because their need for competence, relatedness, and autonomy were being satisfied. Ego-involving peer-motivational climate was also found to indirectly influence athletes' intrinsic motivation and persistent with sport via perceived relatedness over time; however, the authors noted that the indirect effects of ego-involving peer-motivational climate was negative and smaller in magnitude in comparison to the indirect effects of task-involving peer-motivational climate.

2.4   Team cohesion: a conceptual framework

Team cohesion is a multifaceted, dynamic construct which serves an instrumental and affective function in sport (e.g., Carron, Widmeyer, and Brawley 1985). It is 'a dynamic process which is reflected in the tendency for a group to stick together and remain united in the pursuit of its instrumental objectives and/or for the satisfaction of member affective needs' (Carron, Brawley, and

Widmeyer 1998, 213). Carron and colleagues (1985) proposed a conceptual framework whereby team cohesion is reflected in both the group members' perceptions of the group as a unit and of their own attraction to the team. These perceptions are characterised as group integration (GI), which refers to the players' perception of the team performing as a unit, to emotional closeness, and to bonds formed within the group, and individual attraction to the group (ATG), which refers to the players' perception that their needs and objectives are being satisfied by the group and to their personal feelings towards the group (see Carron, Eys, and Burke 2007). Moreover, these perceptions underline two further fundamental foci: task cohesion, which corresponds to players' orientation towards pursuing the groups' common objective/goal, and social cohesion, which reflects players' orientation towards the development and maintenance of social relationships and activities in the group (see Carron et al. 2007). This consequently results in four manifestations of team cohesion, which bind the members to their group (see Lavallee et al. 2004):

- group integration–task (GI-task), which reflects the group members' perceptions about the degree of unity, similarity, and closeness within the whole group as it pertains to tasks;
- attraction to the group–task (ATG-task), which refers to the group members' perceptions about their own involvement with the task aspects of the group, including working towards group goals and objectives;
- group integration–social (GI-social), which captures group members' perceptions about unity, similarity, emotional closeness, and bonds formed within the whole group as it relates to the social aspects of the group;
- attraction to the group–social (ATG-social), which reflects the group members' perceptions about personal involvement, acceptance, and interaction in relation to the social aspects of the group.

2.4.1 Team cohesion: a review of the antecedents and outcomes

Carron (1982) put forward the sport-related factors that affect the development of team cohesion as well as the factors that are affected by team cohesion. Specifically, he postulated that there are four classifications of antecedents that promote the development of cohesion within teams. These include situational, personal, leadership, and team variables. In addition to the antecedents, Carron further proposed that the development of a cohesive team has a positive impact on outcomes for the group and the individual. However, given the research design of the empirical studies that have tested Carron's model, the presumed directionality of the proposed classes of antecedents and outcomes is ambiguous, thus rendering them at best correlates of team cohesion.

2.4.1.1   Team cohesion and situational antecedents

Albeit limited, there is evidence linking situational antecedents, such as performance level and team size, to team cohesion from a series of early studies, with lower-performance-level athletes and smaller groups reporting higher levels of team cohesion (see Carron et al. 2007 for an overview). For example, in a comprehensive study, Widmeyer, Brawley, and Carron (1990) demonstrated that as the size of the team increased, team cohesion decreased, with a team consisting of three basketball players reporting the highest levels of task cohesion (even though they were less successful). However, in terms of social cohesion, Widmeyer and colleagues reported that the smallest basketball team (3 members) and the largest basketball team (9 members) reported lower levels, while the intermediate basketball team (6 members) reported the highest level of social cohesion. Such a trend was also observed in volleyball. During competitions, team cohesion declined as the size of the team increased, with teams consisting of 12 players reporting the lowest level of team cohesion.

2.4.1.2   Team cohesion and personal antecedents

Research has highlighted a number of personal antecedents of team cohesion: motivation, personal responsibility, team sacrifice, team adherence (see Carron et al. 2007 for an overview). Athlete jealousy is a personal variable that has been linked to cohesion by Kamphoff, Gill, and Huddleston (2005). In a study of 236 athletes involved in co-acting and interactive sports, they found athletes who reported higher levels of jealously reported lower levels of both task and social cohesion. The authors further reported that jealousy reduced team cohesion by undermining athletes' satisfaction with the team. Athletes' passion for sport has been identified as another potential personal antecedent of team cohesion, with both harmonious and obsessive passion positively related to task and social cohesion (Paradis, Martin, and Carron 2012). Specifically, student athletes who reported higher levels of harmonious and obsessive passion also reported higher levels of task and social cohesion. This suggests that highly passionate athletes (be the passion harmonious or obsessive) attach high levels of importance to their sport's task and social aspects, such as working towards the same goals, creating a productive and conducive sporting environment, and fostering and maintaining good working social relationships (Paradis et al. 2012).

2.4.1.3   Team cohesion and leadership antecedents

How coaches communicate, behave, interact, and relate with their players has been implicated by a large body of research in the development of a cohesive team (e.g., Callow et al. 2009; Gearity and Murray 2011). For example, Gearity and Murray depicted how poor coaching behaviours, such as encouraging athletes to challenge and confront each other, led to less cohesive teams. One of the athletes Gearity and Murray interviewed said, 'After every game, win or lose, it's like the blame game. Like whose fault is it? It's either the pitchers' fault or it's the batters' fault and they [coaches] really wanted us to like dig into each other. They really encouraged one player to call another player out in front of the whole team, even if that means embarrassing them or like making them feel ridiculous. And if you didn't call somebody out, the coaches would turn on you…so, it was really a hard situation…you're playing against the other team and you're playing against the umpires and you're playing against the coaches and then at the end of day you're working against your teammates too' (217). The athletes further commented that such behaviour generated feelings of resentment, inequality, and lack of unity within the team.

The motivational climate created by coaches has been found to influence team cohesion (e.g., Eys et al. 2013; Horn et al. 2012). For example, in a sample of adolescent athletes, Horn and colleagues reported that a coach-created task-motivational climate predicted high levels of team cohesion. Interestingly, a coach-induced ego-orientated motivational climate was also found to be conducive to the development of a cohesive group provided that a highly task-orientated motivational climate was also present. This suggests that the promotion of an ego-oriented motivational climate may not be detrimental to the development of cohesion. The authors further noted that such patterns did not differ by gender. Eys and colleagues, on the other hand, demonstrated that coach-created task- and ego-motivational climates have distinctive relationships with team cohesion. Specifically, a task-involving motivational climate was associated with high levels of both task and social cohesion, while an ego-involving motivational climate was negatively associated with task and social cohesion. The degree of enjoyment experienced by the athletes was also found to moderate the associations between coach-created ego-motivational climate and team cohesion, with the negative association between ego-involving motivational climate and task cohesion weakened by the degree of enjoyment experienced by the young athletes.

The leadership behaviours coaches exhibit have been associated with the development of team cohesion in a number of studies (e.g., Callow et al. 2009; Smith et al. 2012). Callow and colleagues found leadership behaviours such as fostering acceptance of group goals and promoting teamwork to be associated with both task and social cohesion, while behaviours such as having high-performance expectations and individual consideration exclusively predicted task cohesion. However, players' performance levels moderated the link, with the relationship between fostering acceptance of group goals and promoting teamwork and cohesion being present in the low-performance group (e.g., players who did not qualify for the European Ultimate Club Championships) but dissipating in the high-performance group (e.g., players who did qualify for those championships). When performance level was accounted for, individual consideration predicted task cohesion in the high-performance group but not the low-performance group. This suggests that specific leadership behaviours are not synonymous with cohesion (be it task or social) and such influence on cohesion is dependent on the athletes' performance level. However, some evidence suggests that it is not necessarily the leadership behaviours exhibited by coaches that is predictive of cohesion but rather the quality of the relationship coaches maintain with their athletes (e.g., Cottingham et al. 2010; Jowett and Chaundy 2004). Specifically, Jowett and Chaundy found the quality of the coach–athlete relationship (measured in closeness, commitment, and complementarity) to account for more variance in both task and social cohesion than coach leadership behaviours.

In addition to coaches' behaviours, athletes' behaviours have been found to influence team cohesiveness (e.g., Price and Weiss 2011; Vincer and Loughead 2010). In particular, the findings of these studies suggest that peer leadership behaviours are fundamental to team functioning; they contribute to promoting unity, aligning group members to work towards the same goals, and promoting the development of effective social relationships. For example, Price and Weiss, in their study of adolescent female football (soccer) players, reported that athletes rated by teammates as displaying instrumental and pro-social leadership behaviours reported greater social cohesion. Likewise, athletes who rated themselves as exhibiting instrumental and pro-social leadership behaviours perceived greater task and social cohesion within their team.

2.4.1.4   Team cohesion and team antecedents

In terms of the impact of team antecedents on cohesion, evidence is limited and has primarily focused on the effect of team ability, team position (e.g., starter vs non-starter), and team norms in the development of team cohesion (e.g., Sindik and Vokosav 2011; Verma et al. 2012). Accordingly, findings about the impact of team ability conflict. Sindik and Vokosav found no significant difference in team cohesion levels between high-ability and lower-ability basketball players. However, Verma and colleagues, in their study of high-ability and low-ability elite volleyball players, found that the high-ability players reported greater levels of task and social cohesion than the low-ability players. Another team variable examined in relation to team cohesion is hazing. While hazing is illegal and regarded as unacceptable practice within the sporting context, sport teams frequently argue that hazing operates to promote unity and foster friendships. However, Van Raalte and colleagues (2007) found hazing initiations (e.g., unacceptable team-building activities such as kidnapping, being beaten by or beating up others, drinking games) to be negatively associated with task cohesion and unrelated to social cohesion, while appropriate team-building initiations (e.g., dressing up, taking an oath) were found to be positively related to task cohesion.

2.4.1.5 Team cohesion and group outcomes

The meta-analysis of Carron and colleagues (2002) reported a moderate to large relationship between cohesion and performance. Specifically, an effect size of .655 was found, indicating that more cohesive teams experienced greater team success. Although performance was not synonymous with a particular type of cohesion, social cohesion was found to have a stronger relationship to performance (ES = .702) than task cohesion (ES = .607), suggesting that teams that engage in social activities with each other and have good working relationships report greater team success. However, the impact of cohesion on performance was moderated by gender, with such relationships stronger in female teams (ES = .949) than male teams (ES = .556). Sport type and performance level, on the other hand, were not found to influence the cohesion-performance relationship.

Collective efficacy has been proposed as a group outcome of team cohesion (e.g., Heuzé, Raimbault, and Fontayne 2006; Leo et al. 2010). For example, Heuzé and colleagues found professional basketball players' perception of both task and social cohesion to be related to their perceptions of collective efficacy. Likewise, Leo and colleagues found semiprofessional football and basketball players who reported greater levels of team cohesion also reported a greater shared belief in their team's competence. Marcos and colleagues noted the cohesion-efficacy relationship was evident at the individual as well as at the group level, with individual athletes in teams with high levels of team cohesion reporting greater self-efficacy. However, empirical evidence also indicates that collective efficacy may actually be an antecedent of team cohesion rather than an outcome (Heuzé, Bosselut, and Thomas 2007). Specifically, employing a longitudinal design over two periods (early and midseason) of a competitive handball season, Heuzé and colleagues (2007) found that early season collective efficacy levels predicted task cohesion (ATG) midseason. This effect held even after controlling for confounding variables (prior group performance, group level, early season cohesion levels), suggesting that the players perceptions of the teams' competence at the beginning of the season predicted their feelings about their personal involvement in the teams' goals and objectives midseason. Although the proposed direction of team cohesion and collective efficacy appears to differ from study to study, it is clear that cohesion and collective efficacy are related constructs (Jowett, Shanmugam, and Caccoulis 2012).

2.4.1.6 Team cohesion and individual outcomes

The individual outcomes of team cohesion consist of affective, cognitive, and behavioural variables (Carron et al. 2007). One noted example of an affective outcome of a cohesive team is mood (Henderson et al. 1998; Terry et al. 2000). For example, Terry and colleagues found both task and social cohesion to predict mood on rowing, netball, and rugby teams. In particular, high ATG-task cohesion predicted low levels of tension and anger, while high GI-task predicted low levels of depression. High ATG-social cohesion, on the other hand, was found to predict low levels of tension and depression but high levels of vigour. The GI dimension of social cohesion was found not to be predictive of mood. Interestingly, Terry and colleagues found that these patterns were consistent across the three sport disciplines, despite the substantial variation in group cohesion and mood states exhibited by these sport teams.

Cognitive anxiety reflects a cognitive outcome of team cohesion. Accordingly, a number of studies have demonstrated the effects of cohesion on cognitive anxiety (e.g., Borrego, Cid, and Silva 2012; Eys et al. 2003; Prapavessis and Carron 1996). Prapavessis and Carron found that athletes who reported high levels of task cohesion reported lower levels of cognitive anxiety prior to competition, but they found no relationship between social cohesion and cognitive anxiety. However, the relationship between task cohesion and cognitive anxiety was not direct; rather, it was indirectly determined by athletes' perceptions of psychological costs (e.g., pressure to carry out group responsibilities and satisfy the expectations of the valued members). This suggests that a possible reason why athletes with high levels of task cohesion report lower levels of cognitive anxiety is that they feel less pressure to succeed from their teammates. Furthermore, recent evidence suggests that the relationship between cohesion and cognitive anxiety may be exclusive to male athletes (Borrego et al. 2012). Although female football players reported greater cognitive anxiety than their male counterparts, task cohesion was predictive only of cognitive and somatic anxiety in males, with those reporting lower levels of task cohesion also reporting greater cognitive and somatic anxiety symptoms.

In terms of behavioural outcomes, greater team cohesion has been linked to reduced social loafing (e.g., Everett, Smith, and Williams 1992; Høigaard, Skjekkeland, and Johansen 2003; Høigaard, Tofteland, and Ommundsen 2006), increased effort (e.g., Bray and Whaley 2001; Prapavessis and Carron 1997), and returning to team (e.g., Spink, Wilson, and Odnokon 2010). For example, Høigaard and colleagues (2006) noted that the teams that reported a high level of team cohesion performed equally well (i.e., similar times) under both high (e.g., participants were informed of their individual and team time in the presence of all participants) and low (e.g.. only the team's time was stated) identifiable conditions, whereas those athletes that reported low team cohesion ran slower in the low identifiable condition than in the high identifiable condition. Adding to this, Prapavessis and Carron reported that athletes who perceived their team as high in task cohesion exhibited increased work output (e.g., higher percentage of maximal VO_2). Finally, Spink and colleagues found elite athletes who reported high levels of task cohesion were more likely to return to play for their team the following season than those athletes who perceived their team as lacking in task cohesion.

2.5   Intragroup conflict: definitions and conceptualisations

Conflict is considered inevitable in interpersonal relationships (LaVoi 2007), but it has been reported that athletes most commonly experience more conflict with teammates and other athletes than any other social agents (Mellalieu, Shearer, and Shearer 2013). Conflict between teammates and peers has been associated with undesirable outcomes for the individual and the team (e.g., Carron et al. 2002; Holt et al. 2008; Vazou et al. 2005). Specifically, such conflict is considered to undermine the dynamics of the team and the group's performance (e.g., Sullivan and Feltz 2001). However, the literature on intragroup conflict is limited; only a handful of studies explore the nature, prevalence and correlates of teammate and peer conflict (e.g., Cunningham and Eys 2007; Holt, Knight, and Zukiwski 2012; Paradis, Carron, and Martin 2014). The shortage of studies can be largely attributed to the lack of clarity and consistency in the definitions, theory, and measurement tools used to capture conflict between group members within the sport setting.

Within organisational psychology, intragroup conflict has been defined as 'a dynamic process that occurs between interdependent parties as they experience negative emotional reactions to perceived disagreements and interference with the attainments of their goals' (Barki and Hartwick 2004, 234). A multifaceted construct delineated by cognitive, behavioural, and affective features, intragroup conflict encompasses disagreements (cognitive), negative emotions (affective), and interference behaviours (behavioural) between the parties involved. Barki and Hartwick proposed that two common types of intragroup conflict exist: task (e.g., disagreements and differences between group members about performance or task issues) and interpersonal relationship (e.g., disagreements and interpersonal incompatibility between group members, characterised by emotions such as tension and frustration).

2.5.1   Athletes' perceptions of the nature of intragroup conflict

Congruent with Barki and Hartwick's (2004) conceptualisation, a number of studies have provided support for the multidimensional nature of intragroup conflict within sport (e.g., Holt et al. 2012; Paradis et al. 2014). Holt and colleagues noted that female athletes reported the existence of two types of intragroup conflict: performance (task) and relationship conflict.

Performance conflict related to group members' concerns about practice and competition as well as playing time, while relationship conflict delineated issues related to interpersonal disputes/disagreements unrelated to performance and conflicting personalities. Adding to this, Paradis and colleagues reported that although male and female athletes perceived disagreements as the foundation of intragroup conflict, conflict went well beyond mere disagreement to negative emotional states and feelings of resentment, jealousy, anger, frustration, and irritation, as well as negative body language, avoidance behaviours, silent treatment, verbal and physical fighting, and other behaviours related to interference with goal attainment. Moreover, athletes characterised conflict as manifesting as task (i.e., related primarily to task situations) and social (poor relationships between group members away from the sport, not getting along with group members, confrontation, isolation, exclusion).

2.5.2   Correlates of intragroup conflict in sport

Given the novelty of the topic within sport settings, there is a paucity of data demonstrating the factors that affect and are affected by intragroup conflict. Moreover, though most studies have employed cross-sectional research designs, it is not clear whether the role of intragroup conflict is that of an antecedent or an artefact. In addition, the diversity and inconsistency within the literature in relation to the instruments used to capture intragroup conflict further challenges the understanding of intragroup conflict within sport. For example, employing the Group Environment Questionnaire (Carron et al. 1985) and a conflict-style measure (Canary, Cunningham, and Cody 1988), Sullivan and Feltz (2001) found negative intragroup conflict (e.g., topic shifting) to reduce task and social cohesion (reduced unity, closeness, personal involvement, and social interactions between players), while positive intragroup conflict (integrative tactics) enhanced social cohesion (increased unity, similarity, emotional closeness, personal involvement, acceptance, and interactions between players). In another study, using the Scale for Effective Communication in Team Sports (SECTS; Sullivan and Feltz 2003) and the Athlete Satisfaction Questionnaire (ASQ; Reimer and Chelladurai 1998), Sullivan and Gee (2007) reported that positive conflict (open and constructive methods of dealing with disagreements) related positively to athletes' satisfaction with their ability and the team's social contribution, ethics, team integration, and personal dedication. On the other hand, negative conflict (expression of agitation or anger) related negatively to athletes' satisfaction with training and instruction and the team's task contribution, ethics, and team integration.

Shanmugam, Jowett, and Meyer (2013, 2014) examined the association between relationship quality with significant others such as coaches, parents, and teammates and athletes' eating attitudes and behaviours. In the first study using the Sport-Specific Quality of Relationship Inventory (S-SQRI; Jowett 2009) and the Eating Disorder Examination Questionnaire (EDEQ; Fairburn and Beglin 2008), Shanmugam and colleagues (2013) assessed the link between social support and interpersonal conflict within coach–athlete, parent–athlete, and teammate–athlete relationships and eating attitudes and behaviours among 411 British athletes. They reported that athletes who reported higher levels of conflict and low levels of social support in parental and coach–athlete relationships exhibited greater eating-disorder symptoms. However, social support received from and interpersonal conflict experienced with teammates was not found to be associated with athletes' eating attitudes and behaviours. Expanding upon these initial findings, Shanmugam and colleagues (2014) examined the prospective link between relationship quality with parents, coaches, teammates and athletes' eating attitudes and behaviours over a six-month period among 122 British athletes. Again utilising the S-SQRI and the EDEQ, the authors reported that low levels of social support and high levels of conflict in the coach–athlete and teammate–athlete relationship were associated with greater eating-disorder symptoms six months later (after controlling for their initial eating attitudes and behaviours). Although coach conflict was found to impart the strongest effect on athletes' eating attitudes and behaviours, conflict with teammates was found to be the second strongest temporal correlate, suggesting that intragroup conflict may heighten athletes' risk for eating-disorder symptoms.

In an attempt to further advance the literature on intragroup conflict and bring consistency in the measurement of intragroup conflict, Paradis, Carron, and Martin (2014) developed the Group Conflict Questionnaire (GCQ). The GCQ, guided by the Barki and Hartwick (2004) definition and multifaceted conceptualisation of intragroup conflict, is a 14-item questionnaire which reflects task and social (i.e., relationship) conflict delineated by affective, cognitive, and behavioural features. Using 305 athletes, Paradis and colleagues tested the association of intragroup conflict (as measured via the GCQ), team cohesion, athlete satisfaction, and passion. Task and social conflict were found to be negatively related to social and task cohesion (all four dimensions) and athletes' satisfaction with team integration and team performance, as well as harmonious passion. This illustrates that the presence of conflict, be it task or social, between teammates and peers is not productive for the individual or the team. Paradis and colleagues further tested the influence of team tenure (i.e., new players vs veteran players) and sport type (individual vs team sports) on athletes' perception of intragroup conflict. As expected, athletes with less tenure reported higher levels of both social and task conflict with their teammates than athletes with more tenure. In terms of sport type, it was found that team sport athletes experienced greater levels of task conflict than those in individual sports; however, individual sports athletes reported experiencing higher levels of social conflict than those in team sports.

2.5.3 Can intragroup conflict ever be productive?

It is evident from the aforementioned findings that the presence of intragroup conflict is associated with undesirable outcomes for both individual and team; however, evidence suggests that conflict between group members is not necessarily destructive and in some cases can have a positive effect. For example, in the study by Holt and colleagues (2012), a number of athletes indicated that performance/task conflict could actually be conducive to good performance. Specifically, one athlete said, 'A lot of the [performance] conflict isn't necessarily a bad thing. ... I think a lot of that conflict ends up coming from the will to win ... I don't think that's necessarily a bad conflict or a bad thing to come up. ... I think for me that's a good thing because otherwise I'd be on a complacent team and that's not where I want to be' (143). Likewise, Paradis and colleagues (2014) reported that task conflict was considered beneficial by male and female athletes but only when treated or resolved early. These findings add to the initial findings of Smith and colleagues (2006) that young athletes with high and low levels of intragroup conflict do not significantly differ on anxiety, self-presentational concerns, or self-determined motivation. In fact, athletes with higher levels of intragroup conflict reported greater perceived competence and sport enjoyment.

2.5.4 Creating and maintaining effective group dynamics for optimal performance and well-being

It appears that promotion of a task involving peer-induced motivational climate, unity, and emotional closeness between team members and reducing intragroup conflict is conducive to favourable affective, cognitive, and behavioural outcomes for athletes and their team. Accordingly, a number of strategies can be employed within sport by athletes, coaches, sport psychologists, and other support staff to enhance team members' interpersonal functioning. For example, athletes should be urged to encourage and praise their teammates' improvement (e.g., in skill or performance) and provide constructive feedback to aid further development. Likewise, collaborative group learning could also be employed, wherein athletes work together to develop and enhance their skills (see Ntoumanis et al. 2007). It has been suggested that such practice, which allows them to work together to achieve a collective goal, will create a sense of belongingness, togetherness, and acceptance between team members.

Another method of enhancing unity and togetherness is team building. Team building has been defined as 'a method of helping the group (a) increase its effectiveness, (b) satisfy the needs of its members, and (c) improve work conditions' (Brawley and Paskevich 1997, 13). Accordingly, a number of team-building strategies can be employed to enhance team dynamics (see Carron et al. 2007; Paradis and Martin 2012 for an overview). Setting team goals has been found the most effective team-building intervention to develop or maintain group outcomes (Martin, Carron, and Burke 2009). It requires athletes and coaches to assess their current situation and circumstances (strengths and weaknesses) and appraise the approaches, processes, and resources required to achieve the group objectives. Subsequently, this serves to provide focus, direction, and motivation for athletes, unite members to work towards achieving a common goal, allow them to be more task and action orientated (Bloom, Stevens, and Wickwire 2003; Martin et al. 2009). However, it has been argued that in order for team goal setting to be effective, a combination of long-term and short-term goals, as well as process, performance, and outcome goals, should be set (see Paradis and Martin 2012).

Another team-building strategy to enhance group dynamics is to ensure that all team members understand and accept their role and responsibility on the team (Carron et al. 2007). There are a number of ways to achieve this (see Paradis and Martin 2012), including holding meetings between the coach and individual athletes, wherein both note their perceptions of their roles on the team and discuss and clarify any misunderstandings. Similarly, athletes can take it in turn to discuss each individual athlete's role on the team in a group forum; this can clarify and aid recognition of each member's role on the team. Establishing team norms or rules and boundaries can also serve to increase awareness of athletes' responsibilities, of what is expected from each as a team member. Norms can include unwritten rules about attending practice sessions on time or wearing the appropriate kit for training.

Fostering effective interpersonal relationships between coaches and athletes can improve interpersonal functioning among players. Opening and securing a channel of communication between coaches and athletes is the most critical way to enable athletes and coaches to get to know and understand each other (Jowett 2007). Thus, coaches and athletes should be encouraged to maintain open channels of communication in a supportive and non-judgemental environment, one where they can disclose and discuss concerns about the team (see Carron et al. 2007). Coaches can also maintain good relationships with their team by developing effective coaching behaviours through regular engagement in self-monitoring, behavioural feedback, and similar practices (see Smith and Smoll 2007). Self-monitoring helps raise coaches' awareness of their behaviours and interactions with their athletes. It encourages coaches to keep a record of their behaviours (e.g., number of times they provide reinforcement or encouragement or engage in punitive conduct towards the team) during practice and competitions. Behavioural feedback, on the other hand, consists in coaches' obtaining feedback from other staff members and athletes about their coaching behaviours.

Providing athletes opportunities to socialise and develop meaningful relationships with their teammates outside the sporting environment will also help foster closeness and commitment to the team and preventing social comparison, rivalry, and conflict. Likewise, athletes should be discouraged from making negative comments about each other or blaming each other for poor performances. Coaches and sport psychologists should facilitate structured and supportive forums wherein athletes can constructively raise and discuss concerns and conflicts. These forums can also be facilitated by trained, objective mediators such as sport psychologists or coaches and captains themselves (if they are not involved in the dispute). If the forum approach is preferred, the athletes should be informed and taught about identifying the type and source of conflict, as well as appropriate conflict resolution and management strategies and skills (Holt et al. 2012). Coaches may also want to consider providing a time frame for their players to deal with a conflict. One coach in Holt and colleagues' study revealed that he offers his players 24 to 48 hours to manage and resolve a conflict. Specifically, athletes are advised to wait 24 hours before acting on the conflict and must then discuss and resolve the conflict within the next 24. Moreover, coaches and other supporting staff should also avoid making normative comparisons and evaluating athletes in the public domain; failure to do so tends to reduce effort and enhance tension between team members (van de Pol, Kavussanu, and Ring 2012). Similarly, employing a team motto (e.g., 'we win as a team and lose as a team'), wearing identical team attire, travelling together, and sharing accommodation when playing away, as well as taking social outings away from the training environment, will also serve to unite members, create a sense of belonging within the team, and aid relationship maintenance.

Finally, developing mutual understanding has been suggested as a technique for developing optimal team functioning and preventing lack of understanding about team members' needs, motives, and feelings (see Carron et al. 2007; Pain and Harwood 2009; Paradis and Martin 2012). Athletes should be encouraged to disclose information about themselves to their teammates. Examples of the type of information they could share include how they got started in the current sport and reasons why they continue playing it (Dunn and Holt 2004). Feedback on such approaches has been favourable, with athletes reporting an enhanced understanding of themselves and their teammates and increased closeness and confidence in their teammates (see Dunn and Holt 2004; Pain and Harwood 2009).

The aforementioned strategies, while by no means exhaustive, can be employed either directly (i.e., the coach or sport psychologist implements them with the athletes) or indirectly (the sport psychologist works with the coach, who subsequently implements them). However, as both modes of delivery have been found equally effective, a mode that is compatible with the teams' needs should be employed (Martin et al. 2009; Paradis and Martin 2012).

2.6 Summary

Attention has been traditionally paid to the role of coaches in athletes' athletic and personal development. However, a growing body of research implicates peers and teammates in shaping the quality of athletes' sport experiences (e.g., Carron et al. 2002; Paradis et al. 2014; Vazou et al. 2005). Specifically, peers and teammates appear to have the capacity to positively and negatively influence affective, cognitive, and behavioural outcomes for the individual and the team. However, it is clear that the current status of the peer and teammate literature is limited by the frequent use of cross-sectional research designs. Thus, future endeavours aimed at furthering understanding of the influence of peer and teammate relationships should move beyond examining statistical associations and employ more rigorous methodologies such as experiments and longitudinal studies to ascertain the true nature and impact of peers and teammates on athletic and personal development.

2.7 Case study

2.7.1 Setting the scene

Luke, a 27-year-old lacrosse coach, was promoted to the position of head coach at his local county's men's side last season, after having assisted with the teams' coaching for the prior two years. Having coached the current squad, Luke has several concerns about the upcoming season just two months off. While he felt he got on well with the players last season, Luke is concerned about his squad's current dynamic and the effect it is having on their performance. Before the prior season, a number of well-liked and respected players had retired and were replaced with younger athletes from the reserve team. In his observations during the season, he noticed high levels of tension between the junior and senior teammates. When a number of junior players tried to outdo the senior teammates during training and competitions, the result was often arguments, fights, even injuries. Although Luke tried his best to resolve some of the issues, the younger players found it difficult to integrate with the rest of the team. They reported feeling unwanted and undervalued by the older players. They believed the senior players took an instant dislike to them because they had replaced some of their friends and that they were living in the shadow of the former players. There were often quips like 'Tom would have made that shot if he was here.' The older players, on the other hand, reported that the younger players were not committed to the team and did not adhere to its ethos. For example, the younger players were said to turn up late to training, to travel to competitions as a separate group rather than with the rest of the team, and to miss several arranged group-social activities, preferring to go out on their own or with other friends. Thus, towards the end of the season, Luke noted a clear division in the squad, poor team morale, and a decline in the team's performances, with the team losing several matches to less able teams.

2.7.2   Assessing the situation

Luke's situation, which centres on the functioning of the group, highlights a number of areas of concern. Specifically, it is evident that some level of tension and conflict exists within the group, especially between the younger and older players. It has proven difficult for the new players to smoothly integrate into an already formed team, especially as they have replaced respected and well-liked members. Moreover, it is evident from the comments of the junior players that they are hurt by the comparisons the senior players made to the retired athletes, causing them to feel unappreciated and disparaged. These feelings might be fuelling their subsequent behaviours (not attending social activities, limiting the time spent with the team). However, their actions are interpreted by the senior players as a lack of compliance with the team's ethos and a lack of commitment to the team. Consequently, it seems an 'us vs them' divide has been created within the team, a divide impacting not only the team's performances but also the quality of the team's functioning. Thus, it seems critical to ensure that Luke and his players are equipped with the appropriate strategies to manage and resolve these issues before there is further decline in the team's performance and functioning.

What can Luke, the coaching staff, and the team members do to ensure that they operate optimally as a team so as to prevent further decline in their performance and group functioning?

2.7.3   Specific strategies that can be used to help Luke

Several strategies could be used by Luke, the coaching staff, sport psychologists, and the team members themselves to develop and foster effective group functioning and subsequently enhance performance.

- Raise an awareness of the current ill feelings among the team members in a group discussion forum prior to the beginning of the new season. Forum sessions can be directly facilitated by the coach or indirectly via a consultant. During the sessions team members should be encouraged to disclose and discuss their concerns about the team in a supportive and non-judgemental environment, with a mediator overseeing and controlling the session.
- Develop mutual understanding between team members. Encourage team members to disclose personal information about themselves to the team. For example, share stories about how they got into the sport, what

motivated them to play for the current team, and why they continue to play. The sessions aim to promote understanding about team members' needs, motives, and feelings and foster a sense of unity. When generated, the enhanced unity and closeness could be used to formulate a team motto, one that is inclusive and reflective of all players.

- Establish team norms prior to the season, with the upcoming season being perceived as a 'fresh start' or 'clean slate'. The development of norms raises team members' awareness of what is expected from them and how they should behave. The team, along with the coaching staff, could develop rules that everyone has to adhere to, as well as appropriate punishment for when rules are not followed. They can be referred to as the 'ten commandments'. Norms may include that all players must turn up 15 minutes before the start of the training session (i.e., so they can get changed and be on the pitch on time), travel together to away games, and attend a number of social activities over the course of the season. Those that fail to comply could be financially penalised or required to do 50 burpees prior to the training session or even wash the teams' kit. It is important that no penalties imposed demoralise or demean team members. Agreed norms should be printed and provided to all players for them to sign and keep (a form of contract, as it were). Additionally, printouts of the team norms should also be displayed around the training ground so that players are aware of them.

- Set team goals. Again, this could be done prior to the season's beginning. Together, players and coaches should assess their strengths and weakness as a team. Guided by this, coaches and players should collectively formulate three to five goals, both long and short term, relating to process, performance, and outcome and using the SMART/INSPIRE principles. When formulating goals, it would be advantageous for the players to sit with individuals they may not have much contact with. During these sessions, team members should also be encouraged to think about what is needed to achieve the group objectives (e.g., strategies they are going to adopt, obstacles they face and how they are going to overcome them, resources required to achieve their goal). Once the goals have been formulated, they should also be distributed to the players, as well as displayed around the training ground and in players' lockers. Doing this will serve to remind the players what they are working towards. Additionally, it is important that progress is monitored regularly during the season.

- At the start of the season, Luke should use group discussions to ensure that all team members accept and understand their role on the team. For example, each team member (including Luke) can take the 'hot seat' while the other team members in turn comment on what that person's role is on the team and what that person brings to the team. This serves to clarify the role of every player and to recognise and appreciate each player's unique contribution.

- Encourage Luke to engage in self-monitoring and behavioural feedback over the course of the season. Both these practices can serve to raise his awareness of his coaching behaviours, as it has been reported that coaches are often unaware of how they behave. Luke can keep a log of his behaviours during practices and competitions and record the number of times he exhibited positive reinforcement, acted punitively, ignored mistakes made by players, and the like. Additionally, Luke can gain feedback on his coaching behaviours from other members of the coaching staff. Specifically, using the Coach Behaviours Assessment Scale (CBAS; see Smith and Smoll 2007), his coaching staff can record the number of times Luke engages in positive and negative coaching behaviours. Luke can foster effective relationships with his players by having regular one-on-one meetings with them and discussing their progress or any concerns they have, whether on or off the field.
- Engage in team-building exercises. This can take the form of either attending a two-day or weeklong military-style team-building course or carrying out recognised team exercises under supervision. For example, team members can participate in the so-called birthday balance beam, wherein team members stand shoulder to shoulder on a balance beam and attempt to rearrange themselves in order of birthday without losing their balance and falling off (Bloom, Loughead, and Newin 2008). Such exercises aim to promote communication, problem solving, and teamwork.
- Educate senior members of the team, such as the captain and vice-captain, about how their leadership behaviours affect group functioning – specifically, the significance of working hard, of being able to instruct (i.e., about skills, techniques, tactics), support, understand, and motivate their teammates so as to foster not only a positive team environment but also harmonious relationships with teammates – whereas their engaging in autocratic behaviours negatively influences the team environment.
- Promote engagement in social activities away from the sport and the training ground. Encourage athletes to go out for dinner once a month as a group, go bowling, or play pool. Given the level of conflict and tension evident in the team, it is important that such social outings do not involve alcohol.

2.8   Further study and recommended reading

The following literature is recommended for further reading on key concepts addressed in this chapter.

- Carron, A. V., Eys, M. A., and Burke, S. M. (2007). Team cohesion: Nature, correlates and development. In S. Jowett and D. Lavallee (eds), *Social Psychology in Sport* (91–101). Champaign, IL: Human Kinetics.

- Ntoumanis, N., Vazou, S., and Duda, J. (2007). Peer created motivational climate. In S. Jowett and D. Lavallee (eds), *Social Psychology in Sport* (145–156). Champaign, IL: Human Kinetics.
- Paradis, K. F., Carron, A. V., and Martin, L. J. (2014). Athlete perceptions of intragroup conflict in sport teams. *Sport and Exercise Psychology Review*, 10(3), 4–18.

Additionally, reading of the following relevant documents is recommended. They address factors not covered in this chapter that may be central to understanding the effect of teammates on athletic and psychosocial development.

- Carron, A. V., and Brawley, L. R. (2008). Group dynamics in sport and physical activity. In T. S. Horn (ed.), *Advances in Sport Psychology* (214–237). Champaign, IL: Human Kinetics.
- Harwood, C., Spray, C. M., and Keegan, R. (2008). Achievement goal theories in sport. In T. S. Horn (ed.), *Advances in Sport Psychology* (158–185). Champaign, IL: Human Kinetics.
- LaVoi, N. M. (2007). Interpersonal communication and conflict in the coach-athlete relationship. In S. Jowett and D. Lavallee (eds), *Social Psychology in Sport* (29–40). Champaign, IL: Human Kinetics.
- Smith, A. L. (2007). Youth peer relationships in sport. In S. Jowett and D. Lavallee (eds), *Social Psychology in Sport* (41–54). Champaign, IL: Human Kinetics.

3   Competition

3.1   Learning objectives

This chapter examines the context of competition in sport and the role opponents can play in the quality of athletes' experiences. It focuses on the importance of competition in a variety of forms and how groups' and individuals' subjective perception can increase or decrease athletes' sense of their chances of success or failure – possibly even humiliation, injury, or fame. The key learning objectives are:

- to define competition and understand how competition can be applied to sport as both a process and an underpinning structure;
- to examine how attribution theory can explain how individuals evaluate their own success and the influence this has on their perceptions of sport and their own ability;
- to use the schematic model of person perception to examine how athletes make judgements about their opponents and to look as well at how the continuum model of impression formation and the realistic accuracy model explain the use of information sources to ensure the accuracy of these judgements;
- to investigate the concept of intergroup conflict, drawing upon realistic conflict theory to understand the origin of conflict, and to use social identity theory and relative deprivation theory to explain why competing groups grow to view each other in negative terms;
- to look at how a coach or psychologist can manage a team's expectations to minimise negative consequences of being involved in a one-sided competition.

3.2   Introduction to the context

From playground football with jumpers for goalposts to the FIFA World Cup Final, competition is an integral part of all aspects of sport culture. The term 'competition' is used to refer to a range of different situations in sport. Individuals could be competing against others (either individually or as a team), against themselves, against the stopwatch, or in comparison to a previous record. For example, a gymnast might compete individually, but her score could also contribute to that of her national squad; or in a marathon, while only one runner can cross the finishing line first, other runners might be competing against specific individuals or trying to achieve a personal-best time. What all sports have in common is some level of competition, and competitors generally want to win. The subject of competition and the desire to win have generated lively debate and not a small amount of controversy in academia, physical education, sport development, and elite sport. It has been claimed that competition can generate anxiety and aggression, cause jealousy and conflict, create individuals who value winning over playing, or even cause some individuals to drop out of sport altogether (e.g., Allender, Cowburn, and Foster 2006). Conversely, it has also been suggested that competition in sport can prepare individuals for the real world, build character, and provide an overall positive experience (e.g., Skinner and Brewer 2004).

Competition can be defined both as the process of sport and as an infrastructure that provides the organisation underpinning sport. When defined as a process, competition is the method used to ascertain success through direct comparison of individuals' achievements when they perform the same physical activity under the same conditions (Kohn 1992). Competition is therefore the process that identifies winners and losers. This definition can be further refined by dividing it into zero-sum games and non-zero-sum games (Harrington 2008). A zero-sum game is a type of competition in which the success of one individual or group is exactly balanced by the losses of another individual or group. That is, the gains of one side summed with the losses of the other will equal zero. Sports that fall into this category of competition are termed strictly competitive; typical examples are invasion games such as football and rugby. In these sports there can be only either one winner and one loser or a draw. Non-zero-sum games are a type of competition where the sum of the gains and losses of those involved do not equal zero. Referred to as competitive or, rather confusingly, non-competitive sports, one example is athletics. In a 100-metre race, while only one individual ends in first place, there will often be silver and bronze medal positions, various individuals attempting to achieve qualifying times, and others seeking to attain a personal-best time or a national record.

Competition when defined as an infrastructure underpinning sport equates to the rules determining how rewards are distributed amongst the individuals involved (Kohn 1992). This means that besides determining winners and losers, competition is also the reward structure that determines what individuals can potentially gain from being involved in sport and therefore impacts on the relationships between competing individuals. Resources available in terms of reward are finite; how they are distributed is determined on the basis of how well each individual does compared to others. In the example of the 100-metre race, while those who finished in gold, silver, and bronze medalling positions can all be said to have won, they receive differing amounts of reward in terms of money, prestige, fame, or personal influence. While it is important to understand that competition is a part of sport at all levels, there are situations where the reward structure promotes equality as opposed to inequality (Kohn 1992). In these circumstances individualised standards of achievement are applied. As achievement no longer depends on outperforming others, there is no longer a need for direct comparison. Any perceived rewards from competing are earned by a fixed level of performance. In these circumstances one competitor can help another without negatively impacting his or her own chances of success. This reward structure is most readily applicable to non-zero-sum or non-competitive games and at amateur or recreational levels of sport. For example, in a marathon the majority of runners are not trying to win; instead they most frequently have a specific time they wish to complete the race in. It does not hinder them to share training advice with other runners in the race. In these circumstances individuals can achieve their specific time; everyone can 'win'. An example from professional sport would be a qualifying race in a motor sport, such as Formula 1, where each driver must complete a lap under a fixed time. This type of reward structure is also applied to zero-sum games such as football and tennis. Generally this is done with children to de-emphasise the competitive or comparative elements of sport by, for example, not keeping a running score during a game and rewarding everyone equally for effort and involvement.

3.3   How individuals judge their own success

Determining winners and losers in sport is generally straightforward and based upon the nature of the competition and the rules of the particular sport. Determining the success of individuals is less straightforward. It is possible for individuals to lose a match, game, or competition and still believe they have been successful. Success is a matter of an individual's perception of a range of factors. Attribution theory is a conceptual framework that explains how individuals and teams evaluate levels of success and failure (Weiner 1992); an attribution in sport is the perceived cause for and explanation of the outcomes of a competition. It is important to understand how athletes attribute their success or failure. A given individual's perception of the causes of why he succeeded or failed during competition will in turn determine his levels of motivation to engage in that form of competition in the future. As such, attribution theory enables us to understand the consequences of both success and failure for individuals and teams.

The three-dimensional model of attribution (Weiner 1992) proposes that individuals undergo a cognitive evaluation of the casual properties of an event (see Figure 3.1). This then influences future actions in similar situations. The cognitive evaluation is based upon three categories: stability (stable or unstable), controllability (controllable or uncontrollable), and locus of causality (internal or external). Stability is related to an individual's expectations of the consistency of similar situations in the future; for example, a cross-country run on a particularly rainy day. As there is no guarantee that during the next competition it will also be raining, this would be referred to as an unstable factor. Controllability is related to individuals' expectations of their ability to deliver a similar outcome in the future. For example, before a competition a weightlifter puts in extra training hours and then wins the competition. In the future, as the weightlifter could again choose to put in extra training hours, this would be referred to as a controlled factor. Finally, locus of causality refers to whether individuals believe they themselves caused the outcomes (internal) or others caused them (external). A gymnastics squad member who performed poorly but still received a medal in the group event because of the squad's overall combined score would know he won only because of external assistance. As Figure 3.1 shows, these three categories create a taxonomy for attributing outcomes. In the example of the cross-country run, where a runner wins due to poor weather, we can see all three categories. It is unstable, as the runner cannot guarantee it will rain at the next race. It is uncontrollable, as the runner cannot predict the weather. It is external, as the weather that hindered others runners is external to the actual runner. Due to this, the runner may have doubts about her ability to win the next race. Conversely, in the example where the weightlifter puts in extra training hours before a competition, the three categories appear more positively. It is stable, as the number of hours of training is predictable. The number is controllable, as the weightlifter can decide what he wants to do. Finally it is internal, as the number of training hours is linked with the weightlifter's own motivation and effort. Due to this, the weightlifter is likely to be confident about his ability to win the next competition.

	Internal		External	
	Stable	Unstable	Stable	Unstable
Controlled	Typical effort	Unusual effort	Consistent help/hindrance from others	Unusual help/hindrance from others
Uncontrollable	Ability	Mood	Task difficulty	Luck

Figure 3.1 *An illustration of Weiner's attribution theory*

3.3.1 Egocentric bias

Individuals are not objective in their beliefs and are prone to making subjective errors when they attempt to understand the world around them. Some individuals make consistent and predictable errors in judgement. Known as an attribution bias, this is a systematic error made when individuals attempt to explain their own or others' behaviours (Funder 1987). These biases come in a variety of forms; for instance, the self-serving bias: the tendency of individuals to attribute their success to internal, stable, controllable factors and their failures to external, unstable, uncontrollable factors (De Michele, Gansneder, and Solomon 1998). The self-serving bias has been called a means of protecting self-esteem. An athlete might say he won a competition because of his skill, effort, or fitness and so increase his motivation and confidence. Conversely, another athlete might say he lost a competition because of poor conditions, unfair officiating, or bad luck; by placing the blame on others, he reduces his shame and protects his pride. Additionally, high achievers in sport tend to have a self-serving bias, while low achievers, who tend to attribute success to external factors, find sport to be less satisfying and so become more likely to drop out (De Michele, Gansneder, and Solomon 1998). It would seem to be in athletes' best interest to have this self-serving bias. However, athletes who consistently ascribes losses to external factors may be less aware of their own weaknesses and therefore less likely to listen to criticism, take advice, or put in the required time and training to progress.

A second potential form of bias is the fundamental attribution error. This refers to an error in judgement in explaining the behaviours of other individuals, especially opponents. A fundamental attribution error reflects a tendency to attribute outcomes to internal dispositional factors rather than external situational factors (Funder 1987). An athlete who sees a fellow competitor trip and fall over a hurdle may be more likely to blame the mishap on that individual's clumsiness rather than a wet track or bad luck. While there are a variety of ways of explaining this phenomenon, the most applicable to sport is the just world hypothesis. This theory suggests that individuals make biased judgements because they want to believe people get what they deserve (Lerner and Miller 1977). In sport, individuals want to believe that hard work, training, skill, and a good strategy will allow them to succeed; hence they reason that anyone who does not succeed must not have put in the time and training required. An attribution error of this type can reinforce the belief that the world is controllable and therefore reduce the perceived threat that random factors could impact one's own success. Essentially, athletes do not want to believe that accidents, injuries, and bad luck could happen as easily to them as to their opponents. Another form of bias, hostile attribution bias, reflects a tendency to attribute others' behaviour to hostile rather than benign intentions (Camodeca and Goossens

2005). For example, a rugby player who suffers an injury when he is tackled might believe the opposing player intentionally fouled him rather than accept that it was an accident. Some link this sort of bias to an increase of aggressive behaviour. That is, the injured rugby player might be more likely to respond with abusive language, tackle an opponent harder than necessary, or even purposefully attempt to injure the other player.

3.3.2 Self-efficacy

The outcome of individuals' judgement about success can play a key role in their belief in their ability and in their future involvement in sport. A sprinter who believes she won only because her opponent tripped is unlikely to have as high an opinion of her ability as one who believes she won because she was the better runner. This belief in one's capabilities, termed self-efficacy, is a form of situational confidence; it is what an individual believes he or she can accomplish in specific circumstances (Bandura 1997). It has been argued that individuals are more likely to be involved in sports where they have high self-efficacy and less likely to stay involved in sports where they have low self-efficacy. Self-efficacy therefore has the potential to influence individuals' ability to learn new skills, their motivation to train, and their performance in sport competitions.

According to Bandura (1997), self-efficacy is the result of four sets of antecedents: performance outcomes, vicarious experiences, verbal persuasion, and physiological feedback. Performance outcomes are past experiences; more successful experiences increase self-efficacy, less successful ones decrease it. A high jumper who made a particular height in training is going to be more confident about achieving that height in competition than an athlete who failed to do so. Vicarious experiences come from watching others perform. An individual who sees another succeed may feel more confident about completing the same task. The important factor in this is the perceived similarity between the two individuals. An amateur athlete will be less confident about a task after seeing a professional succeed than she would have been if she had seen another amateur accomplish the same task. Conversely, watching a similar athlete fail can lower self-efficacy but watching a very different athlete fail is unlikely to do so. For example, a professional footballer is unlikely to have lower self-efficacy after seeing an amateur footballer perform a poor training drill. Verbal persuasion pertains to the encouragement and discouragement given by others. This could be a coach telling an athlete that he did well or that losing a competition was not the athlete's fault. Finally, physiological feedback is about how individuals interpret the emotional arousal experienced undertaking a task. Some elite footballers would interpret the elevated heart rate and respiration experienced during an important tournament as anxiety or fear while others would interpret it as excitement.

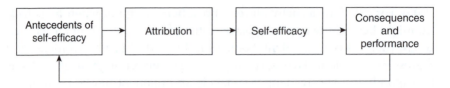

Figure 3.2   *An illustration of Gist and Mitchell's theory: the relationship of attributions, self-efficacy, and performance*

It is important to understand the links between attribution, self-efficacy, and performance. While it has been argued that self-efficacy results from performance outcomes, vicarious experiences, verbal persuasion, and physiological feedback, others think this relationship is moderated by attributions (Gist and Mitchell 1992). The attribution process would therefore play a key regulating role between the four categories of antecedents and self-efficacy, which then affects performance outcomes, which in turn generate a new set of antecedents (see Figure 3.2). For example, an athlete who attributed past performance success to luck or other external factors is likely to have lower self-efficacy than an athlete who attributed past success to skill and fitness. Similarly, vicarious experiences are less likely to increase the self-efficacy of athletes who attribute the performance success of someone they are watching to external factors. Verbal persuasion provides a coach or significant other the greatest opportunity to limit the potentially negative effect of attributions on self-efficacy. A coach should attempt to motivate and encourage the athlete by providing feedback on what he or she does well. Feedback should focus on linking successes to internal, stable, controllable factors, such as telling athletes they performed well because of recent increases in skill or fitness. Verbal persuasion can also be used to alter an athlete's perception of physiological feedback. An athlete who perceives physiological arousal negatively (e.g., as anxiety) is less likely to have positive attributions. A coach or psychologist could work alongside an athlete to positively reframe perceptions of physiological arousal experienced during competition.

3.3.3   Learned helplessness

Athletes are not successful all of the time; no one wins every competition. Some athletes will protect their self-esteem by attributing a loss to bad luck or other unstable external factors. Others may manage their motivation to work harder by attributing a loss to insufficient training or another internal but controllable factor. Although athletes may experience the same or very similar events, how they each explain these events to themselves will dictate how they progress. Not all patterns of attribution are constructive. Learned helplessness is a mental state where individuals have little or no self-efficacy; they explain their failures using stable and uncontrollable factors (Peterson, Maier, and Seligman 1995). They believe they cannot control the situation and therefore cannot influence the success or failure of the outcome. For example, a football player who consistently misses penalty kicks in championship matches may attribute it to an inability to control his nerves. Additionally, 'such individuals will often also attribute their few successes to luck or other external, unstable, and uncontrollable factors; this in turn reinforces belief in their lack of ability and control over the outcome of a competition. This can lead to a self-fulfilling prophecy, where the athlete feels unable to avoid the situation and unable to influence the outcome. The athlete will therefore fail to put in the effort that would allow them to succeed. Learned helplessness can be very general – an individual might believe he is terrible at all sports – but it is more likely to apply to a narrower, more specific area' (Hiroto and Seligman 1975). This could be a particular skill – perhaps a set piece in a game sport or a difficult element of a gymnastics routine – or a specific situation, such as a high-level competition or a match against a particular opponent. Learned helplessness is almost always a consequence of previous bad experiences, where the individual has 'learned' she cannot control the situation (Peterson, Maier, and Seligman 1995). It leads to feelings of embarrassment and a lack of effort; the athlete may even actively work to avoid being placed in a similar situation. Getting athletes to realise that they can exert control over these situations, that failure is not the only potential outcome, can be a long and difficult process and require the input of a dedicated coach and often a sport psychologist.

3.3.4 Self-handicapping

Individuals who believe they are going to perform badly or be unsuccessful will often create excuses to justify their failures. For example, if an athlete feels he is going to perform badly in a competition, he might make up an excuse for his potential failure, such as telling his coach that he feels tired or his muscles are sore from a prior training session. This type of behaviour, known as self-handicapping, is a process used by some individuals to protect their self-esteem from being harmed by lack of success (Leary and Shepperd 1986). But self-handicapping can also be a process by which individuals enhance their standing with others. An athlete who wins a competition when he has already told others he is tired and sore will seem more impressive than one who said he was at his very best. Self-handicapping can thus be seen in a positive light, a bias in attributions to protect individuals from the consequences of failure and enhance the benefits of success. However, self-handicapping is not restricted to claimed handicaps; some individuals go so far as to create a real impediment to performance (Leary and Shepperd 1986). Known as behavioural self-handicapping, this process has significant negative ramifications for performance. For example, a boxer who believes he may fail to make the qualifying weight for a match may actually cheat on his diet, thereby creating an excuse for failing to make weight but at the same time significantly reducing his chance of succeeding. While behavioural self-handicapping still acts as a self-protection mechanism for an individual's self-esteem, its cost is a reduced chance of success. That an individual would engage in this type of behaviour seems strange, especially when the purpose of a sports competition is to achieve success of some sort, be it winning or simply playing to the best of one's abilities (Chen et al. 2008). However, as those involved in sport are required to openly display their physical abilities, any ineptitude or lack of success is readily apparent to an observer (Ommundsen 2001). Thus, sport creates an environment where individuals, feeling pressure to succeed, may be more likely to feel that they need a way to divert blame for any failures. At the same time sport is an environment where many claimed excuses are readily transparent. For example, an athlete claiming an injury may need to have it verified by a physiotherapist or club doctor. Another example would be a footballer claiming to be tired from a previous training session. If other players who completed the training do not complain of tiredness, his claim becomes a weak excuse and might even damage his self-esteem, as he is admitting to a weakness other players do not have. Therefore, as claimed excuses may not justify lack of success, some athletes turn to actual behavioural self-handicapping to create verifiable excuses to explain any potential failures (Chen et al. 2008).

3.4 How we perceive opponents

A key aspect of sports competition is the opponent. This could be another runner in a race, an opposing team in rugby, or the boxer across the ring waiting for the bell. The opponent's skill, fitness, and knowledge obviously play a key role in the outcome of a competition. An opponent who is a faster runner or a stronger power lifter decreases the chance of a successful outcome. However, the opponent's objective abilities are not all that can influence the outcome of a competition. An individual's subjective perception of her opponents' abilities can also significantly influence her chances of success or failure. Known as interpersonal perception, this process is related to how individuals view one another and to the judgements they make based on both verbal and non-verbal information. It has been suggested that individuals who enter a competitive sports environment will actively seek to understand the challenges of that environment so as to adapt to the situation and predict its likely outcome (cf. Fiske and Taylor 1991).

The influence of interpersonal perception on an individual in sport can be understood using the schematic model of person perception (Warr and Knapper 1968). An individual interacting with another can respond in three ways: the attributive response, the affective response, and the expectancy response. The attributive response comes first; it concerns the perceptions an individual has about the characteristics of another. Greenlees (2007) has suggested that in sport the concerns are an opponent's skills, fitness, and mental attitude. The judgements may concern how the opponent is currently behaving (e.g., 'the other runner is putting in maximum effort') or reflect more stable attributes (e.g., 'the other runner is fast and has good endurance'). The affective response concerns how an individual reacts emotionally to the attributive judgement about another; potentially it can directly affect behavioural reaction. Greenlees (2007) suggests that in sport an athlete who perceives an opponent as stronger, faster, or more skilled may react with anxiety, fear, jealousy, or dislike. Conversely an athlete who perceives an opponent as weak, slow, and untalented might react with increased confidence or perhaps derision or contempt for the opponent. Finally, the combination of the attributive and affective responses produces the expectancy response. The individual uses the judgements made about another to predict how he or she is likely to behave and how events are likely to unfold. Greenlees (2007) suggests that an athlete who has judged his opponent to be of a higher standard than himself is likely to believe that the competition will be one sided, overly challenging, and unlikely to be successful. An athlete holding this view might well be less motivated, put in less effort, and be less likely to succeed – regardless of how accurate the judgement of the opponent actually was.

In a sports competition judgements made by one athlete about another can directly influence how the athlete reacts, the effort she puts forth, her expectations of success, and how she evaluates that success. This in turn can influence her chances of victory and enhance or hinder her performance. For example, an athlete who underestimates her opponent may put in only minimal effort and lose when she should have won. Another athlete may overestimate an opponent, put in maximum effort, win, and then feel much more confident and satisfied with her victory because she perceives it to have been against the odds.

The accuracy of the judgements one individual makes about another thus seem an important aspect of interpersonal perception in sport. There are two proposed mechanisms by which individuals make such judgements: schema-driven processes and data-driven processes (Fiske and Taylor 1991). The schema-driven process describes judgements as based upon previously acquired information, schema gathered in the past about the individual being judged or from similar situations with other individuals. For example, a boxer fighting a bigger opponent can infer that the opponent is stronger and more powerful because in the past the boxer has fought bigger individuals who turned out to be so. This process would seem ideal, as the individual making the judgement relies on minimal information and can quickly judge something that may be important in the often time-restricted environment of sport. However, if these schemas are inaccurate, they can have disastrous consequences. For example, a boxer who believes his bigger opponent will be slow and clumsy and bases his tactics on this information may discover, moments after the bell rings, that the other boxer is fast and agile as well as large. The alternative is the data-driven process, which concerns judgements based on information acquired as the interaction with the other individual unfolds. Returning to our example of the boxer fighting the larger opponent; while the boxer might have earlier fought large opponents who were slow or clumsy, in this situation he relies upon actual evidence that this opponent is also slow and clumsy. Using information he gathers from his opponent's posture and movements, the boxer forms the most accurate judgement possible. While this process seems superior to the schema-driven process, it can be slow and require much more thought. Time and concentration may not be abundant resources in a sports environment, and a boxer who spends too much time judging his opponent's abilities might not be able to react quickly enough during the actual competition. However, these two processes need not be mutually exclusive; Fiske and Neuberg (1990) have suggested that individuals use both processes in conjunction. In their continuum model of impression formation, they argue that individuals will first attempt to categorise others using a schema, but an individual with access to sufficient information who is motivated to use a more data-driven process will do so. In competitive situations where desired outcomes depend on successful interaction, such as outperforming an opponent in a sports competition, individuals are more likely to use the data-driven schema (Ruscher and Fiske 1990). In time- or information-restricted environments, however, individuals favour a schema-driven process (Fiske and Neuberg 1990). For example, at the beginning of a game a tennis player may make quick judgements about his opponent based upon previous matches with the opponent or similar situations. As the game progresses and the tennis player gathers more information about his opponent, he will make more refined data-driven judgements.

Although schema-driven processes seem to offer quicker but less accurate judgements than data-driven processes, maximising the accuracy of interpersonal judgements is not so simple as encouraging the use of one process rather than another. The bulk of research on interpersonal perception suggests that, more often than not, interpersonal judgements are wrong (Krueger and Funder 2004). Funder (2012) describes the conditions under which an accurate judgement about another can be made. He suggests that for a judgement to be accurate, four conditions must be met: relevance, availability, detection, and utilisation. This is called the realistic accuracy model (see Figure 3.3). In an accurate judgement the person being judged displays relevant behaviour. For example, a footballer cannot know that the opponent he has been assigned to mark is a skilled player unless he observes the

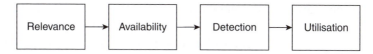

Figure 3.3 *An illustration of Funder's realistic accuracy model*

opponent with the ball. Second, the person being judged must display this behaviour somewhere that is available to the individual making the judgement. If the opponent has displayed skill with the ball only during training or during matches that our footballer has not seen, he will be unable to make use of this information. Next, the information must be detected. If our footballer is not paying attention to his opponent or his perception is impaired (e.g., another player gets in the way), he will not be able to use that information to form his judgement. Finally, the information must be used correctly. If our footballer either knows little about skilled play (lack of knowledge) or fails to give any thought to what he has observed (lack of motivation), he will not be able to make an accurate judgement about his opponent. The realistic accuracy model provides a useful framework for understanding the conditions under which an accurate judgement can be made. If a relevant behaviour is not displayed, not available, not detected, or not utilised, an accurate judgement is simply a matter of luck. All four conditions must be met for purposeful accurate judgements of another individual.

While judgements athletes make about others have a large impact potential on competitive success, relatively little work has been done to understand this. Researchers have shown that individuals hold stereotypes or make schema-driven judgements based on sport type (Sadalla, Linder, and Jenkins 1988), athletes' race (Stone, Perry, and Darley 1997), and gender (Lorimer and Jowett 2010). For example, Stone, Perry, and Darley (1997) have shown that individuals who believe a basketball player to be a black American rate him as having more athletic talent and less sport-specific knowledge than one they believe to be a white American despite the fact that all the other information they were given was identical. Greenlees (2007) has highlighted that while athletes might use similar stereotypes to make judgements during competition, it is important to directly observe how these judgements influence the progress and outcome of an actual sports competition. Greenlees and colleagues (2005) have shown that athletes' body language plays a key role in other athletes' attributive responses. When athletes display positive body language, they are perceived as more assertive, competent, and relaxed. Greenlees and colleagues also suggested that these judgements influence the expectancy responses in athletes during competition. They demonstrated that individuals asked to rate their confidence in defeating different opponents were likely to rate their chance of success lower if the opponent displayed positive rather than negative body language. Additionally they found that those opponents who wore sport-specific rather than general athletic clothing caused individuals to rate their chance of success even lower. This would suggest that presenting the image of a confident athlete who is familiar with the sport has the greatest potential impact on an opponent. Athletes can therefore use body language and attire to create a desired impression in opponents: to impress and intimidate their opponents and hide the individual's own ability in order to encourage complacency.

3.5   Intergroup conflict

Sports competitions are inherently about conflict. Individuals compete for victory, affirmation, fame, trophies, money. Conflicts occur when there is incongruence between the goals or interests of those involved. Nowhere is this more apparent than in team/invasion sports (e.g., football, rugby, hockey) Team/invasion sports are invariably zero-sum games. For one team to win the other team must lose. This type of conflict, referred to as intergroup conflict, is defined as a situation in which two or more groups take antagonistic actions toward one another to control a mutually important outcome (Eidelson and Eidelson 2003). While in sport this is most frequently expressed in team/invasion games, it is not limited to this domain. In many sports where athletes perform individually, they actually compete as part of a squad (e.g., gymnastics). Even in sports where individuals are not part of a squad, they often perform at a competition as a representative of a club, region, or nation (e.g., the Olympic games).

3.5.1   Group identity

To understand how groups work in competitive situations, it is necessary to understand how groups form and function as a whole (see Ch. 2). However, identity, more than any other factor, is what drives group behaviours in these situations. Groups have what is known as a collective identity – one formed from the cognitive and affective connections individuals have with the broader group and their shared ideology, motivations, and goals (Polletta and Jasper 2001). Over time, the individual members of a group develop a series of behavioural norms – shared expectations and evaluations about correct ways of behaving. This collective identity and these behavioural norms underpin the behaviours of the individuals in a group rather than the individual beliefs they may espouse in other contexts. What this means is that an individual's behaviour may differ radically when acting as part of a group and when acting alone. For example, an individual who believes that cheating is wrong will generally be honest in day-to-day life, but when playing football as part of a team, he may regard taking a dive and claiming a foul as both acceptable and appropriate behaviour. Social identity theory (Tajfel and Turner 1979) offers an explanation for such disparate actions. It suggests that individuals' sense of self derives in part from the social groups to which they perceive themselves as belonging (e.g., a sports team, subculture, race, nationality). Once individuals perceive themselves as belonging to a group, they derive self-esteem from membership in the group and will take action to preserve the group and the benefits they gain from it. This social identification has three stages; categorisation, identification, and comparison. Categorisation is the process of defining individuals by putting them into categories and giving them general labels. For example, this individual is a footballer and that one is a gymnast. This includes labelling ourselves; self-image is associated with the labels we give ourselves. Identification is the process whereby we use these labels and categories to associate ourselves with various groups. This creates two groupings: in-groups, groups we identify with, and out-groups, those we don't identify with. Certain footballers will see themselves as belonging to a particular club, the in-group, and will not identify with footballers belonging to a rival team, the out-group. Finally, comparison is the process where individuals compare their in-group to an out-group, most frequently favouring their in-group. For example, a footballer will believe it is better to belong to his team than the rival club, as this promotes a higher level of self-esteem.

3.5.2   Intergroup perceptions

Identifying with a group creates a potential bias in how we view ourselves and other groups, including attributions we make about our group's and other groups' behaviours. The first bias, in-group favouritism, includes allocation of resources and how positively we evaluate the actions of others (Taylor and Doria 1981). For example, a rugby player is likely to judge a fellow teammate's hard tackle as a firm but fair challenge for the ball. Such favouritism also covers how individuals judge the success of others. Athletes are more likely to attribute the success of their team and of teammates to internal, stable, and controllable factors such as talent and skill while ascribing failure to external, unstable factors such as biased officiating. A second bias, out-group negativity, could also influence individuals' perceptions of group behaviours (Tajfel and Turner 1979). For example, the same rugby player is likely to judge an opposing player's hard tackle as an overly aggressive and unfair challenge. While in-group favouritism is based upon a collective identity and underpinned by the need to preserve self-esteem, out-group negativity may be based upon a perceived dissimilarity between groups; the greater the dissimilarity, the greater the negativity (Struch and Schwartz 1989). For example, a team of male footballers might exhibit a degree of out-group negativity to another male football team but is likely to exhibit even greater negativity to a female football team.

The combination of in-group favouritism and out-group negativity creates an increasing bias in intergroup perceptions, reinforcing individuals' self-identification with a group while increasing the perceived dissimilarities between themselves and other groups. This creates polarised perceptions that can lead to increased competition, aggression, even outright hostility. First, individuals perceive their in-group as doing no wrong (Pinter et al. 2003). Group members grow increasingly positive about each other while in conflict with another group. A football team might feel that its own behaviour is beyond reproach, that it is a skilled and talented team, and that officiating decisions against it are unfair. Second, individuals perceive the out-group as able to do no right (Pinter et al. 2003). The players on a football team might feel that their opponents are unskilled and untalented, that the referee is favouring them, and that they are getting away with unacceptable behaviour. The players might then use these perceptions to condone their own borderline or rule-breaking actions. For example, a footballer might believe that diving and claiming a foul is acceptable because the other team is going to cheat anyway, and so the playing field needs to be levelled. This justification may even go so far as intentional fouls or borderline violence against the out-group. Finally, individuals perceive their in-group as superior and most deserving (Eidelson and Eidelson 2003). The footballers might feel they are more talented and have worked harder than everyone else and so deserve to win. Such simplistic thinking can create tension and even anger when these perceptions are not upheld. Players who feel they deserve to win are likely to become frustrated if their team is losing, and this may cause increased aggression as they attempt to exert their perceived dominance over the other team.

3.5.3 Intergroup aggression

Wildschut and colleagues (2003) have suggested that a significantly higher level of competitiveness is displayed between groups than between individuals. This discontinuity effect, as it is called, suggests that the cooperative behaviours individuals exhibit become overshadowed by the competitive orientation of the group. For example, individual gymnasts may be pleasant and friendly towards each other, but when in a competition, such as the Olympics, their identification with their own nationality heightens competition between them and gymnasts from rival nations. Realistic conflict theory states that intergroup aggression arises from the struggle for important resources or conflicting goals (Jackson 1993). So in sport, athletes compete for limited opportunities for victory and the associated recognition and rewards that come with it. This in turn creates greater identification with the team, squad, or national grouping and so increases negative perceptions and potential aggression towards other perceived groups. However, limited resources and dissimilar goals may not themselves be enough to explain why the competitiveness of some athletes and groups becomes aggression and hostility. Relative deprivation theory suggests that it is not the objective reality of winning and losing that causes increased conflict; instead, it is the social comparison between one group and another (Walker and Smith 2001). Unfavourable social comparison, such as individuals' shared belief that their group has not achieved what it deserves due to the actions of another, often more powerful group, can result in increased tensions. For example, a team whose players feel they have worked harder than every other team but have lost out on the championship only because another team has a richer financial backer is likely to feel increased ill will toward that team.

Although realistic conflict theory helps us understand the origin of conflict and social identity theory and relative deprivation theory help us understand how groups can grow to view each other in increasingly negative terms, they do not fully explain the jump between group values and why within a group an individual will display behaviours they would deem unacceptable in other circumstances. These disparate behaviour displays may be due in part to diffusion of responsibility, a phenomenon whereby an individual takes less responsibility for his or her actions or the actions of a group when others are present (Leary and Forsyth 1987). This phenomenon is combined in sport with high levels of group socialisation and group norms; they in turn allow individuals to act in a way that aligns with the groups' needs and beliefs even when they conflict with their own. Vallerand, Deshaies, and Cuerrier (1997) have demonstrated that when presented with a moral choice that will disadvantage their team (e.g., informing an official of a foul on their own side or lending equipment to an opposing team), individuals are less likely to act morally. Instead, they are more likely to choose to act immorally if it leads to a more positive outcome for the team. Additionally, Kavussanu and Ntoumanis (2003) demonstrated that the longer an individual had competed in a team sport such as football, hockey, or rugby, the lower his or her level of moral functioning in terms of judgements, intentions, and behaviours regarding their team. Team sport athletes are likely to experience greater levels of peer pressure to conform to group norms and are less likely to feel personally responsible for their actions, instead diffusing this responsibility to the team and team members. This may be more prevalent in team sports due to the more official and permanent nature of their groupings, stronger group identity (e.g., shared name and uniform), and high levels of socialisation compared to a 'looser' grouping such as a gymnastics squad. However, all groupings to some extent exhibit this phenomenon, and it is evident in sport squads, clubs, and national sides.

3.6   Dark side of competition

It can be argued that competition is not an inherently constructive aspect of sport (Kohn 1992). While the structure of sport cannot be separated from the idea of competition, in that there must be winners and losers, the competitive mindset, where individuals seek to validate their own superiority through defeating others, can produce negative consequences. It has been shown that individuals who focus exclusively on the outcome of sports competitions do well until their competence is challenged, at which point they develop self-doubts and lower self-efficacy, begin to demonstrate self-handicapping behaviours, and eventually drop out of sport (Cervelló, Escartí, and Guzmán 2007). An increase in competitive pressure, such as parents shouting from the sidelines, and an emphasis on winning have also been shown to increase anxiety and decrease enjoyment of sport (e.g., Brustad 1988). Additionally, the focus on competition can create group rivalry and intergroup aggression (Eidelson and Eidelson 2003). Unsurprisingly this is a touchy, personal area for many involved in sport and often a catalyst for heated debate. Some researchers argue that competitiveness is an inherent aspect of life, while others argue that the absence of competition is a prerequisite for real excellence (Kohn 1992). Perhaps an important distinction is that between competitiveness and hypercompetitiveness. Hypercompetitiveness is the need to compete and win at all costs as a means of maintaining self-worth. While competitiveness can promote productivity, efficacy, and efficiency (Mulvey and Ribbens 1999), hypercompetitive individuals will feel threatened if they find themselves losing; their response is likely to be debilitative for themselves and those around them. What is more, the potentially negative consequences of competitiveness can be offset by teaching individuals to be good losers, to accept a loss without allowing it to damage their self-esteem or motivation or prevent them from participating in future competitions (Emmison 1988). The effective use of competition and its potentially negative consequences must be carefully managed as part of the role of a coach (see Ch. 1) and of a team (see Ch. 2), and the desired outcomes of the competition context must be carefully considered (e.g., professional sport or physical education).

3.7   Summary

Competition forms an important part of sport. It is the process by which success is judged and the framework used for the assignment of rewards. How individuals judge their own success has profound implications for their perceived ability, satisfaction, and continued participation in sport. The way competition influences individuals is firmly based upon interpersonal and intergroup perceptions. Those participating in sport need to carefully assess their perceptions of why they and others succeed or fail. Additionally, they must be aware of the subjectivity in how they view teammates and competitors and of the connections between the two. As competition has the potential to be both beneficial and harmful to those involved in sport, it must be carefully managed. This case study discusses specific strategies that a team's coach or a psychologist working with it could utilise in order to maximise the benefits of being involved in a potentially one-sided competition while minimising any negative consequences.

3.8   Case study

3.8.1   Setting the scene

The Raiders are a semiprofessional rugby union squad that competes in the National League 1 (tier 3). The team has had a good season and won its last five games. Currently it looks as if it will be promoted to the RFU Championship League (tier 2). As part of a regional competition organised to promote the sport, the team has the opportunity to play a friendly game against the current leaders of the RFU Championship League. The game looks to be a big event and is expected to draw a large crowd as well as being televised and heavily covered by the local media. The head coach of the Raiders has a number of concerns. First, he worries that his team may be intimated by the higher-level opposition and give a sub-optimal performance. He fears that this will have a negative impact on its media representation and potentially its sponsorship. Second, he is worried that the game against the higher-level squad could tire out or even injure some of his players and so damage their chances in future league games. Thus, he is considering not playing a number of the key members of his first team. Finally, conflicting with his first concern, he is worried that his players will be overconfident. They have been successful and are on the cusp of being promoted to the same league as the team they will be playing in the friendly match. The coach feels that if the players enter the game overly confident and are subsequently soundly beaten, they will play with decreased enthusiasm and reduced confidence in their first season in the new league. If the team's performance does suffer, it could be relegated back to the National League 1 after only a single season in the RFU Championship League.

How can the head coach manage his players' expectations of the upcoming game to maximise any successful outcomes while minimising the risks?

3.8.2   Assessing the situation

The key socialising agent in this situation is the team coach. Although it is the expectations and responses of the individual players and the team as group that are central to this issue, the coach is the one in a position to manage this situation. As the head coach, he can dictate the players' training schedule, which makes assessing individual players easier to accomplish. To accomplish this, the coach could use a questionnaire to assess each player. For example, the sport attributional style scale (SASS; Hanrahan and Grove 1990) is used to assess an individual's explanatory style in sport. The questionnaire is made up of eight hypothetical events (four positive and four negative). For each event the respondent is asked to name its single biggest cause and then rate that cause on five causal scales; internality, stability, globality, controllability, and intentionality. Having a greater knowledge of the individual attributional style of each player could help the coach carefully select his team based upon a player's likelihood of coping appropriately with success or failure. Additionally the coach will need to be aware of the team as a whole and any attributional biases its members have developed. This is difficult to directly assess, and therefore the coach has to attempt to subjectively gauge the group. The coach works on a regular basis with the team and so should be able to draw upon a great deal of information about past experiences with it. However, he should not really solely upon schema-driven information. Instead he must draw upon cues from the players at each training session as the game approaches. This data-driven approach, which relies less upon assumptions about the group, is likely to give the coach a more accurate impression of the team's expectations and probable responses to success or failure.

3.8.3 Specific strategies for key socialising agents

In this situation the head coach plays the most important role in managing the expectations and behavioural responses of the team. However, the head coach must make use of key individuals within the team to assist him. These 'social architects' are the players with greater social influence within the group than the majority of players. This may be an assistant coach, the team captain or even just a particularly charismatic individual whom other players naturally gravitate toward. The head coach needs to meet with these individuals and ensure that they have a common understanding of the head coach's and team's goals and direction. Here are some strategies that could be used by other coaches and teams to manage performance expectations.

- Ensure that all expectations are realistic. This means balancing optimism with realism so that individuals understand their chances of success. For example, in this case study the coach and players could watch video recordings of the opposition's games to establish the probability of winning against them.
- Be aware of how you (as an athlete) or your team (as a coach) explain outcomes in sport. Identify common trends and reflect upon how they influence you and others.
- Focus on linking internal factors and success. If a player or team has achieved its goals, a coach should emphasise internal factors such as

personal skill and fitness and explain why success has been achieved. In training sessions the coach should reinforce the association between effort and outcome and the control an individual has over his or her achievements.

- Where appropriate, attribute failure to external causes. It is important that this is done only in situations where external factors really did influence the outcome. Blaming failure on external causes that do not exist can mean athletes do not take responsibility for the internal control they can exert over outcomes. It is important to retain a positive interpretation of events but also important to confront potential weaknesses if an athlete is to progress.

3.9 Further study and recommended reading

The following literature is recommended for further reading on key concepts addressed in this chapter.

- Greenlees, I., Leyland, A., Thelweel, R., and Filby, W. (2008). Soccer penalty takers' uniform colour and pre-penalty kick gaze affect the impressions formed of them by opposing goalkeepers. *Journal of Sport Sciences*, 26, 569–576.
- Kuczka, K., and Treasure, D. (2005). Self-handicapping in competitive sport: influence of the motivational climate, self-efficacy, and perceived importance. *Psychology of Sport and Exercise* 6, 539–550.
- Mulvey, P., and Ribbens, B. (1999). The effects of intergroup competition and assigned group goals on group efficacy and group effectiveness. *Small Group Research*, 30, 651–677.
- Rees, T., Ingledew, D., and Hardy, L. (2005). Attribution in sport psychology: seeking congruence between theory, research and practice. *Psychology of Sport and Exercise*, 6, 189–200.
- Weinberg, R., and Gould, D. (2006). Competition and cooperation. In R. Weinberg and D. Gould (eds), *Foundations of Sport and Exercise Psychology*. Champaign, IL: Human Kinetics.

4 Audience and Spectators

4.1 Learning objectives

The purpose of this chapter is to examine the significance within the sporting realm of audience and spectators and their role in shaping athletic performance. The key learning objectives are:

- to understand the importance of the audience and spectators within the context of sport;
- to examine the theoretical frameworks that outline the contribution of audience and spectators to athletic performance;
- to consider the empirical evidence that illustrates the dual role of a supportive, encouraging, and motivating audience on athletic performance;
- to discuss the practical strategies and implications that athletes, support staff, and sport organisations can use to reduce the negative impact of the audience on athletic performance.

4.2 Introduction to the context

Since the work of Triplett (1898), which is often credited as the first social psychology study, interest in understanding the impact of spectators and audiences on human performance has only grown. There is no platform where the complex interaction of audience and athletes is more apparent or clearer to scrutinise than the sporting domain (Jones, Bray, and Lavallee 2007). Audiences and spectators are a common feature of high-performance sport. For example, it was reported that 1.4 million spectators attended the 2012 UFEA European Football (i.e., soccer) Championship and that over 7.4 million attended the 2012 Olympic Games in London. Even at lower performance levels, athletes are likely to perform in front of spectators. According to 2013 NCAA men's basketball attendance figures, the University of Kentucky had an average turnout of 23,099 spectators per game, totalling 415,775 over the year. Even Marshall University, listed last, had an average of 5,598 spectators per game.

The significance of a supportive audience on performance outcome is nowhere more evident than in the Olympic Games. Nevill, Balmer, and

Winter (2009) noted that the country hosting the Olympic Games always win more medals than when it does not. For example, China won 100 medals when it was the host country for the 2008 Olympic Games; it won far fewer medals, on average 44, in other Olympic years. Thus, in the build-up to London 2012, using the figures on the medals won by all the countries that had hosted the games post–World War II, Nevill and colleagues predicted that the United Kingdom would win 63 medals (in fact it won 65). Although a number of reasons were suggested for this triumph, including increased funding, the authors stated that the presence and support of the partisan London crowd were what encouraged UK athletes to maximise their effort – and may have influenced the officials to favour the hosting nation's athletes. These sentiments have been echoed by the UK athletes themselves. Jessica Ennis even credited the support of the 80,000 spectators for her personal best in the 200-meter sprint (Doward 2012). Similarly, Katherine Grainger, who secured her first gold medal (after being a three-time silver medallist) in the women's double sculls, said that it was the British people's medal, because of the support they showed her throughout the games (Doward 2012). All did not view the presence of a partisan crowd as positive, however. Rebecca Adlington, a bronze medallist, reported that the crowd presence and supportive atmosphere in the aquatic centre overwhelmed her (Doward 2012). It appears that the supportive audience that pushes some athletes to excel is a source of pressure and anxiety for others.

Accordingly, this chapter outlines the impact of audiences and spectators on athletic performance and well-being. For the chapter's purposes, an audience (following Wallace, Baumiester, and Vohs 2005, 430) is defined as observers or spectators physically present at a sporting event. This chapter draws upon the theoretical frameworks of social facilitation, home advantage, and choking under pressure to understand the productive and detrimental effects of spectators, and it reviews the evidence that underpins these frameworks. Finally, emphasis is placed on practical implications and/or solutions for athletes and those who undertake intervention or support work with them.

4.3 The effects of the presence of others on personal effort: a review of early theoretical processes

Study into the effects of competing in the presence of others has been grounded in and guided by the seminal observations of Triplett (1898). In his analysis of records of cycling outcomes in 1897, Triplett noted that cyclists who competed in events and competitions wherein they raced against other competitors (paced) obtained faster times than cyclists who competed in individual time trials (unpaced). In particular, in the unpaced events, cyclists were found to average 2.30 minutes/mile, while in the paced events against time cyclists averaged 1.56 minutes/mile. It was further noted that when these paced events were in competition, times were considerably faster, with cyclists averaging 1.50 minutes/mile. While Triplett factored in a number of reasons for the difference in performance (e.g., aerodynamics, negative evaluation and worries, the hypnotic effect of watching the wheel of the pacer), he believed that the main cause was the bodily presence of another contestant, which sharpened the competitive instinct (Strauss 2002a). This audience effect on performance was referred to as social facilitation. To test this, Triplett (1898) devised a study wherein 40 children, turning the handle of a 'competition machine' as fast as they could, wound a flag around a circuit of 16 metres. This task was performed in solitary fashion and in competition with another child. The study produced conflicting results: 20 children showed performance increments (i.e., faster times) when competing against another child; however, 10 children's performances declined in the presence of others, and in the remaining 10 the performance difference was minimal. This resulted in a number of subsequent studies, both human and animal, examining the effects of competing against or in the presence of others in cognitive and motor tasks (see Strauss 2002a). These early studies' findings were equivocal as to the effects others had on performance: some demonstrated performance increments; others, performance decrements.

In an attempt to provide a satisfying explanation for these inconsistent results, Zajonc (1965) put forward the drive theory of social facilitation. He proposed that the presence of others increases individuals' arousal level and thereby increases the probability of occurrence of dominant responses (i.e., well-learned reactions to specific stimuli) and decreases the probability of subsidiary responses. He further noted that if a task was simple or well learned, the dominant response would be appropriate and lead to performance improvement in the presence of others. However, if a task was difficult or unlearned, the dominant response would lead to performance impairment in the presence of others. While support for the drive theory was initially provided in a number of studies (e.g., Worringham and Messick 1983; Zajonc, Heingartner, and Herman 1969), since then support for Zajonc's theory has declined. Moreover, doubt was cast on the underpinnings of Zajonc's theory, and various explanations were offered to account for audience effects on performance: evaluation approaches (e.g., Cottrell et al. 1968), monitoring approaches (Guerin 1983), attention disruption models (Sanders et al. 1978), attentional overload models (Baron 1986), and attentional shift models (Carver and Scheier 1981). In fact, a comprehensive review of the studies conducted on social facilitation concluded that 'if any effects of the mere presence are to be found at all, they tend to be weak' (Strauss 2002a, 253).

4.3.1   Presence of others on personal effort: recent developments in theory

Rather than close the door on the effects of social facilitation on performance, Blascovich and colleagues (1999, 2000, 2003) put forward the biopsychosocial model of challenge and threat, a comprehensive framework which they considered to have the capacity to integrate the early fundamental theoretical paradigms of social facilitation. Specifically, the authors proposed that in the presence of others, individuals exhibit two different physiological responses, which depend on their appraisal of the situation. In particular, the motivational state of challenge ensues when an individual evaluates herself (either consciously or unconsciously) as possessing adequate resources (e.g., ability, social support) to meet the demands (e.g., skill, required effort) of a given situation, while the motivational state of threat occurs when the individual considers the demands to exceed her resources. According to Blascovich and colleagues (1999), the presence of an audience increases the goal relevance (the importance) of a performance. Thus, individuals who perform well-learned tasks in the presence of an audience and perceive that they have sufficient resources (e.g., mastery of the task) to meet the demand should experience the motivational state of challenge and display the cardiovascular patterns underpinning challenge (i.e., increased cardiac activity, decreased systemic vascular resistance, little or no change in blood pressure). However, if individuals perform unlearned tasks in the presence of an audience and consider themselves lacking the resources (e.g., sufficient task familiarity) to meet the demand, they should experience the motivational state of threat and consequently display the cardiovascular patterns underlying threat (i.e., increased cardiac activity, systemic vascular resistance, and blood pressure).

The findings of Blascovich and colleagues (1999) appear to support the assertions of the biopsychosocial model. In the study, they manipulated task-relevant knowledge and abilities of undergraduate students by requiring all participants to learn a task, either a number-categorisation or pattern-recognition task, to a predetermined proficiency of 80%. Participants were then randomly assigned to perform the mastered task in the presence of an audience or in a solitary condition, while another group performed the unlearned task in the presence of an audience or in a solitary condition. All participants' cardiovascular responses were monitored during the learning and performing phase. In line with the earlier social facilitation study findings, it was reported that participants who performed the unlearned task in front of the audience displayed a significant depreciation in accuracy scores compared to participants who performed the unlearned task in a solitary condition. Moreover, it was noted that participants performing the learned task before an audience had higher cardiac reactivity and decreased peripheral vascular resistance – physiological responses characteristic of the challenge motivational state. Those performing the unlearned task before an audience, on the other hand, displayed physiological responses characteristic of the threat motivational state.

Harkins (2001), however, argued that the Blascovich group's findings did not fully demonstrate the effects of social facilitation. He argued that they failed to demonstrate whether the physiological responses were causes, concomitants, or the results of performance effects. Moreover, he highlighted that the measurement of cardiac reactivity was limited to the first minute of the test. Therefore, while the participants who performed the unlearned task in the presence of an audience exhibited physiological responses characteristic of the threat motivational state, it was not clear whether they continued to exhibit the response past the first minute and throughout the activity. He further stated that it is not apparent whether the participants performing in this condition 'continued their striving in an effort to perform the task successfully or whether they withdrew their effort' (235). Thus the effects of social facilitation on performance continue to elude precise determination.

4.4 Home advantage

It has been frequently observed in both the scientific literature and popular culture that competitors' performances are vastly superior when they compete on their home ground – that is, compared to 'away' venues. This phenomenon, popularly referred to as 'home advantage' was first documented by Schwartz and Barksy (1977), who found that the home team won more games than visiting teams. This pattern was evident across basketball, baseball, American football, and ice hockey.

The definitions of 'home advantage' vary. For example, it was initially 'the consistent finding that home teams in sports competitions win over 50% of the games played under a balanced home and away schedule' (Courneya and Carron 1992, 13). Recognising that this initial definition accounts only for the home win percentages of competitors and fails to consider teams' away records, Bray (1999) redefined 'home advantage' as occurring when home wins exceeded away wins by more than 5%. Similarly, realising that Courneya and Carron's definition was not applicable in individual sports, whose tournaments often take place in a fixed location, Koning (2005) redefined 'home advantage' as 'the performance advantage of an athlete, team, or country when they compete at a home ground compared to their performances under similar conditions at an away ground' (422).

Regardless of the effect's exact definition, home advantage is ubiquitous and robust across the worldwide sport domain (e.g., Gómez and Pollard 2011; Koning 2011; Pollard 2006). Consequently, the research consensus is that home advantage is present (1) at the professional and amateur level, (2) in team and individual sports, (3) among male and female athletes, and

(4) at international competitions between countries (for a comprehensive review, see Carron, Hausenblas, and Eys 2005). While the magnitude of advantage varies between sports, competitions, and even countries, there is overwhelming evidence supporting the existence of home advantage, with home teams/competitors winning 60% of competitions (Jamieson 2010). However, ever more evidence suggests that home advantage is prevalent only in sports that are subjectively evaluated (e.g., gymnastics, boxing) or that rely on subjective decisions (e.g., team sports), as opposed to sports that are objectively judged (e.g., athletics, weightlifting), wherein there appears to be little or minimal home advantage (Balmer, Nevill, and Williams 2003).

Accordingly, a number of diverse models and theories have been proposed to explain the cause of home advantage. These include but are not limited to biological theories of territoriality and circadian rhythm changes, psychosocial theories of arousal and cognition (e.g., social facilitation, self-presentation), and sociological theories of community celebration (see Carron, Loughead, and Bray 2005; Courneya and Carron 1992; Marcelino et al. 2009). Given the insufficient support for these aforementioned theories, Carron and colleagues put forward a conceptual game location framework of home advantage that incorporated conceptions from a variety of theoretical paradigms (see Courneya and Carron 1992; Carron, Loughead, and Bray 2005). This framework postulates that home advantage is composed of five interrelated components: game location, game location factors, critical psychological states, critical behavioural states, and performance outcomes, with each component influencing the next.

Research employing this conceptual framework to understand the nature and causes of home advantage are plentiful (see Courneya and Carron 1992; Carron, Loughead, and Bray 2005; Nevill and Holder 1999; and Pollard 2006 for a review). However, in general, evidence suggests that the effects of travel are minimal, while the effects of learning and rules on home advantage have received little empirical attention. Much of the research has focused on the effects of the crowd on home advantage (e.g., Goumas 2013; Myers and Balmer 2012; Page and Page 2010; Poolton, Sui, and Masters 2011). While the findings generated are more compelling, research examining the effect of the crowd on home advantage has engendered two lines of thought: (1) that crowd factors (size, density, noise, proximity) directly influence home advantage by positively affecting the home team's performances; (2) that crowd factors inadvertently affect home advantage via creation of officiating bias against the opponents.

4.4.1 Crowd factors and home advantage: athletes' performances

In their seminal 1977 study, Schwartz and Barksy concluded that home advantage 'is mainly attributable to the social support of the home audience' (641). Accordingly, a large body of work has examined the effect of crowd factors, in terms of noise, size, density, and proximity, on performance (e.g., Agnew and Carron 1994; Boyko, Boyko, and Boyko 2007). However, the results generated have disagreed as to whether crowd size, density (the number of spectators relative to the capacity of the arena), or intensity is associated with favourable performance outcomes for the home team (Pollard 2006). Agnew and Carron's study examined the influence of crowd size and density, time of year, and opponents' ability on performance outcomes in junior hockey teams over the course of two seasons. Using archival data, they found that the only predictor of performance outcome was crowd density, which, however, accounted for only 1% of home advantage, suggesting that other factors also influenced the performance of the home team. In a similar vein, Boyko and colleagues examined the effect of crowd size and density on goal differential and game outcome (e.g., home win, loss, or draw) in 5,244 English Premier League football matches. They reported that crowd size but not density had a decisive effect on the performance outcome and goal differential of the home and visiting team. Specifically, for every 10,000-person increase in the crowd, home advantage increased by 0.86 goals.

However, a growing body of evidence suggests that the relationship between crowd size and home advantage isn't so linear or straightforward. Goumas (2013) examined the effect of crowd size on home advantage in major international football leagues across Europe, Asia, and North and South America. Combining data from all four continents, Goumas found performance outcomes in favour of the home team to increase by 1.5% per each 10% increase in crowd size. However, it was noted that although home advantage increased as the crowd size increased, there was a ceiling effect, past which the rate of home advantage increase decelerated as crowd size increased. Specifically, the increase in home advantage started to plateau at crowds of 77,000 in Europe, 42,000 in Asia, 53,000 in South America, and 25,000 in North America. No case of home advantage was observed in crowds of fewer than 1,000 on any continent.

Similarly, equivocal evidence links spectator behaviours to favourable performances for the home team (e.g., Greer 1983; Salminen 1993; Strauss 2002b; Thirer and Rampey 1979). Using a quasi-experimental design, Greer reported that following episodes of spectator booing (directed either at the referee for an incorrect call or at the visiting team), there was an improvement in the home team's performance and a decline in the visiting team's – namely, the visiting team committed more fouls and violations. However, Salminen found that the spectators' vocal support had minimal (or negative) effect on the performance of the home team. In his analysis of football, ice hockey, and basketball games in Finland, when the spectators supported (e.g., cheered) the home team, not only did the home team score more points, but it also made more fouls than the visiting team. Interestingly, he also reported that the home team also scored more points even when the audience supported the visiting team.

4.4.2   Crowd factors and home advantage: officiating bias

Officials, referees, and judges play a critical role in shaping performance and competition outcomes (Unkelbach and Memmert 2010). They have an unenviable task: presiding over emotionally charged competitions and enforcing the sport's rules and guidelines, which are often subject to interpretation, under the scrutiny of spectators, coaches, and the governing sport organisation (Poolton et al. 2011). Fundamentally, judges and referees have to ensure that they remain impartial and do not favour one competitor or team over the other (Poolton et al. 2011). A large body of research has highlighted the crowd's effect (in terms of both size and the noise the home fans produce) on officials and referees, in particular on their decision making, as a strong contributor to home advantage.

Downward and Jones (2007) explored the impact of crowd size on football referees' decision to penalise players via the use of yellow and red cards. Using archival data spanning six seasons of the English FA cup, they examined the number of first yellow cards awarded home and visiting players. They reported a bias towards the home team: the referees awarded more yellow cards to the visiting team. Additionally, the degree of favourable bias increased as the crowd size did, the number of yellow cards awarded the home team decreasing as the crowd grew. However, Downward and Jones reported that the relationship between crowd size and referee bias was not uniform: the bias ceased in games with the largest crowds, suggesting that home bias reaches a ceiling, after which it dissipates. Likewise, Boyko and colleagues (2007) reported that crowd size and density influenced the number of cards and penalties awarded by English football referees. Specifically, they found that larger crowds reduced the number of yellow and red cards awarded the home team but increased the number awarded the visiting team. Crowd size also influenced the number of penalties awarded, with referees favouring the home team in the presence of a large crowd.

These empirical findings have been reinforced by those of Pattersson-Lidbom and Priks (2007) in a real world setting. In 2007, the Italian government forced teams with stadiums with inadequate safety standards to play home matches without spectators. With a total of 24 games played without spectators, comparisons of referees' decision making with and without a crowd present could be drawn. Pattersson-Lidbom and Priks, comparing the number of punishments (fouls, yellow cards, red cards) referees awarded, reported that while the home team was penalised less harshly than the away team in the presence of spectators, with them absent, the home team was penalised more harshly than the visiting team.

The dominant effect of crowd noise on the decision making of referees has also been highlighted in a number of experimental and archival studies (e.g., Myers and Balmer 2012; Myers, Nevill, and Al-Nakeeb 2012; Nevill, Webb, and Watts 2013; Unkelbach and Memmert 2010). Unkelbach and Memmert's comprehensive study consisted of two separate investigations. In the first, they used archival data to examine the effect of crowd noise on the number of yellow cards awarded home and away teams by referees in a German football league. Analysing some 1,530 games where a total of 6,489 yellow cards were awarded, they found that crowd noise and density influenced referees' decisions and thus predicted the number of yellow cards awarded the visiting team. Specifically, they found that on average, the home team was awarded fewer yellow cards (M = 1.89, SD = 1.19) than the visiting team (M = 2.35, SD = 1.27). In the second investigation, 20 male referees were presented video footage of fouls from different football games accompanied by either a high or low volume of crowd noise. Referees were asked whether they would award a yellow card for the foul committed. It was found that more yellow cards were awarded when levels of crowd noise were high. This finding, in combination with the results from the archival data study, suggests that referees may use the volume of crowd noise to judge the severity of fouls committed, which may contribute to home advantage.

The dominant influence of crowd noise on officiating bias has been found to extend to other sports, such as the martial art of Muay Thai. Myers and colleagues, on two separate occasions, demonstrated that crowd noise inflates the scores awarded to competitors with high levels of crowd support and consequently gives the home competitor an advantage (Myers and Balmer 2012; Myers, Nevill, and Al-Nakeeb 2012). For example, Myers and colleagues showed 10 Muay Thai judges video footage of a competition with and without crowd noise. Judges were asked to rate the number of strikes made by the contestants. The presence of the crowd noise was found to have a small, albeit significant, effect on the judges' decisions. Specifically, with the crowd noise the judges awarded 5% more strikes in favour of the home competitor. Extending the study, Myers and Balmer (2012) conducted a controlled experiment wherein 17 Muay Thai judges officiated 30 bouts in a live international tournament. For each bout, the judges officiated under a 'crowd noise' condition or a 'no crowd noise' condition (noise-cancelling headphones and white noise). Myers and Balmer reported that on average, live crowd support produced a half-point advantage for the home competitor. Judges exposed to the crowd noise conditions awarded the hometown competitor the bout in four rounds, while their counterparts in the 'no crowd noise' condition awarded the same bout to the visiting competitor.

While crowd factors seem to have the potential to influence officials' judgement, a number of studies have shown that the extent to which a crowd can influence the process is largely dependent on the individual. For example,

Nevill, Balmer, and Williams (2002) suggested that referees' experience may affect the extent to which crowd noise influences their decision making, with more experienced referees exhibiting less bias towards the home team. Poolton and colleagues (2010), on the other hand, suggested that an official's personality, in particular the tendency to ruminate or reinvest during decision making, can lead to a bias towards the home team. In this study, referees with a propensity for decision rumination (the tendency to reflect on previous poor decisions) were found disproportionally to make decisions favouring the home team, such as awarding the visiting team more fouls.

4.4.3   Perspectives on crowd factors and home advantage: fans, players, coaches and referees

Many sport fans believe that the atmosphere they create is the critical contributing factor of home advantage. Wolfson, Wakelin, and Lewis (2005) examined what football fans thought caused home advantage. In line with the amassed empirical evidence, crowd support was more frequently endorsed as the cause than travel, familiarity, and referee bias. Specifically, 59% of fans suggested that the home crowd could inspire and encourage the home team. Fans further maintained that the noise generated, in terms of boos and taunts, could distract the visiting team and influence the referee to make decisions in the home team's favour. Unlike sport fans, athletes and coaches do not consider crowd support fundamental to home advantage. Rather, familiarity with the ground was named by coaches (Gayton, Broida, and Elgee 2001) and athletes (Bray and Widmeyer 2000) the most significant contributor to home advantage. In a more recent study, Anderson and colleagues (2012) compared perceptions of fans, players, and referees on the precursors of home advantage. Fans endorsed the energising and motivating effect on players of crowd support as a major contributor to home advantage more than players and referees did. Players and referees, on the other hand, pointed to familiarity with the ground as more critical to home advantage. Interestingly, Anderson and colleagues noted that of the three comparison groups, referees alone marginalised the influence of officials on home advantage, as they are trained to be impartial and unbiased.

4.4.4   Minimising the effects of crowd factors on performance

It is evident that crowd factors have some effect on home advantage, either directly or indirectly, by influencing officials' decision-making process. This has implications for athletes, coaches, governing sport organisations, and the training of referees. When playing away, coaches and athletes should, to an extent, expect to be penalised more frequently. Thus it would be advantageous to employ psychological strategies (e.g., simulation training or desensitisation) during training and practice to minimise the impact of crowd factors.

Athletes can learn to focus their attention more explicitly on the competition at hand if they are provided the opportunity to practice in conditions that imitate a competitive environment (Jones et al. 2007). Thus, to alleviate crowd distractions, athletes could train in situations with crowd noise (cheering, booing) playing in the background. Similarly, as crowd factors also influence officials' decision-making process, athletes could prepare by incorporating 'poor official' training (Bull, Albinson, and Shambrook 1996), wherein they face decisions biased against them, in their training and practice sessions for away competitions. This would help athletes not only become desensitised to being penalised by officials but also acquire practice in controlling the resulting negative emotions and behaviours (Jones et al. 2007).

Similar desensitising techniques could be employed in the training of officials to ensure that they are fair and impartial and do not succumb to the protests and pressure of the crowd. Specifically, training programmes should focus on helping referees and judges make critical, game-deciding decisions under conditions such as a packed stadium and loud crowd noise in the background. Like athletes, referees need to avoid being influenced and distracted by the crowd. Moreover, as officials susceptible to decision rumination are more likely to be biased toward the home team, psychological techniques, such as thought stoppage, should be taught for use in situations where they feel their decisions are being questioned by the crowd.

4.4.5 Audience and home disadvantage

A crowd can be a source of support and emotional comfort positively influencing athletes' performances (i.e., home advantage), but a supportive presence can also sometimes be detrimental to athletes' performance. Evidence for the detrimental effect was initially provided by the archival findings generated by Baumiester and Steinhilber (1984). From analysis of data from major league baseball and basketball, they reported that hosting teams had a tendency to lose the decisive game in a championship series. In baseball, 60% of the hosting teams won their matches played in the beginning of the season, whereas towards the end, in particular in decisive games, only 39% of the hosting teams won their matches. In basketball, 70% of the hosting teams were found to win their early-season matches, but this dropped to 39% as the season ended. Baumiester and Steinhilber noted that the decline resulted from hosting teams' performing worse than they had previously, as opposed to visiting opponents' performing better. In particular, the home teams committed more fielding errors (baseball) and showcased a lower percentage of successful free throws (basketball).

These patterns also appear to be supported by studies employing experimental designs. For example, in a series of three experiments, Bulter and Baumiester (1998) examined the influence of a supportive audience, a hostile audience/no audience, and a neutral audience on a skill-based task. Across all three experiments participants performed more poorly on the tasks in front of a supportive audience than in front of a neutral or unsupportive one. However, the authors noted that performances were impaired in front of a supportive audience only when the tasks were challenging or difficult. The presence of a supportive audience did not impair performance when conducting an easy or simple task, however. While the evidence for the link between crowd support and home disadvantage is not compelling, as it is for home advantage, it is not difficult to understand why the presence of a supportive crowd can negatively affect performance. For example, athletes have reported worrying about the home supporters' reactions if they make a mistake (Frost and Henderson 1991). Furthermore, supportive audiences can be a source of distraction; they can cause attentional disturbances, amplify concerns and self-consciousness, heighten pressure to succeed, and elicit anxiety and arousal, all of which can be detrimental to performance and lead athletes to choke under pressure (see Bulter and Baumiester 1998; Wallace et al. 2005).

4.5   Choking under pressure

The debilitating effects on athletes of choking under pressure include under-achieved sporting potential, decreased enjoyment, reduced well-being, and impaired self-identity (Hill et al. 2011). The term refers to an athletic performance that is unexpectedly compromised by anxiety (Lavallee et al. 2004). It is also popularly referred to as the 'yips', 'dartitis', and 'icing' (see Moran 2003). A number of high-profile athletes (e.g., tennis player Jana Novotna, golfer Greg Norman) have reported that they choked in critical high-pressure situations in the course of their career. In each case the athlete suffered extensive deterioration in performance and consequently lost a very commanding lead and eventually the competition (Mesagno and Hill 2013). Choking's symptoms are similar to an arousal state; they include tense muscles, shaky limbs, rapid heart and pulse rate, shortness of breath, butterflies in the stomach, feelings of panic, and 'racing' thoughts (see Moran 2003). Choking also involves difficulty in executing skills, movement, and strokes that are usually automatic (see Lavallee et al. 2004).

While researchers largely agree on the symptoms and consequences of choking under pressure, they differ on the definition of choking. A number of different definitions have been put forward in the past 30 years. These include but are not limited to Daniel's (1981, 70) 'the inability to perform up to previously exhibited standards', Baumiester and Showers's (1986, 362) 'the occurrence of sub-optimal performance under pressure conditions', Masters's (1992, 344) 'the failure of normally expert skill under pressure', and Gucciardi and colleagues' (2010, 79) 'heightened levels of perceived pressure...where incentives for optimal performance are at a maximum [leading] to acute or chronic forms of suboptimal performance or performing more poorly than expected given one's skill level and self-set performance expectations'. In a special journal issue on choking under pressure, Mesagno and Hill (2013, 273), after extensive review of the various operational definitions, proposed 'an acute and considerable decrease in skill execution and performance when self-expected standards are normally achievable, which is the result of increased anxiety under perceived pressure' as a definition.

4.5.1   Models of choking under pressure

While choking under pressure is a persistent problem in sport, no consensus about the theoretical mechanisms that underpin it is evident (Lavallee et al. 2004). Thus, a number of competing models have been proposed, including self-focus/self-consciousness models (e.g., Baumiester 1984; Masters 1992; Jackson, Ashford, and Norsworthy 2006), distraction-based models (e.g., Mullen, Hardy, and Tattersall 2005), processing-efficiency models (e.g., Eysenck and Calvo 1992; Eysenck et al. 2007; Williams, Vickers, and Rodrigues 2002), and self-presentational models (e.g., Leary 1992; Mesagno 2009). While they are competing models, these theories agree that in high-pressure situations, anxiety impairs performance by triggering an athlete's reversion to an earlier stage of skill acquisition (Lavallee et al. 2004).

The most empirically researched model of choking is the self-focus/self-consciousness model, which postulates that pressure increases athletes' self-consciousness and concerns about executing performance correctly, resulting in increased attention to the mechanics and procedural nature of skill execution. In particular, heightened pressure seems to direct athletes' attention toward consciously processing explicit rules and toward how the skills were learned (Masters 1992). The increased conscious attention to the specifics of skill execution is thought to disrupt the habitual character of the learned performance. Distraction-based models see high-pressure situations as creating a distracting environment, which causes attentional shifts from task-relevant to task-irrelevant cues such as worries about performance and outcome. As arousal levels increase, athletes become more preoccupied with these task-irrelevant cues and so fail to focus on relevant cues, such as the task at hand (Mesagno, Harvey, and Janelle 2011). Moreover, choking's effects are thought to occur when attention paid to these cues exceeds the level of attentional capacity athletes need to maintain optimal performance (Mesagno, Harvey, and Janelle 2011; Mullen, Hardy, and Tattersall 2005).

The processing-efficiency model states that choking results from a reduction in the processing capacity of working memory due to levels of anxiety and/or the completion of cognitively demanding tasks (Hill et al. 2010). Specifically, the model states that when tasks place very little demand on working memory, the negative effects of anxiety and heightened pressure are eliminated as athletes increase their levels of effort and use available auxiliary processing resources and strategies. However, if the task at hand overburdens the processing and storage capacity of working memory, high anxiety levels lead to decrements in the efficiency and effectiveness of working memory and to subsequent performance impairment (see Eysenck et al. 2007). The final model, the self-presentational model, has received limited attention in sport. Self-presentation, a goal-directed behaviour, aims at conveying a positive image of self to others and influencing how others treat and view the self (Mesagno, Harvey, and Janelle 2011). If athletes successfully portray themselves in a positive and desirable manner, the effects of anxiety on performance will be minimised. However, if athletes feel they are unsuccessful in the attempt to portray themselves positively, their levels of anxiety will increase and subsequently impair performance. Accordingly, this model postulates that choking is a result of athletes' self-presentation concerns and fear of negative evaluation. In particular, athletes' concerns about being discredited or perceived as incapable of performing successfully under pressure cause them to direct attention toward the self-monitoring techniques promoted in the self-focus and distraction models of choking (Mesagno, Harvey, and Janelle 2011).

4.5.2 Choking under pressure: the effect of audience and spectators

Studies examining observer and audience effects on choking fall into one of two strands: those that employ an actual audience and those that manipulate the presence of others or are observed and evaluated via a video camera. Observation's influence on choking has been the subject of a number of studies (e.g., Hill and Shaw 2013; Mesagno, Harvey, and Janelle 2012). For example, several early studies reported that in gymnastics (Paulus and Cornelius 1974) and squash (Forgas et al. 1980), experienced, skilful performers choked more under audience scrutiny than did novice or low-skilled performers. Navarro and colleagues (2012) examined choking in simulated penalty kicks by 31 participants in solitary conditions and in front of a large participative audience. Their findings highlighted that in the presence of the audience, participants reported increased stress and took longer to make motor decisions and respond to goalkeeper movements. Specifically, participants exhibited higher cortisol levels and heart rates, as well as taking significantly longer (30%) to respond to the goalkeeper's movement when in the presence of the audience. However, the authors noted that this effect was present in only a third of participants, thus suggesting that individual differences played a role in how participants responded to the presence of the participative audience.

Support for the adverse effect of spectators on choking also stems from studies in which observer effects have been manipulated artificially via videotaping. For example, Krendl, Gainsburg, and Ambady (2012) examined the effect of stereotypes and observer effects captured through videotaping free throws by 81 male white participants. These participants were exposed to one of three recordings: one showing white basketball players as the best free throwers in the NBA (positive stereotype), one showing black basketball players as the best (negative stereotype). or one neutrally depicting major league soccer (MLS) players scoring penalty kicks. Half the participants then performed free throws under an observer condition (videotaped) and no-observer condition (not recorded). Results revealed that being exposed to negative stereotypes impaired performance in both the observer and no-observer condition, while being exposed to positive stereotypes improved the free throwing performance of participants in the no-observer group. However, in the observer condition positive stereotypes impaired participants' performance. These findings suggest that adding observer pressure caused participants to feel that they needed to conform to the stereotypes of their group and excel. Subsequently, this expectation caused the participants to choke.

In a more comprehensive study, Mesagno, Harvey, and Janelle (2011) randomly assigned 45 competitive field hockey players to groups, including a performance-contingent monetary incentive group (participants were informed that they would get a monetary reward for every successful shot), a video camera placebo group (participants were informed that the video camera would be facing and taping the target), a video camera self-presentation group (participants were informed that performances would be taped and shown to the coach to further aid their development and potential penalty stroke selection), an audience group (participants' performances were observed by five teammates), and a combined pressure group (involving all the other high-pressure situations) before taking a penalty stroke in low- and high-pressure induced situations. Mesagno and colleagues reported that the presence of others (either an actual audience or a video camera) caused an increase in anxiety (cognitive and somatic) and a decrease in performance under high pressure. Moreover, they reported that cognitive anxiety mediated the relationship between observation and performance, suggesting that the presence of a live or videotaped audience increased athletes' worries and negative evaluations and caused their performance to decline to a substandard level.

4.5.3 Minimising the effects of audience on performance

It is evident that the presence of others disrupts the automaticity of athletic performance. Accordingly, the findings these studies generated present implications that highlight various psychological strategies that athletes can use to help them cope with the pressure of performing in front of others and avoid being distracted by their presence. It would be advantageous for athletes to incorporate such strategies during their skill-acquisition phase, in training or competition, to reduce the impact of observer effects on athletes' attentional focus and levels of anxiety. These include but are not limited to desensitisation, attentional cues and triggers, performance routines, cognitive restructuring, and relaxation techniques.

Desensitisation, or simulation training, can serve to reduce the impact of observer effects on athletes' attentional focus by demoting the novelty associated with performing in front an audience during competitions. By mimicking the presence of an audience in training, either having team-mates observe the performance or using a video camera, it allows athletes to become more aware of their sensations and reactions to being observed, to be trained to manage and overcome them – in short, to become acclimatised to observation. Athletes can thus eventually inoculate themselves against the distracting effects (Jones et al. 2007).

Using attentional cues or triggers has been advocated as a strategy to direct athletes' attention to task-relevant factors (e.g., Bull et al. 1996; Wilson, Peper, and Schmid 2006). Verbal, visual, or physical cues can help athletes attain or regain concentration and focus in a situation. These triggers can be employed prior to or during competition. Verbal cues include short, vivid, positively framed buzzwords – words relevant and meaningful to the athlete, that focus on specific skill and techniques, images, physical feelings, emotions. Visual cues include directing attention to a specific object (again, something mean-ingful and relevant to the athlete). Examples of visual cues might be a tennis player focusing on the strings of their tennis racket or a golfer looking at a spot on their golf club. Finally, action cues consist of brief actions or behav-iours that help one avoid distraction. Examples might include a tennis player tapping their shoe with their racket prior to each point.

Pre-event and pre-performance routines have been postulated to be the two most effective types of performance routines to help athletes cope with being observed (see Jones et al. 2007; Lavallee et al. 2004; Mesagno, Marchant, and Morris 2008). Pre-event routines are tasks or behaviours that athletes per-form in the lead-up to an event or competition. The pre-event routine serves to direct athletes' attention and focus toward what needs to be done, as well as create a relaxed and confident frame of mind (Jones et al. 2007). Examples of a pre-event routine for athletes are having a meal prior to competing, checking the equipments and grounds, performing a warm-up routine, and mentally rehearsing the performance. A pre-performance routine involves sequences of mental and physical activities that athletes may engage in prior to executing specific skills or tasks (Shaw, Gorely, and Corban 2005). A pre-performance routine serves to combat the effects of being observed by direct-ing athletes' focus to task-relevant cues and being in the present moment, as well as distracting athletes' attention from the techniques and mechanisms underlying their performance (Moran 2004).

Cognitive restructuring involves the interpretation of habitual thinking. In particular, it allows athletes to restructure negative or threatening situ-ations into positive or manageable ones by drawing on the positives and recognising that the perceived threat is not a fact but, rather, a result of the individual's perception (Lavallee et al. 2004; Shaw et al. 2005). For example,

reinterpreting a high-pressure situation as an exciting challenge or changing negative thoughts or concerns about an upcoming performance into
positive thoughts. The most commonly followed method is the ABC cognitive restructuring (Ellis and Dryden 1987). This procedure is aimed at elimi-
nating destructive and irrational thoughts and replacing them with rational
responses (Zinssler, Bunker, and Williams 2006). Finally, other techniques
that athletes can utilise to cope with observer effects are relaxation techniques, which attempt to regulate and lower athletes' anxiety and arousal
level by relaxing the body and relieving tension (Williams and Harris 2006).
The relaxation techniques that can be used include progressive muscular
relaxation, centring, meditation (see Williams and Harris 2006 for an overview and guidelines), and the black box (Syer and Connolly 1998).

4.6   Summary

The mere effect of the presence of an audience on athletic performance was
first noted by Triplett over a hundred years ago. While evidence indicates
that the presence of an audience enhances performance by increasing the
effort athletes invest and creating officiating bias against competitors, findings also demonstrate that the presence of an audience can cause athletes'
performances to deteriorate. The presence of others can undermine performance by increasing athletes' arousal state or enhancing their apprehension that the audience might negatively evaluate them. Although evidence
largely derives from archival data or cross-sectional research designs, which
prevent the cause-and-effect distinction from being made, the findings that
derive from controlled laboratory experiments are promising and clearly
demonstrate audiences' causal effect (supportive or unsupportive) on performance outcomes.

4.7   Case study

4.7.1   Setting the scene

Ryan, a 17-year-old professional footballer, has recently been selected to play
for his first international cap in the forthcoming World Cup football tournament. Ryan is regarded by his coaches, teammates, and sport fans as a talented young striker with a promising career in front of him. However, some
football pundits have questioned whether, given his age and experience, he is
physically and psychologically ready to start an international career in such
an important tournament. Ryan is also worried about his upcoming performance, what with the eyes of the world on him. Although he is accustomed to
playing in front of crowds of over 40,000 every week, the idea of playing in
a packed stadium, with spectators and cameras watching his every move and

analysing and evaluating his performance, fills him with dread. He is also worried because the tournament is not on home ground but in a foreign country, away from the family and friends upon whom he relies for emotional support. He has become very anxious and preoccupied about not making 'silly' mistakes. To avoid them, Ryan has analysed his performances over the past few months and has made a record of every mistake he made during play – every mistimed tackle, every misplaced pass, every shot not on target. As a result, he has started to wonder whether he is any good or ready for this opportunity. Every time he thinks about the upcoming tournament, he reports feeling tense and jittery; his stomach is full of knots, and he has even vomited on several occasions. Furthermore, it seems his worry and preoccupation with the tournament, his not wanting to let others – coaches, family, fans – down and wanting to exhibit a positive image of himself, has had an effect on his current performance, as he failed to score in the last four matches of the season.

4.7.2 Assessing the situation

Ryan's case highlights a number of areas of concern, all of which revolve around his selection for a major football tournament. Playing in a major tournament can be daunting for any player, let alone a young athlete who has yet to make an international debut. Ryan is exhibiting not only signs and symptoms of increased physiological arousal (feeling jittery, tense) but also cognitive anxiety (fear of being judged or negatively evaluated, worries about making an error). It also appears that his heightened anxiety and worries are causing a decline in his performance, a decline likely to affect his confidence. The signs and symptoms – high levels of self-consciousness or self-presentational concerns; high levels of cognitive, somatic anxiety, and concentration disruption – indicate that Ryan is potentially a choking-susceptible athlete. Therefore it is critical to ensure that Ryan is equipped with the appropriate strategies to cope with these pressures so that he does not choke during the upcoming tournament, as doing so would be a further detriment to his athletic development.

What can Ryan and those working with him do to help him cope with the pressures of playing his first international game so that he does not choke under the spotlight?

4.7.3 Specific strategies that can be used to help Ryan

The following strategies could be used by Ryan, his coaches, and sport psychologists to alleviate the impact on his performance of the increased pressure and physiological and psychological arousal, as well as to ensure that he is prepared for the upcoming tournament.

• Develop an awareness that this situation should be perceived as an exciting rather than intimidating situation, as an opportunity to showcase his talent at the highest level against the world's best players. This can be achieved by implementing cognitive restructuring with Ryan. He should be encouraged to seek out the positives, such as being the youngest player ever to be selected to represent his country. He has been selected to play because the national coach believes that he is an excellent player, one who is able to hold his own against other world-class players. Furthermore, he should be encouraged to perceive this opportunity as a challenge that is within his control if he is appropriately prepared both physically and mentally.

- During practice sessions in the training camp, mimic the presence of an audience by having teammates and coaches cheer and boo during play. Alternatively, during training play a recording of an audience and have cameras set up off the pitch to mirror real-life settings. In these sessions, Ryan can also be trained to manage his emotions and reactions to foul play or being unfairly penalised by the referee. This will help reduce the novelty associated with playing on foreign turf and in front of a large unfriendly audience.
- Implement the use of attentional cues or triggers in competitive matches to direct Ryan's attention to the task at hand. Encourage the use of short, positively structured verbal, visual, or action cues. Be sure, however, that the cues are relevant and meaningful to Ryan. These cues could also be used in practice sessions and simulation training to facilitate automaticity.
- Incorporate relaxation techniques such as progressive muscular relaxation, centring, and meditation into Ryan's training to reduce physical symptoms of anxiety. One technique that may be of dual benefit is the black box, which involves relaxation and a visual symbolic image of leaving or placing worries behind you for the performance at hand and facilitates being in the present, ready and focused for the game. Promote the use of performance routines with Ryan. These can include pre-event, in-event, and pre-performance routines. Pre-event routines should focus on what needs to be done in preparation for the competition or match. This can incorporate checking and packing kit, walking around the stadium, performing warm-ups, using other psychological strategies such as relaxation techniques and affirmations. In-event routines should be guided by the recognised crucial moments in the match and should stipulate what Ryan's focus should be at these moments. A pre-performance routine could also prove to be fruitful for Ryan, especially if he is to take penalties in the tournament. The routine should include a sequence of mental and physical activities he can engage in before taking the shot. For example, his routine could incorporate the following sequence: (1) pick up the ball and walk forward with head held high; (2) during the walk to the penalty box, take deep breaths and repeat positive affirmations or decide where the ball is going to be placed; (3) place the ball on spot, look up, and

visualise placing the ball as intended and scoring; and (4) walk backwards from the spot, facing the goalkeeper at all times, taking deep breaths and visualising the perfect shot.

- Consider delving further into Ryan's fear of negative evaluation and where it stems from; then educate Ryan about the consequences of fear of failure.
- Endorse regular communication between Ryan and his family and friends so that he has a support system away from the football squad.

4.8 Further study and recommended reading

The following literature is recommended for further reading on key concepts addressed in this chapter.

- Carron, A. V., Loughead, T. M., and Bray, S. R. (2005). The home advantage in sport competitions: Courneya and Carron's (1992) conceptual framework a decade later. *Journal of Sports Sciences*, 23(4), 395–407.
- Hill, D. M., Hanton, S., Matthews, N., and Fleming, S. (2010). Choking in sport: a review. *International Review of Sport and Exercise Psychology*, 3(1), 24–39.
- Jones, M. V., Bray, S. R., and Lavallee, D. (2007). All the world's a stage: impact of an audience on sport performers. In S. Jowett and D. Lavallee (eds), *Social Psychology in Sport*, ch. 8 (103–113). Champaign, IL: Human Kinetics.
- Strauss, B. (2002). Social Facilitation in Motor Tasks. *Psychology of Sport and Exercise*, 3, 237–256.

Additionally, reading of the following relevant documents is recommended. These address factors not covered in this chapter that may be central to understanding the effect of an audience on athletic performance and provide guidelines for implementing psychological strategies that may alleviate the pressure of being observed.

- Lavallee, D., Kremer, J., and Moran, A. P. (2004). *Sport Psychology: Contemporary Themes*, ch. 6 (118–138). London: Palgrave-Macmillan.
- Williams, J. M. (2006). *Applied Sport Psychology: Personal Growth to Peak Performance*, chs 14–19. New York: McGraw-Hill.

5 The Family and Significant Others

5.1 Learning objectives

The purpose of this chapter is to examine the function of the family and significant others within the sporting realm and their role in athletes' sporting experiences. The key learning objectives are:

- to understand the importance of the family and significant others in the sport context;
- to examine the theoretical frameworks that outline the contribution of the family and significant others in shaping athletes' sporting experiences;
- to consider the empirical evidence that illustrates the changing influence and involvement of families and significant others in the athlete's sporting career;
- to discuss the practical strategies and solutions that athletes, support staff, and sport organisations can use to reduce the negative impact of familial involvement on athletic performance and psychosocial development.

5.2 Introduction to the context

In social and developmental psychology it has been frequently suggested that human behaviour, attitudes, beliefs, and values are a result of the interaction between individuals and the significant others embedded in their social environment (e.g., Bronfenbrenner 1993; Lewin 1934). Athletes' involvement in sport stretches from early childhood to late adolescence or beyond (Partridge, Brustad, and Stellino 2008). Consequently, over the course of their athletic involvement athletes form multiple relationships with various social agents, including coaches, teammates, parents, siblings, and romantic partners (see Côté 1999; Jowett and Cockerill 2002), each exerting varying influence on athletes' sporting experiences, either independently or collectively across the trajectory of athletes' development. Families, in particular parents, represent powerful social agents in children's socialisation into sport. Parents are regarded as the catalyst for initiating young athletes' involvement in sport and physical activity (e.g., Brown, Frankel, and Fennell 1989; Lewko and Ewing 1980). In addition to introducing children to sport, parents remain highly involved in children's sporting participation by investing time and effort, purchasing training equipment, and providing transportation to training and competitions (Horn and Horn 2007).

Such parental behaviours and sacrifices have been highlighted as critical in shaping athletes' development. For example, long jumper Greg Rutherford attributed his success at the 2012 Olympic games to all the support and help his parents had given him over the years. He viewed the medal as their reward for all their involvement in helping him find a sport he enjoyed and driving him to competitions and training in various UK locations (*Telegraph Sport* 2012). Likewise, diver Tom Daley commented that his parents supported his sporting development by ensuring that he had access to provisions and facilities to develop his talent. He specifically recalled that he received a trampoline for his tenth birthday so that he could practice somersaults and twists (*Telegraph Sport* 2012). However, parental influence isn't always viewed as positive by all athletes. In his autobiography eight-time Grand Slam champion and Olympic gold medallist Andre Agassi described how his father's pressure and determination to ensure that Agassi was the number one tennis player in the world made him hate tennis (Agassi 2010). Agassi claimed that tennis was not a sport he chose to play; rather, he was pushed into it by his father. He further described how this father attached ping-pong paddles to his wrists as a baby and made him hit a mobile composed of tennis balls; when he was six his dad forced him to hit 2,500 tennis balls a day on a self-constructed court. Agassi also recalled that his father created a ball machine, nicknamed the Dragon, that threw balls out at 110 mph. Thus it seems that the way in which athletes interact with their families, in particular parents, can have a profound impact upon their experiences of competitive sport, influence such factors as their satisfaction, enjoyment, and motivation, and directly or indirectly affect their well-being and performance.

Despite the clear impact that families have on athletes' sporting experiences, it is only recently that researchers in sport psychology have examined the influence of the family and significant others in sport (Fraser-Thomas, Strachan, and Jeffery-Tosoni 2013; Fredricks and Eccles 2004). Accordingly, this chapter outlines the varying social influence of parents, families, and significant others on athletes' sporting experiences across the sporting lifespan. The chapter draws upon the theoretical frameworks of Eccles's (1993) expectancy value theory, Bloom's (1985) and Côté's (1999) developmental model of sport participation, and Wylleman and Lavallee's (2004) lifespan model to understand the functional and debilitative effects of families and examine the changing involvement of such relationships in athletes' development. Finally, emphasis is placed on practical implications and solutions for athletes and for anyone undertaking intervention or support work with them.

5.3 Promoting athletic involvement: the role of parents

Eccles and various colleagues (Eccles and Harold 1991; Eccles, Wegfield, and Schiefele 1998; Fredricks and Eccles 2004) proposed the expectancy value model to understand the influence of social agents on achievement and behaviours. They postulated that children's achievement-related choices, such as motivation, persistence, increased effort, and performance, are influenced directly by two factors: their expectations of success and the value they assign to the task. Expectations of success are influenced by their perception of their own competence and the task's difficulty, while the task's value is based on evaluations of its perceived intrinsic value, its usefulness in achieving future goals, the importance of executing it successfully, and its negative aspects (Wegfield and Eccles 2000). This model suggests that children – who perceive themselves as highly competent, enjoy participating in a sport, believe that sport is of great significance in both the short and long term, and perceive more benefits as a result of involvement – are likely to enhance the effort they put into sport, as well as continue their participation. The original model posited that multiple social agents (parents, siblings, teachers) would influence children's expectations of success and task values through their own beliefs and behaviours; however, more recently, Eccles and colleagues (1998) and Fredricks and Eccles (2004) put forward a model wherein parents lie at the core, significantly shaping children's expectations of success and task value and consequently their persistence, effort, and performance (Fredricks and Eccles 2004). Parents have been identified as influencing and shaping their children's outcomes through serving as a provider, an interpreter, and a role model of experiences.

5.3.1 Parents as providers of athletes' sporting experiences

As providers of athletes' experiences, parents are assumed to introduce their children to the sport, act as a source of encouragement, provide emotional, practical logistical, and financial support, and ensure that the children have a variety of sport-related opportunities and experiences both in and away from the home and sporting environment. The model indicates that parents who expose their children to sporting experiences by purchasing equipment, taking them to sporting events, giving encouragement and feedback on their performances, and enlisting them in special courses positively influence their children's motives, efforts, and skills. These theoretical contentions appear to be largely supported within the literature, with parents noted as providing financial support for resources such as magazines, books, membership fees, and extra training (e.g., Gould et al. 2008; Wolfenden and Holt 2005), providing transportation services to and from training and competitions (e.g., Dixon, Warner, and Bruening 2008; Gould et al. 2006), volunteering their own time to help the team or sport club with administration, acting as an additional coach, official, or referee, and fund-raising (e.g., Dixon et al. 2008; Fredrick and Eccles 2005). Moreover, parents have been reported to change their work life and schedule, give up free time on weekends, and rearrange family holidays and outings around competitions and tournaments (Harwood and Knight 2009; Young and Pearce 2011). Such sacrifices and adjustments are mostly endured by mothers, who adjust their social life and careers to manage their children's training and competition schedules and provide transportation. Fathers mostly provide financial support (e.g., Dixon et al. 2008; Hayman et al. 2011; Young and Pearce 2011). Beyond providing tangible and instrumental support, parents also shape young athletes' sporting experiences by providing emotional and informational support, in particular via their involvement, communication, feedback and parenting styles (e.g., Fraser-Thomas et al. 2013; Fredricks and Eccles 2005). Parenting styles reflect the emotional environment created by parents (Holt et al. 2009). While initial studies produced inconsistent findings as to whether certain parenting styles were associated with successful athletes and outcomes (e.g., Csikszentmihalyi, Rathunde, and Whalen 1993; van Rossum and van der Loo 1997), more recent studies have suggested that rearing styles do contribute to athletes' experiences (e.g., Holt and Black 2007; Holt et al. 2009; Jõesaar and Hein 2011; Juntumaa, Keskivaara, and Punamäki 2005; Sapieja, Dunn, and Holt 2011). Collectively, these findings suggest that athletes who grow up in demanding yet supportive family environments are more involved in decision making, more satisfied with their sport, and more engaged in sportspersonlike behaviours. These athletes also reported healthy perfectionist cognitions and persisted with sport.

Hellstedt (1987) proposed a continuum of parental involvement in sport ranging from underinvolved to overinvolved. Underinvolvement characterises parents who are uninterested in their children's sport and skill development and do not invest financially, emotionally, or functionally. Nor do they attend games or competitions or volunteer to help out. Moderately involved parents are characterised as supportive, interested in their child's sport participation and skill development; they volunteer to help at training and competitions. Overinvolvement, on the other hand, characterises parents who take an excessive interest in their children's sport in terms of providing financial support and even coaching their children. They are also unable to distinguish between their own needs and desires to succeed and their children's (see Ede et al. 2012; Knight, Boden, and Holt 2010).

A number of studies that focused on quantifying the optimal level of parental involvement for children's participation in sport produced conflicting results (Fraser-Thomas et al. 2013). For example, Wuerth, Lee, and Alfermann (2004) reported that higher levels of parental involvement were related to greater athletic success among soccer players. However, Kanters, Bocarro, and Casper (2008) found that parental overinvolvement or high levels of parental involvement resulted in children losing interest in their sport or feeling trapped to continue participation, while low levels of parental involvement were associated with reduced levels of sport enjoyment and interest. Moderate levels of parental involvement, on the other hand, were related to positive attitudes to sport; this aligns with a number of other studies (e.g., Ede et al. 2012; Wuerth et al. 2004). Furthermore, the involvement of mothers and fathers appears to impact children's sporting experiences differently (e.g., Stein, Raedeke, and Glenn 1999; Wuerth et al. 2004). For example, Stein, Raedeke, and Glenn found high levels of maternal involvement associated with higher levels of enjoyment, while high levels of paternal involvement were associated with increased stress. Furthermore, the nature and quality of parental involvement has been linked to athlete outcomes such as success (e.g., Lauer et al. 2010; Woodcock et al. 2011), enjoyment (e.g., Ede et al. 2012), anxiety (e.g., Bois, Lalanne, and Delforge 2009), well-being (e.g., Jowett and Timson-Katchis 2005; Nunomura and Oliveira 2012), cheating (e.g., Casper 2006), injury (e.g., Podlog et al. 2012), coping strategies (e.g., Lafferty and Dorrell 2006), burnout (e.g., Strachan, Côté, and Deakin 2009), and dropout (e.g., Atkins et al. 2013; Keegan et al. 2009). Collectively, these studies indicate that supportive parental involvement is linked to increased enjoyment, sport competence, self-esteem, well-being, and continuation in sport, while increased parental pressure and controlling parental involvement is associated with lowered self-esteem, increased anxiety, burnout, and dropout from sport.

However Lauer et al. (2010) argued that parents who push, who are forceful and demanding (i.e., negative parental involvement), can still make successful athletes. In their interviews with professional tennis players they found three pathways to the development of talent, expertise, and competence. These pathways consisted of the smooth (supportive, good parent–child relationship, emphasis on effort, fun, and enjoyment), difficult (strained parent–child relationship but conflict often resolved, emphasis on winning and tennis), and turbulent (pressure to perform, strained relationship with parents, with high levels of conflict, increased perception of conditional love dependent on tennis performance). This indicates that parents don't have to be supportive and positive to encourage development of talent, but the authors noted that being forceful and demanding, although beneficial for athletic development, had detrimental effects on the parent–child relationship, resulting in increased conflict, frustration, and sadness.

Consequently, the quality of parent–child relationships and the interactions between parents and their children have also been examined in relation to shaping athletes' sporting experiences (e.g., Fraser-Thomas and Côté 2009; Knight et al. 2010, Knight, Neely, and Holt 2011; Ullrich-French and Smith 2006). Ullrich-French and Smith found that soccer players who maintained relationships characterised by positive and harmonious interactions and low conflict with their parents reported greater sport enjoyment, competence, and motivation and lower levels of stress. Jowett and Cramer (2010) examined the role of parental and coach–athlete relationships in young athletes' sense of self. They reported that athletes' perceptions of performance, sport skill, body, mental competence, and physiology were predicted only by their interactions with coaches, not parents. However, interaction was noted between conflict in the parental and coach–athlete relationship and athletes' sport skill and body development. Specifically, athletes who experienced lower levels of conflict in their parental relations reported lower levels of conflict with coaches and subsequently higher perception of skill and body development. However, athletes experiencing high levels of conflict in parental relations reported higher levels of conflict with coaches and lowered perceptions of skill and body. This suggests that parent–child interactions directly influence not just performance outcomes for the athlete but also the quality of their interactions with significant others.

The final area of research examining parents' role as providers of athletes' sporting experiences has focused on parents' behaviours and the nature of the sport-related feedback they give during and after competitions (e.g., Knight and Holt 2013; Knight et al. 2010, 2011; Omli and LaVoi 2012). Research indicates that parents generally tend to spend a large proportion of their time providing praise and supportive comments, cheering, and giving encouragement; however, they also make negative and derogatory comments, shout instructions, provide performance-contingent feedback, and engage in angry, aggressive, and humiliating behaviours such as swearing, yelling at referees and coaches, and encouraging athletes to engage in unsportspersonlike behaviours (e.g., Holt et al. 2008; Kidman, McKenzie, and McKenzie 1999; Shields et al. 2007; Omli and Wiese-Bjornstal 2012). Such behaviours have been identified as a source of both support and stress, as well as reduced enjoyment and sense of self-worth (e.g., Atkins et al. 2012; Keegan et al. 2009, 2010; Omli, LaVoi, and Wiese-Bjornstal 2008). In a series of qualitative interviews with young athletes, Keegan and colleagues (2009) showed that parents' feedback and behaviours can either promote or diminish athletes' sporting experiences. Demonstrating positive behaviours during competitions and providing sport-related feedback balanced with encouraging play or practice were related to enhanced motivation and competence. Providing conflicting advice to the coach or too much technical instruction were seen as 'confusing', 'overloading', and essentially detrimental to motivation (Keegan et al. 2009). Yelling and shouting instructions during competitions was also seen as detrimental. One young athlete remarked, 'It's alright if they're there and being supportive, but if they're like shouting at you what to do or like being really over the top, then it gets really wrong' (Keegan et al. 2010, 99).

5.3.2 Parents as interpreters of athletes' sporting experiences

Functioning as an interpreter, parents transmit messages relating to an athlete's ability and competence and the value of sport participation through their beliefs, values, expectations, and behaviours. In particular, parents who hold high expectations for their children's success, as well as high value for sport participation, are regarded to have children with more favourable outcomes (Fredricks and Eccles 2004). A number of studies have highlighted that parent's perceptions of a child's sporting ability and competence, as well as the value they place on sport participation, corresponds with the child's perception of his or her own ability, value for sport, and prolonged sport participation (e.g., Fredricks and Eccles 2002, 2005). For example, Fredricks and Eccles (2005) found that mothers' and fathers' ratings of a child's sporting ability was positively related to the child's beliefs about competence, value of sport, and engagement in sport participation, both concurrently and over time, during the child's elementary sport participation. Interestingly, evidence suggests that fathers may play a more important role in shaping athletes' perceptions of their skill and competence. Fredricks and Eccles (2002) found fathers' perceptions of the children's ability and competence was more strongly related to the children's own ratings of competence and sporting ability than mothers'. Adding to this, Kanters et al. (2008) noted that fathers' perception of children's skill was a stronger predictor of their children's perception of skill in a sample of young hockey players.

Dixon et al. (2008) further illustrated that female athletes' value for sport participation stemmed from their parents' beliefs about its value. In their interviews with female athletes, mothers and fathers were perceived to create an atmosphere that normalised and promoted the importance of sport participation for females. One female athlete remarked, 'I think my views just stemmed from the way I was raised, and the opportunities that I had, without people saying, "You're a girl. You can't do that"', while another female athlete said, 'I remember growing up I used to throw the football with my dad, and my dad always raised me [to think that] the girls can do anything that boys can do' (Dixon et al. 2008, 551). Moreover, the female athletes believed that their parents' expectations, which focused on encouragement rather than pressure to excel, led to their continuing in sport. One athlete recalled, 'My parents were completely supportive; if I wanted to do gymnastics, [it was] wonderful. If I didn't want to do gymnastics, [that was] wonderful also. ... If I wanted to quit, there would have been no ramifications. Because of that I ended up really enjoying my gymnastics experiences' (Dixon et al. 2008, 552).

In contrast, high parental expectations and pressure to excel has been linked to negative sport outcomes such as reduced sport enjoyment and satisfaction, feelings of uncertainty, lack of motivation, psychological problems, athletic injury, and sport discontinuation (e.g., Fraser-Thomas and Côté 2009; Gould et al. 2006, 2008; Hamstra, Cherubini, and Swanik 2002; Kanters et al. 2008). Collins and Barber (2006) examined the association between parents' beliefs and expectations, competitive state anxiety, and performance expectations among hockey players. Athletes who perceived their parents to hold high expectations about their future performances were more confident than those athletes who perceived their parents to hold lower expectations. However, Collins and Barber noted that athletes whose parents placed higher levels of importance on success (winning) reported greater levels of cognitive anxiety. This suggests it is not necessarily the possession of high expectations about the task at hand that results in unfavourable outcomes for athletes but rather the emphasis on ego (Collins and Barber 2006). Another study found the parent-initiated motivational climate to moderate the association between perceived parental pressure and trait anxiety both concurrently and over time. O'Rourke and colleagues (2011) found that swimmers exposed to high parental pressure and a high mastery motivational climate reported lower levels of performance anxiety than swimmers whose parents placed high pressure but low emphasis on mastery. In contrast, swimmers exposed to high parental pressure and ego motivational climate reported higher levels of performance anxiety than swimmers exposed to high parental pressure and low ego-involving motivational climate. This suggests that the impact of parental pressure to excel is not necessarily negative; rather, it is dependent on the motivational context that accompanies high parental pressure.

Correspondingly, an extensive body of recent evidence suggests that parents' motivational orientation is also associated with their child's motivational orientations (e.g., Kavussanu et al. 2011; Sánchez-Miguel et al. 2013) and psychosocial outcomes, including motivation (Gutiérrez, Caus, and Ruiz 2011), perfectionist cognitions (e.g., Appleton, Hall, and Hill 2011), good sporting behaviours (e.g., LaVoi and Babkes Stellino 2008), trait anxiety (e.g., O'Rourke et al. 2011), and sport discontinuation (e.g., Le Bars, Gernigon, and Ninot 2009). For example, LaVoi and Babkes Stellino demonstrated that a positive sport climate created by parents, in terms of promoting learning and enjoyment, significantly contributed to task-motivational orientation and athletes' engagement in sportspersonlike conduct. Athletes were more likely to report greater concern for opponents and demonstrate graciousness regardless of outcome (i.e., win or loss) if parents provided positive feedback and responses to good performances, encouraged mastery of skill and enjoyment, promoted mistakes as part of learning, and lessened pressure to win and outperform opponents.

5.3.3   Parents as role models of athletes' sporting experiences

As role models, parents influence athletes' experiences through providing models of appropriate and non-appropriate behaviours and normalising involvement in sport. In particular, parents who compete in sport them-selves, show composure during competition and in interactions with oth-ers, and promote a work ethic appear to enhance their children's beliefs and values and consequently their performance. However, support for this assumption has been inconsistent. Positive associations of parents' physical activity involvement and children's physical activity involve-ment have been found in qualitative studies and epidemiological studies employing electronic monitoring devices to capture physical activity (see Fredricks and Eccles 2004; Dixon et al. 2008), with children found to be more physically active when their parents were currently or previously active (e.g., in high school and college). However, a number of other studies failed to find associations between parents' sporting involvement and their children's (e.g., Babkes and Weiss 1999; Fredricks and Eccles 2005). Moreover, recent studies have demonstrated that the dropout rate is also associated with parents' previous engagement with sport as well as level of athletic involvement (Fraser-Thomas, Côté, and Deakin 2008a). Athletes who ceased participation more often had parents who had previously been athletes who competed at a high performance level (county and higher) than athletes that continued sport participation. Follow-up interviews with the dropout ath-letes indicated that thy dropped out because they felt pressure to succeed and reach their parents' performance level (Fraser-Thomas, Côté and Deakin 2008b). However, it was noted that such pressure came not from the parents themselves but internally from the athletes.

Parents' influence as role models also extends to the conduct and compo-sure they exhibit during competitions. In particular, athletes model their own sports conduct on their parents'. Shields et al. (2007) reported that poor sports conduct exhibited by parents, such as teasing, or yelling at ath-letes, coaches, other parents, and referees, was positively related to poor sporting conduct by young athletes. Children of parents who teased ath-letes, yelled at athletes, coaches, other parents, and referees, and were more accepting of cheating, aggressiveness, and hurtfulness towards opponents and sports officials engaged more frequently in poor conduct such as cheat-ing, intentionally hurting opponents to help the team win, and arguing with officials. Adding to this, Arthur-Banning and colleagues (2009) found that while positive parental and coach behaviours significantly predicted positive sporting conduct in players, negative parental conduct significantly predicted negative conduct among third, fourth, fifth, and sixth graders. This suggests that athletes are more likely to engage in good sporting conduct if their parents and coaches did so, too, but they are more likely to demonstrate poor sporting conduct if their parents argued with referees or yelled at teammates.

5.4   The changing role of parental involvement in athletes' sport participation

Bloom (1985) first underscored the changing role of parents' involvement in athletes' sport participation, as well as in other domains, including science and arts. Bloom suggested that athletes' engagement in sport is composed of three distinct stages: the early years, the middle years, and the later years. During the early years of participation, parents tend to be heavily involved and supportive, introducing the child to the sport, supporting the choice to participate in the sport (or not) with an emphasis on fun and effort. Following this, during the middle years, parents encourage specialisation and greater engagement in training and competition. During this stage, parents also make sacrifices and change family schedules and environment to give their children financial, logistical, and informational support. Finally, in the later years, as the child-athlete's engagement becomes more competitive, parental involvement seems to dissipate, with parents becoming less involved in providing practical, informational, and logistical support; rather, they act as a source of financial and emotional support and help athletes cope and manage with the demands of competitive sport.

While Bloom's (1985) framework was initially considered to capture the involvement of the family in athletes' sport participation, it neglected the role and influence of other family members, such as siblings, on athletes' sporting experiences. Thus, Côté (1999) advanced Bloom's model to incorporate these additional social agents and psychosocial influences on athletes' sporting career. In the developmental model of sport participation, Côté, like Bloom, postulated three stages of sport development: the sampling years (6–12 years of age), the specialising years (13–15), and the investment years (16 and up). During the sampling years, parents are responsible for introducing the child into the sport, providing opportunities for the child to experience fun and excitement, as well as supporting all family members' desire to engage in extracurricular activities. During the specialisation phase, athletes reduce their engagement in other extracurricular activities, commit to one or two sports, and focus on developing their skill. In this stage a number of social agents influence children's sport participation experiences: parents, coaches, siblings, friends. Parents support the child's engagement in sport by becoming more actively involved, committing their time to the child's sport (e.g., by helping out during training or competitions), and providing tangible support (cost of registration, equipment, supplies, travel expenses). Older siblings, on the other hand, were deemed to influence athletes' sport participation by acting as role models and promoting cooperation and hard work. Finally, during the investment years, children commit their time to achieve elite status in one sport. In this stage the role and influence of parents may intensify, with parents increasing the provision of tangible and emotional support (e.g., by helping children cope and deal with injury, fatigue, pressure, or failure). Although the model has been modified (see Côté and Fraser-Thomas 2011; Fraser-Thomas et al. 2013), the modified model still emphasises the changing influence of multiple social agents, such as parents and siblings, across children's sport participation trajectory.

In a similar vein, Wylleman and Lavallee (2004) proposed the lifespan model, which described the developmental stages and transitions faced by athletes at the individual, psychosocial, and academic/vocational level. This model postulated four stages of athlete development, which are loosely related to athletes' age; (1) the initiation stage, wherein the child is introduced to competitive sport participation around 6 or 7; (2) the developmental stage (12–13), wherein the child athlete engages in increased training and competition after being recognised as talented; (3) the mastery stage (18–19), during which athletes compete in their sport at the highest competitive level; and (4) the discontinuation stage (28–30), wherein athletes transition out of competitive sport (see Wylleman et al. 2007). Embedded in these transitions are the athletes' psychological development (childhood, adolescence, adulthood), academic/vocational development (primary, secondary, and higher education; vocational training or professional occupation), and the psychosocial context perceived as significant to athletes' development (parents, siblings, peers, coaches, partners, family). The model stipulates that across the sporting career, different social agents are significant for athletes' involvement and development. At the initiation stage, parents, siblings, and peers are salient in influencing athletes' sporting experiences. At the developmental stage, parents are still influential alongside coaches and peers. However, during the mastery stage, coaches and partners are the only social agents salient in shaping athletes' experiences. Finally, during the discontinuation stage, the family and, to a lesser extent, the coach are significant.

Collectively, all three models highlight the significance of parents in the sporting development of athletes. However, these models indicate that the involvement and influence of parents change during athletes' sporting development. Parents appear to be predominantly situated in the initial stages, wherein they introduce the child to the sport and support the development of skill and talent. Beyond this initial stage, parents' involvement and

influence decline substantially, while simultaneously the involvement of significant others (coaches and peers) increases as athletes enter the transition to
the investment/mastery stage. There is empirical evidence to support parents'
changing role in athletes' sporting experiences (for a comprehensive review of
the literature, see Fraser-Thomas et al. 2013; Harwood, Douglas, and Minniti
2012; Wylleman et al. 2007). For example, in reviewing the literature examining the influence of parents, coaches, and peers across athletes' sporting
trajectory, Keegan and colleagues (2014a) reported that in the initiation stage,
parental involvement was high, with parents providing significant instrumental and material support. However, during the specialisation and investment stage, the involvement of parents was reduced as athletes became more
independent. Parents became indirectly involved in athletes' development;
they were spectators or in some cases provided emotional and financial support. Simultaneously, the role and involvement of coaches and peers changed
across the three sporting trajectories. During the initiation stage, peers were
partially involved, facilitating athletes' socialisation into sport. As athletes
transitioned into the specialisation and investment stages, peers' influence
and role became more dominant; they were the main source of support of
athletes' emotional needs. Likewise, the influence of coaches became more
central following the specialisation stage; they became the main providers of
feedback, behavioural reinforcement, authority, advice, and instruction.

In addition to being more involved, coaches and teammates/peers also
appear to have more impact on athletes' outcomes at the specialisation and
investment stages than do parents (e.g., Chan, Lonsdale, and Fung 2012;
Keegan et al. 2014b; Rottensteiner et al. 2013; Shanmugam, Jowett, and
Meyer 2014). Keegan and colleagues (2014b) conducted a series of interviews
with young elite athletes to examine the role and function of parents, peers,
and coaches in athletes' motivation. In this study, parents were sources of
emotional and moral support; however, coaches and peers were regarded by
athletes as the main and focal influencers of their motivation towards sport,
through the provision of instruction and leadership (coaches), emotional
support, and promotion of collaborative/competitive behaviours (peers).
Expanding upon these findings, Chan and colleagues examined the influence of parents, coaches, and peers on children's and adolescents' enjoyment, effort, competence, and anxiety. The authors noted that in childhood
(i.e., the initiation stage) mothers had a more salient influence on athletes'
effort invested in swimming, on their enjoyment, and on their perceived
competence and anxiety level than did coaches and peers. Children of mothers who provided encouragement and praise, emphasised effort, and did not
criticise their children for mistakes or poor performance reported increased
enjoyment, effort, and competence and reduced levels of anxiety. However,
during adolescence (i.e., the specialisation and investment stages) coaches
and peers had more influence on athletes' competence, anxiety, enjoyment,

and effort. Specifically, athletes who trained with coaches and peers who provided encouragement and praise and did not react negatively to athletes' mistakes reported greater sport enjoyment and competence, invested more effort into swimming, and reported lower levels of anxiety. In a similar vein, Rottensteiner and colleagues examined the influence of coaches, parents, peers, and siblings on adolescent athletes' decision to withdraw from sport participation. Their findings indicated that coaches and teammates had a more significant influence on the decision than parents and siblings.

5.5 Significance of siblings in shaping athletes' sporting experiences

As noted in the models of both Côté (1999) and Wylleman and Lavallee (2004), siblings play a critical role in shaping the sporting experiences of athletes. Although empirical evidence examining the effects of siblings is limited in quantity, the research largely indicates that siblings have both a positive and negative effect (e.g., Davis and Meyer 2008; Côté 1999; Fraser-Thomas et al. 2008b; Weiss and Knoppers 1982). In an early study, Weiss and Knoppers found that siblings, in particular brothers, were the main influence on female athletes' socialisation into sport participation during childhood and college. In a later study, Weissensteiner, Abernethy, and Farrow (2009) reported that healthy competition between siblings (and friends) facilitated the development of psychological attributes such as competitiveness, strategising, coping, and mental toughness in elite cricketers. One cricket player noted, 'I think the most important thing really in the whole development process was the backyard test matches [test match means international match], the test matches in the street or in the park or down the beach with our mates, that's where we learned to compete. ... Having an older brother, I had to learn to compete with him ... I had to struggle to keep up there and those coping skills that I learned at that stage were absolutely critical for what happened later on' (Weissensteiner et al. 2009, 282).

Côté (1999), on the other hand, demonstrated the functional and adverse influence of siblings on sport participation across athletes' sport trajectory. During the specialising stage of athlete development, older siblings were perceived as role models transmitting a strong work ethic, which the athlete attempted to match. Moreover, athletes noted a lack of sport competition with their siblings; rather, their relationship was characterised by cooperation. However, as athletes progressed into the investment phase, the nature and quality of the sibling relationship changed. Athletes reported feelings of tension, bitterness, and jealousy from younger or twin siblings as a result of the increased attention and involvement from parents. This has been further highlighted in more recent findings (e.g., Knight and Harwood 2009; Wolfenden and Holt 2005). In a series of interviews with elite junior tennis players, parents, and coaches, a number of parents and athletes commented on the impact that the investment of time and resources on a talented young athlete had on the siblings. A female tennis player remarked that 'I think my sister is a little bit jealous that I get taken everywhere and she's had to give up stuff for me. I do feel a bit sorry for her, because she just gets carted around wherever I am or has to stay with other people' (Wolfenden and Holt 2005, 120).

Apropos of this point, Fraser-Thomas et al. (2008b) reported that feelings of resentment, increased competition, sibling rivalry, and jealousy could lead athletes to drop out of sport. In their interviews, swimmers who ceased participating and those who continued differed in their experiences with their siblings. In particular, the former characterised their sibling relationship as negative, competitive, and full of silent jealousy. Swimmers that continued commented more favourably about their relationship with siblings. They reported that they couldn't pinpoint the siblings' true influence but found their mere presence and involvement in the same sport a model to be emulated. For example, one swimmer remarked, 'That's what they do. That's what I do. I didn't choose to go into swimming when I was five. I just kind of did what everyone else in the family did. They went to the pool and worked hard – that's what I did. They went to swim meets and tried their best – that's what I did' (Fraser-Thomas et al. 2008b, 656).

5.6 Significance of romantic and marital partners

Although some anecdotal evidence indicates a salient effect of romantic partners on athletes' sporting experiences (e.g., Paula Radcliffe, Victoria Pendleton), as with the literature examining sibling influence on athletes' sport participation, only a handful of studies examine how romantic or marital partners shape athletic participation (e.g., Dionigi et al. 2012; Jowett 2003; Jowett and Cramer 2009). In a comprehensive study, Dionigi and colleagues examined the influence of spouses on Masters athletes' sporting experiences. Interviews with 14 married couples highlighted both the critical role of romantic partners (and to a lesser extent their children) in supporting the athletes continued sport participation and the effect of sport participation on their relationship's functioning. Although Masters athletes reported receiving and requiring less support from spouses and children regarding sport participation compared to their younger competitive counterparts, they described their spouses as influencing their involvement in a number of ways, including providing emotional support (encouragement, understanding), logistical support (taking care of children while athletes compete), engaging in training or physical activities with them, being a role model and generally allowing the Masters athletes to continue their participation without questioning it or complaining about it. For example, a male runner commented, 'My wife has always been encouraging, but not really influential...she hasn't stopped me, put it that way...just [by] kind of leaving it alone and not saying, "Why are you doing that [running] instead of doing this?" She recognizes the importance of it...[or] resigned herself [to the fact that her husband is a runner][laughs]' (Dionigi et al. 2012, 374). However, the Masters athletes also acknowledged that sport participation, in particular their training schedule and time restriction, was a source of tension and conflict in their romantic relationship. However, many of the athletes said they manage, often negotiating their schedule with their spouse in order to minimise conflict and maximise their time together. One swimmer commented, 'For the most part I keep [training] to two evenings a week and I go early on Saturday and Sunday mornings [i.e., while his wife is still in bed]....She usually sleeps in, so it doesn't interfere with our time together that much' (Dionigi et al. 2012, 376).

Jowett and Cramer (2009) examined the influence of romantic relationships on athletes' performance and well-being. Their results initially revealed that athletes who fostered effective relationships, in terms of enhanced interpersonal commitment, communication, and reduced hostile interactions, reported greater satisfaction with their sport participation. Subsequent analysis revealed that negative spillover (i.e., negative feelings, attitudes, or behaviours that emerge in one domain and carry over into another) mediated the effects between romantic relationship quality (commitment, negative transactions) and the athletes' satisfaction with sport and depressive symptoms. Specifically, the findings suggest that higher levels of romantic commitment and negative interactions indirectly increase depressive symptoms and reduce sport satisfaction because they increase athletes' perception of negative spillover in their romantic relations.

5.7 Optimising athletes' sporting experiences by cultivating their social relationships

The manner in which the family and significant others communicate, behave, and interact with athletes appears to have a substantial impact on both athletic development and athletes' affective, behavioural, and cognitive experiences. A number of relevant strategies can be employed by parents, coaches, sport psychologists, and sporting organisations to enhance athletes' sporting experiences (the examples that follow are by no means exhaustive and are predominantly meaningful for those engaged in youth sports). When introducing children into sport participation, parents should encourage and praise the child's development and improvement in sport (rather than performance outcome), focus on having fun and on learning new skills and techniques (Smoll, Cumming, and Smith 2011). Rather than criticise or react in a negative or hostile manner following mistakes or poor performances, they should provide the athletes constructive and honest feedback, which should be limited to technical and tactical information if the parent possesses a good understanding of the child's sport (Knight et al. 2010). Moreover, during competitions parents should not engage in hostile and negative encounters with other parents, coaches, referees, and athletes. Rather, they should encourage and cheer the team as a whole (Ede et al. 2012; Knight et al. 2011). Parents should encourage children to engage in other activities away from their chosen sport and create a balance between sport participation and other family and social activities (Genevois 2011). In particular, parents should not discuss sport-related topics during family time, especially if they have other children not invested in sport. Such practices will produce a more rounded athlete and limit the potential for sibling conflict, tension, resentment, and jealousy.

Coaches should foster open channels of communication with parents to allow for constructive and meaningful relations and provide a forum for parents to discuss their concerns and ask questions about their child athlete's sport participation and development (Smoll et al. 2011). Coaches should have preseason meetings with parents to outline their coaching philosophy, expectations, and rules of engagement (Harwood 2011). Thereafter, coaches should arrange regular meetings with parents, away from the training or competition environment (but with the athlete present), to discuss the child's development. Such practices serve to reduce conflict between parents and coaches, which is associated with negative athletic outcomes. It allows coaches and parents the time and means to listen and discuss the child athlete in a meaningful manner; it also allows the opinions, comments, and observations of all parties – parents, coaches, athletes – to be heard in a supportive and non-judgemental environment. A sport psychologist might also be involved in these discussions to act as a mediator or facilitator, to reduce or minimise any potential conflict or hostility, and to contribute to the conflict resolution process (Smoll et al. 2011).

In addition, coaches should work with parents to enhance athletes' sporting experiences. Rather than assume that they serve distinct purposes and functions in the athlete's life, coaches and parents should form a partnership or a support team (Wolfenden and Holt 2005) to reinforce each other's contribution. For example, if a coach is not able to attend a competition, parents can act as an excellent source of feedback for the coach, provided that the coach has adequately informed the parents what to observe and report on (Harwood 2011).

Finally, sport organisations and national governing bodies should develop guidelines, set up workshops, and provide information booklets aimed at educating families, enhancing their understanding of their role in the athlete's development, and providing strategies on how they can maximise their positive contribution. Such an initiative has been implemented by the Football Association, whose *Official FA Guide for Football Parents* (2004), a booklet which covers the code of conduct for parents and highlights their role in the development of young football players. They have also launched an online scheme called 'Respect: A guide for parents and carers'. Like the booklet, it provides guidelines on how to behave on the sideline, act as a role model, and prolong their child's engagement in the sport. Similarly, coaches should also receive education in how to interact, communicate, and relate with parents in an effective manner and learn tools and strategies to manage unhelpful or problematic parents.

5.8   Summary

Although family members are often the social agents that initiate a child's involvement in sport, research examining their influence in shaping athletes' sporting experience is in its infancy, especially beyond the initial introduction. Only since the 1990s have we seen a surge in research dedicated to the family's contribution to athletes' affective, cognitive, and behavioural outcomes. The findings generated highlight the critical role of family members, in particular parents, in shaping young athletes' sporting experiences, as well as their function in athletes' development and specialisation in sport. Parents are seen as crucial social agents, acting as the source of tangible, emotional, social, and logistical support during the early years of sport participation. Similarly, during this stage siblings also influence athletes' experiences, acting as a role model and promoting hard work, on the one hand, but also being a source of rivalry manifesting as tension and jealousy. As athletes progress and develop their sport, skill, and talent, the role and function of parents and siblings is taken by coaches and peers, who influence athletes' enjoyment, motivation, anxiety – even withdrawal from sport.

Much of the literature has been limited by employment of cross-sectional, retrospective, or qualitative research designs that confine examination of the experiences of athletes to a particular stage in the sporting trajectory (initiation, specialisation, investment, etc.). There is a paucity of data following athletes as they transition from one stage to the next. To gain a more comprehensive understanding of the function and role of families, future studies need to incorporate these methodologies and broaden the scope of investigation to include other significant social influences, including siblings and romantic partners.

5.9   Case study

5.9.1   Setting the scene

Sebastian has been coaching Elijah, a 13-year-old tennis player, for the past four years. Sebastian spotted Elijah four years ago, while he was playing with his friends on the court; he believes that Elijah has the talent and skill to become a promising tennis player. Elijah, an only child, has two parents who are heavily involved in his tennis. Both played tennis competitively when they were younger, although not to an elite standard, and are members of the tennis club. One parent or both always attend his competitions and observe his training sessions, during which they are not afraid to voice their opinions of Elijah's performance. Initially, when Sebastian started coaching Elijah, his parents were generally positive and supportive about his development and performance; however, in the past year there have been more and more incidents during competitions where they nitpicked his performance, questioned umpires' decisions, and attempted to coach him beforehand (to Sebastian's annoyance) by providing advice and instructions on what he should be doing. Coincidently, in the past six months, Sebastian has noticed a change in Elijah's attitudes and behaviour towards tennis. Whereas he was once a happy, sociable, and extroverted individual who perceived mistakes and errors as areas for improvement, in the past few months he has become socially withdrawn, spending more time training alone (i.e., hitting serves) after the squad practice, and has reacted with frustration, hostility, and even aggression after making mistakes or errors during competitions and training. Following his recent outburst during the final practice of the winter season, Sebastian had a chat with Elijah about the recent change in his behaviour. During this chat, it became evident that Elijah felt a lot of pressure to succeed from his parents. Specifically, Elijah said that over the past year or so, his parents regularly made comments (1) about how much money they had invested in him and tennis and not feeling that they were getting a return on their investment; (2) about how they had changed family schedules, gave up holidays, and made sacrifices to accommodate his involvement in tennis; and (3) about how at his age they were performing at a higher standard and how other tennis players on his squad were playing better than he was. These and other comments and related conduct during and after competitions had caused a lot of conflict between him and his parents. Elijah also reported feeling anxious and frustrated about his recent form, but he thinks that it will improve if he invests more time and effort into tennis. When asked whether he still enjoyed playing, Elijah only shrugged and commented that he needed to work harder so that his parents' investment was not a waste.

5.9.2   Assessing the situation

The situation faced by Elijah reflects a number of areas of concern – including the lack of sport enjoyment, increased levels of anxiety and frustration, intensive training, and narrow focus on success and winning. If things continue thus, sport withdrawal or athlete burnout could result. The issues seem to be responses to the behaviours and comments of Elijah's parents.

It is clear that their comments regarding making sacrifices, investing financially and emotionally, and making social comparisons and their providing technical and tactical advice prior to competitions and engaging in bad sporting conduct during them are placing pressure on Elijah to ensure that his performance is always first rate. Although it is not clear whether his parents are making these comments purposely or only in passing, it is evident from Sebastian's observations that they are having an impact on Elijah's performance and interpersonal functioning. Thus it seems critical to ensure that Sebastian, Elijah, and Elijah's parents are equipped with appropriate strategies and solutions to manage and resolve these issues before there is further decline in Elijah's performance and psychosocial development.

What can Sebastian, Elijah's parents, and those working with Elijah do to ensure Elijah continues his sport participation and has more positive sporting experiences?

5.9.3   Specific strategies that can be used to help Elijah

The following strategies could be used by Elijah, Sebastian, and sport psychologists to develop and foster effective parental involvement, which subsequently can enhance Elijah's performance and sporting experiences.

- Encourage Elijah to have conversations with his parents about their comments and behaviours, as well as the impact they are having on him. It is likely that his parents are not aware of the negative consequences of their comments and behaviours and perceive their actions as a way of demonstrating their support. Through these discussions, his parents may become more aware of how their behaviours are being interpreted by Elijah. Moreover, the discussions can help both parties identify behaviours they should manifest, those that are helpful and beneficial to Elijah (e.g., not providing technical and tactical support, respecting the tennis etiquette). During these discussions, it may be appropriate for the sport psychologist to act as a mediator.
- Encourage Elijah and his parents to engage in family time and social activities away from tennis during his time off and on weekends; they should have non-tennis-related conversations during these times. They can serve to improve the quality of the relationship between Elijah and his parents and help create a balance between tennis and other aspects of their life.
- The sport psychologist, coaches, and tennis club should establish ground rules for appropriate parental conduct and interactions and inform all parents prior to the start of the new season (so as not to single out Elijah's parents). Appropriate information includes how to behave during competitions, what coaches and the organisation expect from parents, when to approach coaches, and how to raise concerns about players. This can be

communicated first via a group meeting with parents and athletes at the start of the season, so that all members are aware of the ground rules, and in a booklet emailed to all parents thereafter. In both cases, the consequences of inappropriate conduct should also be included (e.g., washing the whole team's uniform for minor violations; then verbal warnings, written warnings, and suspension). It would also be beneficial for all parents to sign this booklet, agreeing to the code of conduct.

- The sport psychologist, coaches, and tennis club should develop and provide educational workshops, booklets, and resources for parents that illustrate the impact of their conduct on athletes' sporting experiences and contain strategies for how they can enhance the sporting development and experiences of their children. Such content should focus on the importance of parents creating a task-orientated motivational climate with an emphasis on effort and learning and stressing the importance of not placing pressure on athletes (either directly or indirectly through comments about sacrifices). In doing so, parents will get a better understanding of their function in shaping the child's sport experience.

- The tennis club should provide constant updates and resources for parents. Even though most parents will likely believe that they have a good level of understanding, it would be beneficial to share resources (mental skills training, nutrition and diet, player development) which guide the coaches' practice with parents so that parents are educated and on the same page. Using the same resources will prevent coaches and parents providing athletes with conflicting technical advice and instruction.

- Sebastian should provide time for meetings with Elijah and Elijah's parents at the beginning of the season to discuss Elijah's performance and development, as well as realistic goals and expectations (developed with Elijah's input) for training and competition in the coming season. During these meetings, Elijah's parents' role in facilitating achievement of these goals can also be discussed. Besides providing the parents with an understanding of what to expect, this would also create a sense of teamwork, with parents and coaches working together to enhance the child athlete's sporting experience.

- Sebastian should provide sufficient time to have regular meetings with Elijah's parents throughout the season (with Elijah present) to discuss his progress in a supportive and non-judgemental environment. This would allow Sebastian and the parents time and scope to voice opinions and comments, give feedback from observations, and help identify areas that need more attention or thought. Engagement in these meetings will ensure an open channel for communication and foster effective interpersonal relationships and mutual understanding.

5.10 Further study and recommended reading

The following literature is recommended for further reading on key concepts addressed in this chapter.

- Côté, J. (1999). The influence of the family in the development of talent in sport. *Sport Psychologist*, 13, 395–417.
- Fraser-Thomas, J., Strachan, L., and Jeffery-Tosoni, S. (2013). Family influence on children's involvement in sport. In J. Côté and R. Lidor (eds), *Conditions of Children's Talent Development in Sport* (179–196). Morgantown, WV: Fitness Information Technology.
- Fredricks, J. A., and Eccles, J. S. (2004). Parental influences on youth involvement in sports. In M. R. Weiss (eds), *Developmental Sport and Exercise Psychology: A Lifespan Perspective* (145–164). Morgantown, WV: Fitness Information Technology.
- Harwood, C. G., Douglas, J. P., and Minniti, A. M. (2012). The role of the family in talent development. In S. Murphy (ed.), *Handbook on Sport and Performance Psychology*. New York: Oxford University Press.
- Wylleman, P., De Knop, P., Verdet, M. C., and Cecič-Erpič, S. (2007). Parenting and career transitions of elite athletes. In S. Jowett and D. Lavallee (eds), *Social Psychology in Sport* (233–247). Champaign IL: Human Kinetics.

Additionally, reading of the following relevant essays is recommended. They address factors not covered in this chapter that may be central to understanding the effect of families and significant others on athletes' sporting experiences.

- White, S. A. (2007). Parent-created motivational climate. In S. Jowett and D. Lavallee (eds), *Social Psychology in Sport* (131–144). Champaign IL: Human Kinetics.
- Partridge, J. A., Brustad, R. J., and Babkes Stellino, M. (2008). Social influence in sport. In T. S. Horn (ed.), *Advances in Sport Psychology* (270–291). Champaign IL: Human Kinetics.

6 Schools

6.1 Learning objectives

The purpose of this chapter is to examine the social context of the school setting and its importance in relation to shaping physical activity behaviour in children and young adults. The key learning objectives are:

- to explore the leadership role of physical education (PE) teachers in creating an appropriate motivational climate to enhance physical activity behaviour and establish theoretical links to the self-efficacy theory and achievement goal theory;
- to consider the importance of peers as social agents who influence the perceptions of physical competence of others and establish links to the competence motivation theory and the big-fish-little-pond effect;
- to examine the contribution of parents as potential role models and sources of social support for children and young adults to engage in an active lifestyle within the school environment;
- to discuss the practical implications for PE teachers, peers, and parents to create an optimal social environment for physical activity in schools with specific strategies outlined.

6.2 Introduction to the context

Between the ages of 5 and 16 years, children and young adults spend the majority of their time at school. The school day encompasses several opportunities for them to be physically active, including active travel to and from school, PE lessons, and break and lunchtime activity, in addition to opportunities for extracurricular physical activity. Data from a Department for Education report on participation in PE and out-of-hours school sport in the United Kingdom (Quick, Simon, and Thornton 2010) estimated that children across years 1 to 11 (aged 5–16) spend approximately 123 minutes per week participating in PE. Consequently, the school environment can make a significant contribution to the amount of physical activity children and young adults need to achieve physical and psychological health benefits. There is substantial research quantifying the time spent in physical activity in the school environment, particularly in PE lessons, yet relatively limited attention has been given to the social effects and social psychology evident within this environment. According to Gustafson and Rhodes (2006), social variables are among the most important modifiable factors for increasing physical activity in children and young adults. Within the school environment, socialising agents play an important role as gatekeepers to the physical activity choices and behaviours of children and young adults. PE teachers, peers, and parents are all considered influential in a variety of ways; for example, through shared attitudes, values, modelling, psychological support, encouragement, and reinforcement.

Prior to and since the 2012 London Olympic Games, there has been a focus on creating a lasting legacy for sport and physical activity in the United Kingdom. In 2007 an independent charity, Legacy Trust UK, was set up to support communities and organisations across the nation to create projects that celebrated London 2012 in a way that was relevant to them and would leave a lasting legacy. Following the games' success, the government published a ten-point plan for securing such a lasting Olympic legacy (HM Government 2013). The points included providing 125 million pounds of funding for elite athletes until 2016; 1 billion pounds investment into the Youth Sport Strategy through to 2018; linking schools with sports clubs and encouraging sporting habits for life; and ensuring more is done to make PE in schools available to all. Although encouraging, the plan appears to be centred on sport and competition rather than encouraging a physically active lifestyle. Furthermore, one of the key objectives of the Youth Sport Strategy (2012) is to build a lasting legacy of competitive sport in schools. This is contrary to the change in the school curriculum in recent years, where PE has developed a more prominent role in health promotion. There has been a shift that reduces the focus on increasing fitness levels of children and young adults in favour of a holistic approach of encouraging continued participation, motivation, and enjoyment of a physically active lifestyle. Consequently, PE teachers play a key leadership role in developing an appropriate learning environment to foster these positive feelings and behaviours. This can be created through more straightforward social processes such as verbal persuasion, instructional support, and feedback. Additionally, PE teachers can enhance the learning environment further through more complex social processes such as appropriate modelling behaviours, cultivating a task-oriented climate, developing a sense of relatedness, and reinforcing self-referenced competence.

These factors may be more salient in enhancing the physical activity experience for individuals who lack perceived competence, need additional time for skill development, or experience self-presentational issues. In addition to these responsibilities, PE teachers also need to manage the social interaction of peers in the PE lesson and the influence peers can have on shaping the learning environment for others. Peers have emerged as pivotal contributors to the creation of an appropriate motivational climate for physical activity through their perceptions of physical competence, social comparison of ability, and modelling behaviours. Finally, parents, although not directly related to in-school physical activity, play a central role in shaping the physical activity attitudes, values, and behaviours of their children. They also provide essential social support for engaging in physical activity through logistic support (e.g., transportation, financial support) and verbal encouragement. Parents may also act as role models for physical activity, particularly for younger children, who often emulate individuals from their immediate environment; it may be that at this developmental stage, parents are vital in shaping physical activity behaviour and choices.

6.3   The role of PE teachers

Although some researchers argue that PE lessons do not contribute substantially to the overall physical activity levels of children and young adults (Fox, Cooper, and McKenna 2004), others claim that the *experience* individuals gain during PE lessons influences their attitudes, values, and choices regarding physical activity and sport. This is likely to translate to establishing lifelong habits and behaviours in relation to their volitional physical activity. Consequently, PE teachers need to create a positive, enjoyable experience during PE lessons. Traditionally, a PE teachers' role was to provide instructional support to develop specific skills (e.g., outline the key stages of performing a handstand), demonstrate the skill itself (perform the handstand in front of the class), provide instrumental support to pupils trying to learn a skill (physically support them in a handstand position), and provide emotional support during skill development (verbal encouragement to the pupil whilst attempting a handstand). Yet since the early 2000s, there has been a shift in the UK's PE curriculum to a focus beyond skill development. Key aims of the PE curriculum are not only to develop a wide range of skills and abilities through use of tactics, strategies, and compositional ideas but to develop pupils' competence and confidence to participate in physical activity. There is also a clear emphasis on providing pupils with an environment where they are able to make informed choices about lifelong physical activity and to value a healthy, active lifestyle. Therefore, the PE teacher's role is considerably more than simply supporting the development of sport skills and abilities in children and young adults. They are key socialising agents in the attitudes, values, choices, and behaviours that young adults make. These decisions, formulated at a critical time in their lives, may translate to a lifelong active or inactive lifestyle.

6.3.1   Modelling behaviours of PE teachers

Socialisation is the process by which one learns about others' attitudes, values, cultures, and beliefs through observing and experiencing their behaviours (Bandura 1977). Eventually, the socialisation process is used to formulate one's own attitudes, beliefs, and behaviours. Role models are central in the socialisation process; a role model can be defined as anyone an individual comes into contact with, either directly or indirectly, with the potential to influence decisions and behaviours. Adolescence is a period of identity exploration, development, and consolidation; consequently, developing an affiliation with certain role models could be particularly important at this time. During adolescence, young adults typically emulate individuals from their immediate environment – for example, friends, parents, and teachers (Kirby 2009). Within a PE lesson, the teacher is a central role model; according to Bandura (1986), the more alike the role model and the observers are, the more likely modelling will facilitate the observers' behaviour and their self-efficacy in performing that behaviour.

Self-efficacy is defined by Bandura (1986) as 'people's judgements of their capabilities to organise and execute courses of action required to attain designated types of performance. It is concerned not with the skills one has but with judgements of what one can do with whatever skills one possesses' (391). Bandura further differentiates between 'efficacy expectations' and 'outcome expectations'. Efficacy expectations relate to an individual's belief that he or she can perform a specific behaviour, whereas outcome expectations refer to his or her belief that behaviours will produce certain outcomes. For example, in a PE setting a pupil's efficacy expectation relating to performing a handstand may be that she feels she is capable of doing it, but the outcome expectation is that when she performs the handstand, she has straight legs and is able to hold the handstand for a long time.

A more user-friendly definition of self-efficacy is 'situation-specific self-confidence', where an individual assesses his or her confidence in performing a behaviour in a specific situation. For example, a pupil may feel capable of doing a handstand by himself at home but if asked to perform the handstand in front of others in the PE class, his self-efficacy may be reduced. According to Bandura's social learning theory (1977), an individual's perceived self-efficacy can be generated from four primary sources:

- performance accomplishment
- vicarious experience
- verbal persuasion
- judgement of physiological and affective states

Performance accomplishment, the most influential source of self-efficacy, is based on personal mastery. If individuals have successfully mastered a behaviour in the past, their mastery expectations are increased, and they are likely to be able to perform that behaviour or a similar one in the future. For example, pupils who have successfully mastered a handstand in three consecutive PE lessons are more likely to try going from a handstand into a forward roll in the next session. However, individuals with several unsuccessful mastery attempts have decreased expectations; consequently, they are less likely to attempt that behaviour in the future. A pupil with several unsuccessful handstand attempts in three consecutive PE lessons is unlikely to try that behaviour again or advance to a more complex one, such as a handstand into a forward roll. Bandura (1977) emphasised that individuals do not rely solely on performance accomplishment as a source of self-efficacy. Many efficacy expectations derive from vicarious experience. Vicarious experience, also called modelling, refers to a situation where an individual observes someone performing a behaviour successfully and bases his or her efficacy on the idea that a similar outcome to the model's can be achieved. For example, if a PE teacher demonstrates a handstand successfully in class, the pupils' mastery expectations of achieving a similar outcome are likely to increase. This source of self-efficacy is more influential if there is a perceived similarity between observer and model. The third source of self-efficacy information, verbal persuasion, involves others encouraging individuals to believe they are capable of performing a specific behaviour; for example, a PE teacher providing verbal encouragement to a pupil prior to and during a handstand attempt. The last source of self-efficacy is the individual's judgement of emotional arousal in relation to physiological and affective states. If an individual negatively perceives an increase in heart rate and anxious thoughts prior to performing a behaviour (e.g., a handstand), the self-efficacy for that performance is reduced. However, if an individual perceives these symptoms positively, in that the body and mind are preparing to perform, self-efficacy is increased.

Verbal persuasion and vicarious experience are key social sources of self-efficacy that can be gained through an individual's social environment. Observing PE teachers in lessons can enhance children's and young adults' vicarious experiences. This can be done in a variety of ways. PE teachers can demonstrate the behaviour or skill to the pupils successfully, they can communicate their values and beliefs about engaging in a physically active lifestyle to the pupils, and they can portray the benefits of being physically active through their own physical appearance. Early research by Melville and Maddalozzo (1988) examined the effect of a male PE teacher's physical appearance on the perceptions of 850 secondary school students. They were asked to view one of two videos of the teacher conducting a PE lesson. In one video he wore a fat suit to manipulate his physical appearance. Students who saw the 'non-fat' teacher rated him significantly more knowledgeable and a better role model than those who watched the video of him in the fat suit. More recent focus group research conducted by Nicholson (2008) explored the needs of adolescent girls in PE and the characteristics they wanted from their PE teachers. Findings highlighted that adolescent girls favoured young, sporty looking PE teachers who actively participated in the sessions with them. They also reported criticism of male teachers and their conduct towards them in mixed-gender classes.

PE teachers view themselves as role models for children and young adults and accept this as a key responsibility of their chosen profession. A case study conducted by O'Bryant, O'Sullivan, and Raudensky (2000) examining the beliefs and expectations of trainee PE teachers revealed that the trainees considered themselves physically active role models who should contribute to developing the self-esteem and motivation of children and young adults. Overall the research supports the concept that PE teachers are key role models for children and young adults during PE lessons and beyond, particularly in developing their self-efficacy levels for engaging in PE lessons. In an article examining why some people are physically active and others are not, Bauman and colleagues (2012) concluded that self-efficacy is one of the few psychosocial variables that is a consistent correlate and determinant of physical activity behaviour in children and adolescents. Therefore, if PE teachers can contribute to enhancing their pupils' levels of self-efficacy to be physically active in PE through the social sources of vicarious experience (modelling) and verbal persuasion, they are increasing the likelihood of informed lifelong physical activity choices and behaviour for these individuals.

6.3.2   Motivational climate in PE

Creating an optimal climate for children and young adults to maximise their potential in PE is another task PE teachers should undertake. Individuals strive to achieve goals in achievement settings, whether in a science lesson or a PE lesson, and these goals can provide a cognitive structure that defines an individual's perceptions of success and failure and their effort and motivation. Development of the achievement goal theory (AGT; Ames 1992a; Dweck 1986; Nicholls 1989) originated in educational settings; extensive research based on this theory has been carried out in physical activity settings, particularly PE. Central to AGT is the concept of competence; individuals' ability to demonstrate competence is strongly related to their achievement in a specific setting. According to Braithwaite, Spray, and Warbuton (2011), the term 'motivational climate' has been adapted to encompass study of environmental factors that lead people to construe competence in different ways. For some individuals competence is self-referenced, focuses on personal mastery of skills, and is defined by self-improvement. For other individuals competence is other-referenced, focuses on outcome (i.e., winning), and is defined by being the best in a salient reference group. It is important to note that within the AGT literature, theorists use different nomenclature. Ames

(1992a) refers to a mastery versus performance motivational climate, Dweck (1986) to a learning versus performance climate, and Nicholls (1989) to a task versus ego climate. Positive adaptations of a mastery/learning/task climate, where the emphasis is on self-improvement and personal mastery of skills, are confidence, enjoyment, and sustained participation. However, if a performance/ego climate is developed, where the emphasis is on comparing ability to others and winning, maladaptive consequences that can occur include boredom, anxiety, and increased risk of dropout for some individuals. In their review of 22 studies examining motivational climate interventions in PE, Brathwaite and colleagues found that there was an overall positive treatment effect in PE lessons for intervention groups exposed to mastery motivational conditions. Outcome analyses identified that the most consistent and largest overall treatment effects were for behavioural outcomes, including skill development and health and fitness measures. Affective outcomes (e.g., attitudes and anxiety) and cognitive outcomes (e.g., commitment, competence, and confidence) were also found to be more favourable in PE lessons exposed to mastery motivational climates. Conversely, negative outcomes associated with PE lessons exposed to ego motivational conditions were anxiety, competitive strategies, and boredom.

A central element that underpins successful manipulation of a mastery motivational climate is the PE teacher and his or her creation of this environment. Yet it is also important to remember that some individuals who define their own competence through comparison to others' ability and by trying to compete to be the best will not always display maladaptive outcomes such as boredom, anxiety, and dropout. On this basis, within the AGT researchers have trichotomised the AGT framework to distinguish those individuals with 'performance-approach' tendencies from those with 'performance-avoidance' tendencies. Individuals who are focused on performance-approach goals are oriented towards demonstrating competence relative to others, whereas individuals focused on performance-avoidance goals are oriented towards avoiding looking inferior and demonstrating a lack of competence in relation to others. It is suggested that performance-approach goals may also elicit positive outcomes alongside mastery-oriented goals. To further examine this concept within a PE setting, Carr (2006) explored different 'goal profiles' in relation to pupils' motivation for PE. After a sample of 185 11-year-old children completed the Patterns of Adaptive Learning survey (Midgley et al. 1996), they developed four goal profile clusters:

1. high mastery/high performance approach/low performance avoidance
2. high mastery/high performance approach/high performance avoidance
3. low mastery/high performance approach/high performance avoidance
4. high mastery/low performance approach/low performance avoidance

Their findings indicated that the most maladaptive outcomes were exhibited by individuals in cluster 3 and the most positive outcomes in relation to PE motivation were exhibited by those in cluster 1. It would appear that ensuring a high mastery-oriented environment is essential if you want to create an optimal motivational climate, regardless of orientation of performance-approach goals or performance-avoidance goals. Although cluster 1 was associated with positive outcomes, high mastery acts as a buffer if the performance-approach or performance-avoidance orientations become jeopardised. In other words, not everyone can win and be the best in an achievement setting like PE; if this is the only climate created, the risk of pupils becoming demotivated and bored and eventually dropping out is significantly increased. There are also gender differences evident in the criteria children and young adults use to assess their physical competence in physical activity settings. Girls tend to use more internalised, self-referenced information, such as skill improvement and achievement of personal goals, whereas boys predominantly use social comparison of ability (Ebbeck 1990; Horn, Glen, and Wentzell 1993). Therefore, if PE lessons' criterion for physical competence is via social comparison, girls are more likely to be at a disadvantage in maximising their perceptions of physical competence. In order to ensure positive behavioural, affective, and cognitive outcomes for all pupils, PE teachers need to aim to develop a broader base of competence, one not always based on winning and social comparison of physical ability.

6.3.3   Managing behaviours of PE teachers

According to Treasure and Roberts (1995), PE teachers can successfully create an optimal motivational climate in their lessons by examining the combined influence of pupils' dispositional goal orientation (i.e., whether they are task or performance oriented) and the social environment, which can be dictated by certain social agents – in this situation, peers in the PE lesson. Teachers need to develop an awareness of the importance of peer influence in shaping perceptions of competence. Peer interaction and group dynamics can also impact upon others' competence and motivational orientations. Consequently, the PE teacher's role becomes that of a manager who oversees the exchanges of dyads, triads, and groups in the lesson to ensure that an optimal motivational climate is created for all those in the class.

6.3.4   Practical guidelines for PE teachers

An important framework that PE teachers can use to emphasise the importance of specific goals in developing an optimal motivational climate is the TARGET framework (Task, Authority, Recognition, Grouping, Evaluation, Time), developed by Ames (1992b). This framework identifies six areas where a task- or performance-oriented climate can be created. 'Task' refers to the design of the activities in the session; 'authority' to the location of the decision making residing with pupil as well as teacher; 'recognition' to how

Table 6.1   *Using Ames's TARGET framework to develop a task or performance climate in PE*

	Task climate	Performance climate
Task	Challenging yet achievable	Repetitive and unachievable
Authority	Pupils given choice	Teacher-led choices
Recognition	Praise and feedback provided privately to individual pupils	Praise and feedback provided in public in front of peers
Grouping	Mixed ability groups	Rank order of ability to designate groups
Evaluation	Standards of performance are self-referenced	Standards of performance are peer-referenced
Time	Variability of learning pace accommodated	Slow learners not allowed sufficient time to master skills

rewards, such as praise, are distributed; 'grouping' to criteria used for selecting groups; 'evaluation' to standards of performance considered important; 'time' to the pace of learning. Table 6.1 shows how a task and performance climate can be created with the TARGET framework.

Use of a TARGET framework to manipulate an environment to favour a task climate in PE lessons has been shown to have small to moderate positive effects for affective, behavioural, and cognitive outcomes (Braithwaite et al. 2011). However, in their review Brathwaite and colleagues identify the need for a validated and reliable measurement tool to fully address the TARGET framework in physical activity settings.

Based on the TARGET framework and the ideas and concepts discussed, practical strategies that teachers could use within their PE lessons include the following:

- avoiding the creation of highly competitive environments and developing assessment tasks that encourage pupils to pursue their own goals, thereby expanding the basis for selection criteria away from performance measures;
- providing feedback in a confidential manner when it relates to criterion standards and personal improvement as opposed to comparison to other pupils;
- designating groups of mixed ability to enhance feelings of relatedness and cohesion within the group and to reduce the likelihood of social isolation of those with lower levels of ability.

6.4   The role of peers

Within the school setting, Valentine (2000) suggests there are two social worlds that children and young adults experience. First is the school itself, controlled by adults who develop formal social structures – timetables, class groups, lessons – for pupils to follow. Then there is the informal world of the pupils themselves, controlled by them and composed of social networks and peer-group cultures. The two worlds socially interact and impact on one another; in PE lessons the social environment created by the pupils can have a significant influence on the behavioural, affective, and cognitive outcomes of all pupils. Fundamental to understanding the role of peers in relation to physical activity behaviour is having a conceptual understanding of the term 'peers' and how it is differentiated from the term 'friends', particularly in the PE setting. Useful definitional guidelines on peer-related constructs have been provided by Smith (2007) and Smith and McDonough (2008), who suggest that 'peers' relates to individuals who are of a similar chronological age to the population sample of study. For example, pupils in the same class or children on the same sports team would be considered peers. According to Sullivan's (1953) interpersonal theory of psychiatry, peer groups, as opposed to friendship groups, should be viewed as having a distinct social influence on physical activity behaviour. Bukowski and Hoza (1989) define 'friendship' as a dyadic relationship characterised by closeness and mutual understanding. Based on this, we need to understand that for children and young adults involved in a physical activity setting, peer groups and friendship groups may function as different socialising agents, acting in a complementary or distinctive way to influence the affect, cognitions, and behaviours of others in their group.

6.4.1 The big-fish-little-pond effect

For the majority of children, the transition from primary to secondary school represents a major life event (Sirsch 2003) and is characterised by a shift toward larger class sizes, unfamiliar peer groups, and specialist subject teachers. This change in the sociocultural context can have significant effects on the individual in relation to such sociopsychological processes as self-efficacy and perceptions of competence when demonstrating physical ability in PE lessons. In an educational context, Marsh (1987) proposed a frame of reference model known as the big-fish-little-pond effect (BFLPE), stating that individuals compare their abilities to those of classmates and use this social comparison as a basis for forming their own concept of self (i.e., a sense of who they are) and of their abilities. The BFLPE occurs when equally able students have lower perceptions of their ability when they compare themselves with more able students and higher perceptions when they compare themselves with less able students. Marsh (1987) stipulated that the BFLPE is most prevalent in primary school, where children have no standard of comparison except the classmates they have been familiar with for the prior six years; they may not even know the average ability level of their classmates to use as a frame of reference. In contrast, the academic ability amongst classmates in secondary school is often known, particularly when classes are grouped according to academic ability. The BFLPE is posited to be domain specific; therefore, in the physical domain it could be argued that individuals compare their physical ability with that of their classmates and use the comparison as a social basis for their own physical self-concept.

Although extensive research on BFLPE has been conducted in educational settings, research examining frame of reference effects in the PE setting is limited. Unlike any other educational achievement domain, performance and achievement in PE is visible to others; it is common for ability rankings to be made explicit – for example, by being picked for a team (Trautwein, Gerlach, and Ludtke 2008). To address the limited research, Chanal et al. (2005) examined BFLPE and social-comparison processes in PE lessons during a ten-week block where 430 pupils had to develop gymnastics-based skills. Results indicated that the pupils' physical self-concept for gymnastics was positively predicted by their own gymnastics skills (i.e., self-referenced competence) yet negatively predicted by the average level of skill of others in the PE class (other-referenced competence). The findings provided preliminary support for BFLPE in a sport and physical activity setting. In 2008 Trautwein and colleagues conducted a longitudinal study examining frame of reference effects on grades awarded in PE, physical self-concept, and volitional physical activity in 1,095 9- to 12-year-old pupils. Their findings indicated that frame of reference effects on these outcome measures were evident in the domain of sport and exercise and also in children as young as nine. Specifically, pupils who were members of a PE class with high class-average physical ability were graded lower than if they had been members of a class with low class-average physical ability, and vice versa. Furthermore, membership in a class with high class-average physical ability led to lower physical self-concept and reduced volitional physical activity behaviour.

BFLPE has important practical implications in the PE setting. It suggests that peer comparison is a key factor young adults use in assessing their own physical competence. This could change during the school transition period, adding further disruption to the formation of their physical competence and physical self-concept. In primary school, children's basis of social comparison of their competence remains stable; they have had the same peers for six years, and consequently their perceptions of physical competence and physical self-concept are likely to remain relatively consistent during this time. In secondary school, they are no longer using the same basis for social comparison; they have new peers alongside them in PE lessons, and the basis of social comparison of physical competence changes. With this change in frame of reference, the role of peers in developing perceptions of physical competence in PE becomes increasingly important. PE teachers need to be aware of this frame of reference that children and young adults commonly use in assessing physical abilities. Furthermore, PE teachers should strive to minimise the amount of social comparison used in the PE lesson, as outlined in the TARGET framework (Ames 1992b), to ensure where possible that perceptions of competence are self-referenced as opposed to referenced against other class members.

6.4.2   Competence motivation theory

Children and young adults who feel well regarded by others in physical activity settings (e.g., PE lessons) are more likely to seek challenges, exert effort, and increase persistence and motivation. One early theory of motivation is White's (1959) model of effectance motivation, which aimed to fully consider the motivational aspect of competence. In his model White considered competence to be the most singularly important determinant of motivation. In 1978, Susan Harter tested, refined, and extended White's effectance motivation model by specifying domains of competence perceptions, addressing the implications of success and failure, outlining the function of rewards in the control of socialising agents, and stating the relative influence of intrinsic and extrinsic motivation. Central to Harter's development of the effectance motivation model, also known as Harter's (1978, 1982) competence motivation theory, is that children and young people strive to demonstrate mastery attempts in a particular achievement domain (academic, social, or physical) in which they feel competent.

Within the model, mastery attempts are defined as opportunities to develop a skill, via personal effort and hard work, through repeated practice attempts. In these mastery attempts, the degree of approval or disapproval via positive or negative reinforcement from significant others both directly and indirectly contributes to an individual's perceived sense of competence and control. Successful performance or positive reinforcement from significant others (socialising agents) is likely to lead to high perceived competence and effectance motivation. Successful mastery attempts can lead to intrinsic pleasure in the activity itself, which further contributes to high levels of perceived competence and effectance motivation. This then results in an increase in attempts at mastery at various tasks, leading to further positive reinforcement, high perceived competence, and enhanced effectance motivation. Therefore, the model is considered circular in nature, with a continuous positive effect on perceived competence and effectance motivation through repeated successful mastery attempts. However, a lack of reinforcement from significant others and a degree of disapproval of mastery attempts directly and indirectly contribute to low perceived competence and effectance motivation. In addition, failure at mastery attempts can lead to anxiety in mastery situations, which further contributes to a lack of perceived competence and a decrease in effectance motivation. The result is fewer attempts at mastery of tasks and the possibility of eventual dropout from that particular behaviour.

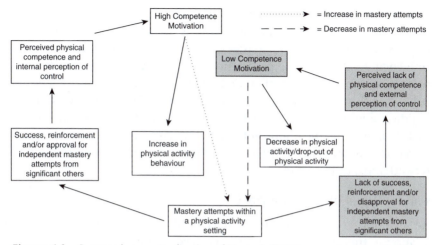

Figure 6.1 *Proposed conceptualisation of Harter's (1978) competence motivation theory in relation to physical activity behaviour*

In relation to physical activity settings – for example, PE lessons – perceptions of competence can be facilitated by providing children and adolescents with positive mastery experiences. During PE lessons, pupils will inevitably attempt to demonstrate mastery and ability of specific tasks (e.g., hitting a tennis ball). (A proposed conceptualisation of Harter's (1978) competence motivation theory in relation to mastering a physical skill is shown in Figure 6.1.) Successful mastery attempts at hitting a tennis ball and/or positive reinforcement and approval from significant others (e.g., peers in the PE lesson) can lead individuals to perceive themselves as more competent at hitting a tennis ball. This results in an overall increase in the level of competence motivation, increasing the likelihood of further mastery attempts at hitting a tennis ball and playing tennis. Increased success can further enhance perceptions of competence and motivation through positive reinforcement from significant others, leading to still more mastery attempts. However, if individuals are unsuccessful in attempts at hitting a tennis ball and/or receive negative reinforcement and disapproval from significant others (their peers), they may well perceive themselves as lacking competence at hitting a tennis ball. This will lead to low levels of competence motivation and result in a subsequent decrease in mastery attempts to hit a tennis ball. The circular nature of the process suggests that if these negative outcomes persist over time, the individual may drop out of playing tennis completely.

The role of peers in the model is central: they act as key socialising agents, either reinforcing or approving the physical behaviour in the PE lesson or disapproving of the individual's attempts, influencing their perceptions of physical competence and potentially their motivation for that specific task in the future. As earlier outlined for BFLPE, children and young adults tend to use social comparison as a basis for perceptions of competence. Therefore, if their social network in the PE setting is not reinforcing perceptions of physical competence, the likelihood of competence decreases, negatively influencing future effort, persistence, and motivation. In reviewing the sources of information children and adolescents draw upon to judge competence within physical activity settings, Horn (2004) suggested that older children and adolescents shift towards peer and social comparison. This further highlights the important role peers play as a frame of reference and as verifiers for others as to whether they approve or disapprove of their mastery attempts in PE lessons.

6.4.3   Types of peer support

A range of peer-related constructs have been examined in the literature in relation to their social influence on physical activity behaviour in children and young adults. Smith and McDonough (2008, 301–303) provided a useful categorisation and description of these constructs into three areas. These categories relate to the peer group (e.g., peer acceptance, peer rejection, peer support), specific peers (friendship, peer modelling), and peer referencing (social goals, impression management). Although the research evidence consistently suggests the importance of peers as socialising agents, the majority of the research has been conducted in volitional physical activity settings as opposed to PE lessons and with a focus on peer support and peer modelling. In PE lessons, social interaction is central to the delivery of the lesson; consequently, social groups can have a significant impact on affect, cognitions, and behaviours of group members. Examining these specific peer-related constructs in the PE environment and viewing peers as agents of social change and influence could provide a clearer understanding of their impact on physical activity choices and behaviours of pupils in PE. As outlined earlier and advocated by developmental psychologists (Rubin, Bukowski, and Parker 2006; Sullivan 1953), considering differences in the psychosocial relevance of peers and friends to young adults in physical activity environments may also be worthwhile. As with conceptualisation of the coach–athlete relationship in a sporting context (Jowett and Meek 2002; Jowett and Ntoumanis 2004), examining the closeness, complementarity, and commitment in friendship dyads, triads, and groups in physical activity settings such as PE lessons could be fruitful in developing appropriate intervention strategies to enhance this relationship. Research by Jago and colleagues (2009) has shown that a number of diverse friendship groups (at school, in the neighbourhood, during extracurricular activities) could mediate higher levels of physical activity due to the larger number of peer physical activity resources available to draw upon. Examining the importance of the physical activity context for social interaction among peers and friends is a research area that needs addressing.

Recently, research has pointed to the need for PE teachers to recognise the importance of peers and group interaction as influential socialising agents in several ways. First, they can be role models for others in relation to their attitudes towards PE and their physical abilities. According to Bandura (1986), the more role models and observers are alike, the likelier that modelling behaviour will occur. During adolescence, young adults have similar interests and ideas, which translate to shared norms in a cultural peer group. Peers and friends emerge as role models in social groups. In the United Kingdom, the PE curriculum varies across the four nations, yet a common key outcome is providing all pupils opportunities for cooperation and leadership. At Key Stage 4 (14–16 years), PE officiating and coaching positions allow pupils this opportunity and give them a sense of autonomy and responsibility for others in the class. Although these roles can develop important social skills, they have to be appropriately managed by PE teachers, as pupils can grow increasingly influential in disseminating their attitudes and beliefs about being active and in judging others' physical ability. Peers also serve as an important frame of reference for others' perceptions of physical competence and ability. Finally, reinforcement and approval from fellow peers, either verbally or visually during mastery attempts of a PE skill, can impact individuals' perceptions of competence, motivation, and long-term engagement with PE.

6.5 The role of parents

Although not directly involved in the social environment of the typical school day, parents are also remote key socialising agents of their children's physical activity behaviours in the school setting. They influence the development of their children's values and attitudes towards physical activity participation in school and also their actual physical behaviour through assistance in active commuting to school and extracurricular physical activity. In both the social learning theory (Bandura 1977) and the competence motivation theory (Harter 1978), parents are key sources of self-efficacy and perceptions of physical competence in a physical activity setting. As identified earlier, an individual's perceived self-efficacy can be generated through four primary sources: performance accomplishment, vicarious experience, verbal persuasion, and judgement of physiological and affective states. Seen from this basis, parents are important sources of vicarious experience and verbal persuasion to enhance their children's levels of self-efficacy in a physical activity setting.

Parents play a central role in shaping the attitudes, values, and behaviours of younger children towards a healthy lifestyle (Glover 1978). Focus group research conducted by Anderson and Cavallaro (2002) examined the influence of role models in young children (8–13) and found that they most frequently identified their parents (34%) as their role model. According to Bandura (1977), parental modelling is primarily achieved by the child's observational learning; some research supports the concept that if parents are active, their children will replicate this behaviour (Cleland et al. 2011; Freedson and Evenson 1991; Moore et al. 1991). Yet other studies have shown that being an active parent does not necessarily translate to having active children, therefore contradicting the role claimed for observational learning in increasing children's self-efficacy in a physical activity setting (Jago et al. 2010; Kimiecik and Horn 1998). It may not be the actual behaviour of parents that influences children's physical activity patterns but rather their beliefs and attitudes towards the children being active. Based on their review of the literature examining role models, Payne and colleagues (2003) suggested that parents with positive attitudes and beliefs about being physically active were more likely to act as a catalyst for their children to engage in physical activity. This has important implications for the school setting, where the physical activity values held in the home environment could translate to the PE environment in school.

Harter (1978, 1982) suggests that the number and content of competence areas increases from early childhood through to adolescence; from the age of eight onwards, children can differentiate perceptions of competence in the physical domain from other domains (e.g., social, academic). Younger children tend to use parents as sources of judgement for perceptions of physical competence, yet as they become older, this reliance shifts towards peer sources. To explore this concept, McKiddie and Maynard (1997) conducted research examining perceived competence in PE in two groups of children: 11- and 12-year-olds and 13- and 14-year-olds. Findings suggested that younger children preferred parental sources to judge perceptions of competence despite being assessed on their physical competence in PE, a social environment where parents are not present, whereas older children used peer sources more frequently. This can be linked to Harter's (1978) competence motivation theory, where parents play a key role as socialising agents who reinforce their child's mastery attempts in a physical activity setting and provide approval of their competence at particular tasks. If this takes place in a positive manner and the message is consistently reinforced outside the school setting, according to the theory (Figure 6.1) the child is more likely to continue with that behaviour. This could translate to mastery attempts in PE where the child has already gained approval of physical competence from the parents and so may be more motivated to master new skills. This has been supported by Bois et al. (2005), who demonstrated in a sample of 8- to 10-year-old children that a father's perceptions of his child's physical competence directly influenced the child's physical activity behaviour and a mother's perceptions indirectly influenced it. As gatekeepers to their children's, particularly younger children's, perceptions of ability, parents who encourage self-referenced perceptions of physical competence and so reinforce their child's ability can impact their physical activity behaviour and motivation in the PE environment as well as outside it.

6.5.1   Parents, active commuting, and extracurricular physical activity

Suggestions have been made in the literature regarding the importance of parents providing logistic support (transportation, financial support) for physical activity behaviour, with recent research evidencing that maternal logistic support can be critical for girls' physical activity levels and paternal logistic support equally central for boys' (Jago et al. 2010). This type of social support and provision from parents is essential in ensuring that children have the opportunity to engage in extracurricular physical activity after school. Parents can also be key socialising agents for extracurricular activity via leadership roles: they often volunteer to run extracurricular clubs for the school. In so doing they can influence the physical activity behaviours of other children as well as their own, where key social processes (e.g., appropriate modelling behaviours, cultivating a task-oriented climate) need to be adopted to maximise children's enjoyment and continued participation in volitional physical activity.

Active commuting to and from school provides another opportunity for children to be active, and this behaviour is predominantly determined by such social-environmental factors as the distance between school and home, work patterns of parents, and the convenience of driving children to school prior to starting work. However, Biddle and Mutrie (2008) note that while the social psychology of parents towards active commuting is also important, it is a limited research area. A review of children's active commuting by Davison, Werder, and Lawson (2008) found that besides the social-environmental correlates of active commuting (distance to school and parents' commuting activity), how parents viewed active commuting and social interaction opportunities during the commute was a key social correlate of the activity. This further emphasises the important social role parents can play in their children's physical activity behaviour through encouraging active commuting to and from school.

6.6   Summary

PE teachers, peers, and parents all contribute to the social processes involved in youth physical activity behaviour in the school setting. They can be achieved through positive attitudes, placing value on being physically active, appropriate modelling behaviours, and verbal encouragement and reinforcement. They should be delivered by a range of socialising agents via a task-oriented climate to maximise current and future physical activity behaviour. The case study discusses specific strategies PE teachers, peers, and parents can use to create an optimal social environment for physical activity in schools.

6.7 Case study

6.7.1 Setting the scene

During their time at primary school, a group of 11-year-old children all enjoyed their PE lessons together, participated in all of the activities that were offered by the teacher, and felt competent in being physically active around each other. As the primary school was just around the corner from their homes, every day they walked to and from school together and participated in a number of after-school clubs together. At the end of their last year in primary school, they had to move to different secondary schools and were timetabled into different classes for PE. Since the start of the school year, the PE teacher has noticed that their enjoyment of PE seems to have decreased; they lack confidence in their ability to perform skills in front of others and isolate themselves from others in the class. The PE teacher has also noticed that there are other pupils in the class who enjoy PE, have developed friendship groups, are willing to perform any skill, and always want to be the best at every activity carried out.

How can the PE teacher and other key socialising agents in the PE environment ensure optimal enjoyment and participation for all pupils in the class?

6.7.2 Assessing the situation

The primary socialising agent in this situation is the PE teacher. Developing an awareness of those pupils in the class who are not engaging, not participating, or seem demotivated is the first stage of addressing the situation. This should be apparent in their conduct during the PE lesson; for example, if they isolate themselves from the rest of the class and avoid voluntary opportunities to demonstrate physical ability in front of the class. The PE teacher can also identify and monitor different friendship groups and peer interaction to determine if these negative behaviours towards PE and physical activity are common to all group members.

6.7.3 Important role of key socialising agents in behaviour change

In this situation, several socialising agents play an important role and can all contribute to ensuring optimal enjoyment and participation for all PE pupils. The main facilitator in this is the PE teacher, who needs to ensure that the motivational climate is task-oriented through both the behaviours adopted and management of pupils' behaviours. The teacher's own modelling behaviour needs to demonstrate a willingness to participate in the activities; he or she must appear to be physically active and have positive attitudes and beliefs in a physically active lifestyle. This will ensure the maximum potential for 'buy-in' from all pupils. Finally, the teacher needs to ensure that a broad base for assessing physical competence is created to encourage self-referenced competence as well as social comparison. This allows the teacher to account for any gender differences in the criteria young adults use to assess their physical competence or to encourage those with lower levels of perceived competence to judge their ability based on self-improvement over time as opposed to improvement compared to others.

Although not directly involved in the PE lesson itself, parents can also be a key social influence on encouraging behaviour change in this situation. Ensuring positive attitudes and belief in a physically active lifestyle in the family environment will maximise the buy-in from their children as to being active and participating in PE. Thus, a consistent message about the importance of physical activity, in both physical and social contexts, will be delivered by all relevant social influences. Awareness of the potential influence of their modelling behaviour on their children, particularly younger children, is needed, as this could be replicated in PE lessons. Finally, their role as facilitator of their children's active commuting should also be considered by parents; they should aim to incorporate active commuting in the family routine.

6.7.4 Specific strategies for key socialising agents

The following strategies could be used by PE teachers, parents, and peers in the PE class to ensure optimal enjoyment and participation for all pupils in the class.

- Develop an awareness that for some children, the transition from primary to secondary school can impact their perceptions of physical competence in PE, as there are changes in their frame of reference and their social environment (PE teachers and parents).
- Provide verbal encouragement, approval, and positive reinforcement for attempts at self-improvement in physical ability (PE teachers, parents, peers).
- Provide instructional support for mastery attempts at a specific PE skill. For individuals who do not improve initially, break the skill down into more manageable tasks where praise is more likely to be warranted (PE teachers and peers).
- Endorse a physically active lifestyle through the sharing of positive attitudes and beliefs (PE teachers and parents).

- Encourage a physically active lifestyle through modelling behaviours achieved through one's own appearance and engagement in physical activity (PE teachers, parents, peers).
- Adopt an inclusive attitude towards peers in PE regardless of their ability (peers).
- Consider restructuring work patterns and one's own commute to work to incorporate active commuting to and from school (parents).
- Develop a task-oriented climate in PE using the TARGET framework to provide self-referenced feedback in confidence rather than in front of the rest of the class (PE teachers). This could be achieved through the use of modern technology (video feedback on a smartphone or tablet);
- allow for some pupil choice of activities in PE (PE teachers);
- develop groups in the PE class based on mixed ability to minimise social isolation and enhance relatedness and group cohesion (PE teachers and peers);
- allow sufficient time for all pupils to master a new skill at their own pace (PE teachers);
- provide a range of tasks for pupils that will be challenging yet achievable for each individual rather than one task for the group that only a few can master successfully (PE teachers);
- develop standards of performance criteria based on individual improvements, not comparison to others in the class (PE teachers).

6.8   Further study and recommended reading

The following literature is recommended for further reading on key concepts addressed in this chapter.

- Biddle, S. J., and Mutrie, N. (2008). *Psychology of Physical Activity: Determinants, Well-Being and Interventions*, 2nd ed. (317–325). London: Routledge.
- Smith, A. L. (2007). Youth Peer Relationships in Sport. In S. Jowett and D. Lavallee (eds), *Social Psychology in Sport*, chs 11–13. Champaign, IL: Human Kinetics.

Additionally, reading in the following relevant areas is recommended. The materials address social aspects of the school environment that are not covered in this chapter but are central to physical activity behaviours in children and adolescents.

Social processes involved in break time and lunchtime (recess) physical activity:

- Pellegrini, A. D., and Bohn, C. M. (2005). The role of recess in children's cognitive performance and school adjustment. *Educational Researcher,* 34(1), 13–19.

Pellegrini, A. D., Kato, Blist K., Blatchford, P., and Baines, E. (2002). A short-term longitudinal study of children's playground games across the first year of school: implications for social competence and adjustment to school. *American Educational Research Journal,* 39(4), 991–1015.

Class cohesion and developing a sense of relatedness in PE:

- Cox, A., and Williams, L. (2008). The roles of perceived teacher support, motivational climate, and psychological need satisfaction in students' physical education motivation. *Journal of Sport and Exercise Psychology,* 30(2), 222–239.
- Ntoumanis, N. (2001). A self-determination approach to the understanding of motivation in physical education. *British Journal of Educational Psychology,* 71(2), 225–242.

7   Workplaces

7.1   Learning objectives

The purpose of this chapter is to examine the social and organisational context of the workplace setting and its importance in relation to shaping physical activity behaviour in employees. The key learning objectives are:

- to explore the role of the employer in facilitating the social processes needed to enhance the physical activity behaviour of employees. Links to goal-setting theory and socio-ecological theory are established to underpin physical activity behaviour change in the workplace;
- to consider the importance of colleagues as social agents who can facilitate, encourage, and motivate physical activity behaviour through team-based activities. Links to Caron's model of group cohesion and the transtheoretical model (TTM) are used to understand the intrapersonal and interpersonal processes involved in workplace physical activity;
- to discuss the practical implications for employers and employees in creating an optimal social and organisational environment for physical activity in the workplace, with specific strategies outlined.

7.2   Introduction to the context

Approximately 60% of the world's population is accessible, either directly or indirectly, through the workplace. According to the Office of National Statistics, there are currently 29.7 million people in employment in the United Kingdom. It is estimated that members of the UK workforce spend more hours at work than the majority of their European counterparts and have less paid annual leave. This could have a detrimental effect on physical activity participation in the United Kingdom, with lack of time commonly reported as a key barrier to adults being physically active. The UK workforce is socially and organisationally diverse in nature due to different sector types (public, private, voluntary), organisation sizes, and types of employment contracts. Consequently the workplace provides access to a range of individuals and an opportunity for sustained peer and employer support for physical activity.

Encouraging and supporting a healthy workplace can result in a range of mutual benefits for both employer and employee. In 2006, the Health and Safety Commission stated that the main causes of absenteeism in the United Kingdom were musculoskeletal disorders, stress, anxiety, depression, breathing problems, and hearing difficulties. The majority of these health issues could be substantially reduced or even prevented if a physically active lifestyle were adopted. Cox, Griffiths, and Rial-Gonzalez (2000) found several psychosocial factors associated with workplace stress, including organisation culture and function, identified role in the organisation, career development, decision making and control, interpersonal relationships, work environment, workload and pace, and work schedule. Incorporating physical activity in the workplace through social processes could reduce these psychosocial stressors for a large proportion of employees. In the United Kingdom, the Well@Work initiative, funded by the British Heart Foundation (Bull, Adams, and Hooper 2008), aimed to assess the effectiveness of workplace health interventions across several sectors with over 10,000 employees. Physical activity interventions, accounting for half of all initiatives, were considered the 'easiest sell' to employees (Batt 2009) and could lead to long-term physical activity behaviour change.

How to go about developing a healthy workforce has been clearly outlined through evidence-based findings from a social responsibility perspective, yet providing a strong financial case for the importance of workplace health initiatives often holds more gravitas with employers and their stakeholders. The financial case for incorporating health and wellbeing in the workplace setting was outlined in a report by Pricewaterhouse Coopers in 2008. The report estimated that in 2006 workplace absence totalled 175 million working days, equating to 13.4 billion pounds lost to the UK economy. The concept of presenteeism (in addition to absenteeism) has also been shown to have financial implications. Presenteeism, a relatively new concept in workplace health, is where an individual is at work yet performs below par due to ill health (Cooper and Dewe 2008). Encouraging a healthy workforce through physical activity could reduce the number of workdays lost due to absenteeism and increase the relative productivity of employees who regularly engage in presenteeism.

The workplace is a distinctive setting in which to promote physical activity in that it provides access to a captive and diverse group of adults. Modes of communication, both formal and informal, are already established, and peer group networks have been formed in the working community (Naidoo and Wills 2002). Making best use of the social processes and cultural norms of employees in the workplace is essential to achieve physical activity behaviour change at the interpersonal and intrapersonal levels. Yet the true potential of workplace physical activity can be realised only if there is clear management endorsement and 'buy-in' from the top down through the organisational structure.

7.2.1   Ecological workplace physical activity model

The workplace has been identified by various governments as a key setting to promote physical activity and reduce sedentary behaviour. Research examining workplace physical activity interventions has shifted its focus to adopt ecologically based approaches to increase physical activity of employees by centring on how individuals interact in their sociocultural setting; for example, home or workplace. Based on work by McLeroy et al. (1988) and Sallis and Owen (1999), Plotnikoff et al. (2005) developed an ecological workplace physical activity model. This model was developed alongside a workplace physical activity audit tool to evaluate workplace physical activity programmes using the ecological model as a framework. The model identified six overlapping levels in the workplace environment: individual, social, organisational, community, policy, and physical environment. Although developing strategies for physical activity behaviour change at all six levels is recognised in the model and overlap across levels is acknowledged, the social level is the key focus of this chapter. This level aims to incorporate the social processes in the workplace setting that can influence physical activity behaviour change; for example, the influence of organisational culture, peer relationships, and employer-employee relationships. In order to change physical activity behaviour in the workplace, numerous strategies based on social processes have been suggested and subsequently tested. These include counselling, tailoring, goal setting, self-monitoring, feedback, education, motivation, incentives, and team competition.

7.2.2   Management endorsement of physical activity programmes

In 2008, the National Institute for Clinical Excellence (NICE) developed guidelines for employers on how to encourage employees to be physically active. The guidelines, based on a systematic review of workplace physical activity interventions conducted by Dugdill and colleagues (2008), advocate a top-down approach to physical activity behaviour change in the workplace, emphasising the importance of management endorsement of physical activity strategies. Several recommendations were highlighted in the guidelines:

- Policy and planning – employers are encouraged to develop an organisation-wide plan or policy to encourage and support employees to become more physically active.

- Implementing a physical activity programme – employers are encouraged to introduce and monitor an organisation-wide, multicomponent programme to encourage physical activity.
- Development of components of a physical activity programme – employers, in consultation with employees, are encouraged to develop components of such a programme, including travel plans, decisional prompts at key locations in the workplace (e.g., lifts, stairs), goal setting, and informational support.
- Supporting employers – employers are encouraged to seek support and advice to implement and sustain physical activity in the workplace. Support should be provided by public health authorities, local partners, and agencies and stakeholders.

The NICE guidelines also recommend incorporating physical activity behaviour into continued professional development activities for employees and link these to organisational goals where possible. Furthermore, the guidelines encourage incentives to be physically active in the workplace to be tailored and appropriately linked to the workload of employees where possible. (The NICE guidelines are discussed in further detail in Section 7.6.)

7.3 The role of the employer

Based on the findings of their systematic review in 2008, Dugdill and colleagues found that the majority of evidence on the effectiveness of workplace physical activity interventions came from larger private-sector companies. Research evidence from the public and voluntary sectors is limited, particularly in small-to-medium enterprises (SME). This poses a potential challenge to fully understanding the applied context of workplace interventions, as most of the UK workforce is employed in the SME sector. Furthermore, Wright, Marsden, and Antonelli (2004) state that workplace intervention research is particularly difficult to conduct in the SME sector due to constraints on managers' time and mistrust of health and safety professionals, who have predominantly adopted enforcement of strategies for health in the workplace as a model of practice. Thus, encouragement as opposed to enforcement might be a more appropriate social process for employers to adopt to enhance workplace physical activity in all sectors. Employer-led approaches can enhance employees' social attributes; for example, communication, productivity, and cohesion via physical activity promotion.

7.3.1 Informational support

The workplace is an ideal setting for disseminating physical activity–related information thanks to its numerous established communication channels:

emails, newsletters, bulletin boards, and the like. Providing this type of informational support for behaviour change can be viewed as a relatively easy and low-cost method for employers to increase awareness of the physical activity opportunities in the workplace and highlight the physical, social, and psychological benefits of being regularly active. This type of approach can be targeted at individuals who would be classed as the hard-to-reach population in the workforce, those who are typically in the pre-contemplation and contemplation stages of the TTM (Prochaska and DiClemente 1983). Pre-contemplators are individuals who are currently inactive and not thinking about becoming active in the near future. Contemplators are also currently inactive but are thinking about becoming active and contemplating change. Increasing awareness of the benefits of being physically active, the opportunities to be active, and the risks of being inactive are appropriate cognitive processes of change that could help pre-contemplators and contemplators move towards physical activity behaviour change (DiClemente et al. 1991). It is essential to use motivational messages that target their reluctance to becoming physically active (this matter is discussed in further detail in Section 7.6.2).

Employees in office-based work settings often have regular access to email, which provides the most accessible channel for disseminating physical activity-related information. For employees without such access (e.g., postal workers and labourers), alternative channels can be used, including bulletin boards and payslips. However, the research evidence for the effectiveness of these channels of communication in relation to physical activity behaviour change is limited. In 2005, Plotnikoff and colleagues (2005) conducted a large-scale study examining the efficacy of an email intervention promoting physical activity and nutrition behaviour in a workplace context in Alberta, Canada. Three government and two large private-sector worksites were recruited for the study, and of the 16,750 employees, 2,121 were assigned a personal email address and randomly assigned to an intervention group or a control group. Weekly email messages related to physical activity and nutrition were sent to employees in the intervention group over a 12-week period. The messages were based on key social-cognitive theories, including the social learning theory (Bandura 1998), TTM (Prochaska and Velicer 1997), the theory of planned behaviour (Ajzen 1991), and the protection motivation theory (Rogers 1983). No other health-promotion campaigns were implemented in the workplace during the intervention period.

Findings from the intervention were encouraging, with an increase in self-reported physical activity for the intervention group workers. The intervention also impacted on social-cognitive constructs, which could have been potential mediators for the increase in physical activity through the email intervention. Participants reported an increase in self-efficacy (situation-specific self-confidence) for engaging in physical activity and a firmer intention to participate in physical activity and perceived more advantages and fewer disadvantages of being active. This intervention was considered highly unobtrusive and cost effective for the employer whilst targeting positive physical activity behaviour change in a large number of individuals. The employer's role is to provide endorsement support in these informational approaches, which may also impact other social processes in their workforce, including self-efficacy, cues to action, and the intention to be active.

Recent years have seen a significant increase in the use of social media (Facebook, Twitter, blogs, etc.) to disseminate information to a large and diverse audience. It is estimated that Facebook and Twitter have, respectively, 1 billion and 500 million registered users worldwide. Accessing this audience to raise awareness and spur physical activity behaviour change has promising and far-reaching potential. This medium of communication has the capacity to be used in a workplace setting by employers to provide informational support for physical activity to their employees. In addition to increasing awareness of the benefits of being physically active and the opportunities to be active in the workplace, social media might also create a sense of relatedness and belonging amongst colleagues who could be posting, tweeting, and blogging with one another about their physical activity behaviours, goals, and progress (for discussion in detail, see Section 7.6).

7.3.2   Motivation of employees in the workplace

Motivation is a central component of behaviour change. To change employees' physical activity behaviour, goal setting has been used in the workplace setting. In 2002, Locke and Latham proposed a theory of goal setting and task motivation that has been the basis for workplace physical activity interventions utilising goal setting. Their theory focuses primarily on motivation in work and postulates that goals affect performance through four mechanisms:

1. directive function – goals direct attention away from goal-irrelevant activities;
2. energising function – more difficult goals lead to greater effort than easier goals;
3. persistence – ensuring there is a balance between time spent on goals and intensity of effort;
4. increased arousal – discovery and/or use of task-relevant knowledge and strategies.

The goal-setting theory is fully consistent with social-cognitive theory in that it acknowledges the importance of conscious goals and self-efficacy, as highlighted in the high-performance goal-setting cycle (see Figure 7.1).

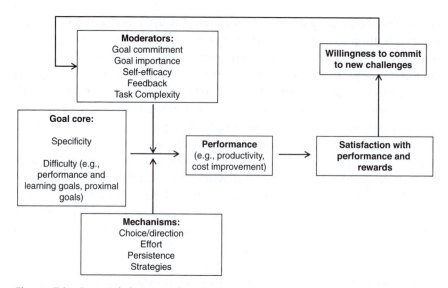

Figure 7.1   *Essential elements of goal-setting theory and the high-performance cycle*

Source: From Locke, E. A. and Latham, G. P. (2002). Building a practically useful theory of goal setting and task motivation: a 35-year odyssey, *American Psychologist*, 57(9), 705–717. Reprinted with permission from the American Psychological Association.

In the cycle, several social processes are identified as moderators in the relationship between the goal core and performance. Of particular relevance to physical activity goal setting in the workplace are the social constructs of self-efficacy, goal commitment, and feedback on goals. Based on Locke and Latham's work, these have been incorporated in several workplace interventions. Research by Dishman and colleagues (2009; 2010) attempted to address the dearth in goal-setting intervention research lacking a theoretical under-pinning and combine the approach with an ecologically derived organisational action component that identified a clear role employers should adopt in implementing workplace programmes. Included was senior management endorsement of the intervention, a joint employee-management steering committee responsible for implementing specific intervention components and providing employee incentives at both the group and individual level. Incentives such as free lunches and T-shirts were also used by employers to increase employees' motivation to attain weekly step-count goals, enhance the key mechanisms of effort and persistence required to achieve goals, and provide employees with extrinsic motivation to continue their behaviour. These organisation-level actions were designed to demonstrate the importance of management support, allow employees to be involved and self-determined in implementing the intervention, and utilise facilitative environments and naturally occurring social relationships in the workplace setting. The goal-setting component included both team and personal goal setting through pedometer step counts during the 12-week intervention. Findings supported using a social-ecological intervention in a workplace setting to increase physical activity behaviour of employees, with an increase from 31% to 51% in the number of workers achieving physical activity guidelines for health during the last six weeks of the intervention. The findings also indicated that social constructs in the goal-setting theory were modified as a result of the workplace intervention. Participants who set more difficult goals sustained higher levels of self-efficacy, had increased goal commitment and intention about attaining their goals, and exhibited a greater increase in moderate to vigorous physical activity (MVPA) and step counts.

Overall, employers have a pivotal role to play in promoting physical activity in their workforce. NICE guidelines support the research evidence highlighting that employers are key in developing an appropriate workplace ethos and culture regarding physical activity and that this can be achieved through several strategies. Senior management endorsement and involvement in physical activity promotion is essential to allow a top-down approach to behaviour change to permeate the organisation's workforce. Discussion with employees regarding plans or policies they would like to implement will allow them to become more self-determined and autonomous in their behaviour change. Employers should also monitor any programme implemented and be involved in specific components of an intervention wherever possible. Doing so will provide validation support to their employees and help develop social relationships between senior management and the general workforce.

7.4   The role of the employee

Workplace employees have the potential to act as key socialising agents in relation to the physical activity behaviour change of their colleagues. Existing patterns of formal and informal communication, established social relationships, and norms naturally created in the workplace can be used as social support mechanisms for physical activity. For example, employees can offer (1) companionship and verbal support to colleagues whilst engaging in physical activity behaviour, (2) instrumental support through leadership behaviours relating to physical activity in the workplace, and (3) validation support via a sense of competition and achievement amongst colleagues. As highlighted earlier, individuals in the workplace will have varying attitudes towards being physically active and will also have varying levels of physical activity. This range of attitudes and abilities must be kept in mind in developing specific targets for employees in order to influence behaviour change. Having an initial consultation with the employees themselves to ensure that they are engaged and involved in implementing the physical activity intervention will maximise its effectiveness.

Phipps and colleagues (2010) recognised the importance of consultation to ascertain employee interest in workplace physical activity programmes, identify employees who would benefit most from these interventions, and assess work-related barriers to implementing an intervention. Using a combination of focus groups and surveys, they collected data on a range of hospital employees (N = 434) at all levels (executives and managers; physicians; nurses and support staff). Interestingly, some of the employees felt that having a workplace physical activity programme meant that their employers cared for their well-being, creating a sense of value and appreciation. One of the study's salient findings was that individuals at the earlier stages of the TTM (i.e., pre-contemplators, contemplators, and preparers) were significantly more interested in workplace physical activity programmes than the already regularly active. Based on the survey findings, participants voiced interest in an on-site physical activity programme, with particular attraction to walking groups, team-based competitions, exercise classes, and access to personal trainers. That having a physical activity buddy was cited as important by two-thirds of the sample highlights the importance of social support networks for workplace physical activity. Half the participants identified incentives as an extrinsic motivator to participation. Personal safety, workload, lack of suitable walking paths in the workplace vicinity, and limited time for breaks and lunch were the key barriers identified by the workers. The authors concluded that for this workplace sample, structural changes to promote a safe walking environment with use of a walking buddy and employer-led enforced policies on breaks for physical activity may encourage participation by the at-risk groups (sedentary, low-activity individuals) in the workplace.

7.4.1   Development of team cohesion among employees

Developing a cohesive workforce can have numerous benefits for employers: increased productivity, increased job satisfaction, reduced conflict, reduced absenteeism. There is a wealth of data in the management literature to suggest that employee cohesion leads to better work, either as a directive function or an antecedent to performance (Chang and Bordia 2001; Evans and Dion 1999; Mullen and Cooper 1994). The workplace has naturally established teams that collaborate in operations and tasks on a daily basis. They can serve as a platform for team cohesion to be enhanced through physical activity. Carron, Brawley, and Widmeyer (1998) consider cohesion 'a dynamic process that is reflected in the tendency for a group to stick together and remain united in pursuit of its instrumental objectives and/or for the satisfaction of member affective needs' (213). To conceptualise cohesion in a sport and exercise context, Brawley, Carron, and Widmeyer (1987), Carron, Widmeyer, and Brawley (1985), and Widmeyer, Brawley, and Carron (1985) have proposed a model for team cohesion based on three fundamental assumptions:

1. Cohesion is a group property that is reflected in and can be assessed through the perceptions of individual group members.
2. Members develop perceptions associated with the level of bonding within the group as well as the way the group satisfies personal needs and objectives.
3. Task and social concerns represent two general foci for the group members' perceptions and personal needs and objectives.

These researchers further suggested that the three assumptions form the basis for the proposal that the majority of variance in team cohesiveness can be accounted for by four constructs. (They are explained using an example of a walking group with weekly team step-count goals).

1. Individual attractions to the group – task (ATG-T). This relates to the individual member's perception of personal involvement with the group task; for example, the contribution to reaching a weekly team step-count goal.
2. Individual attractions to the group – social (ATG-S). This relates to the individual member's perception of personal acceptance and social interaction; for example, the walking group's members all socialise during breaks and lunchtimes at work.
3. Group integration – task (GI-T). This relates to the individual member's perception of the similarity, closeness, and bonding that exist as a totality around the group's collective task; for example, the members discuss their weekly step-goal target regularly, and all value its importance.
4. Group integration – social (GT-S). This relates to the individual member's perception of the similarity, closeness, and bonding that exist as a totality around social concerns; for example, the walking group's members socialise outside work as a group.

Team goal setting seems to be effective at enhancing both task and social cohesion in a group. Goal setting is a powerful approach to changing direction, regulation, and persistence of effort; several workplace physical activity interventions have utilised both team and individual goal setting to increase team cohesion and, subsequently, physical activity behaviour. As already noted, Dishman and colleagues (2009, 2010) conducted a randomised 12-week workplace multicomponent intervention to examine its efficacy on physical activity behaviour. A key social-cognitive component was team and individual goal setting with the use of pedometers. To facilitate participation and goal attainment, individuals were assigned to teams with a team captain. Each captain was responsible for motivating members to set goals and earn points for the team. The captain gave verbal, instrumental, and companionship support to the team throughout the intervention to develop task and social cohesion. Team goal attainment was displayed on a weekly basis in the workplace to develop task cohesion.

The personal goal-setting component of the intervention focused on setting and attaining personal goals that adopted key principles of a SMARTER (specific, measurable, attainable, realistic, time-phased, evaluated, recorded) approach to goal setting (Doran 1981). The goals were self-determined, specific regarding performance and time, challenging but realistic and attainable, and easily assessed. The primary personal goals involved gradual increases in accumulation of daily pedometer steps and ten-minute blocks of MVPA during the 12 weeks of the intervention. Personal goals were targeted toward meeting or exceeding established public health recommendations for physical activity, including accumulating 10,000 or more pedometer steps each day or 150 or more minutes each week of MVPA. Findings related to personal goal setting indicated that individuals who set more difficult goals, sustained higher levels of self-efficacy, and had greater commitment to and intention about attaining goals exhibited more of an increase in MVPA and step counts during the intervention. This suggests that a social process such as self-efficacy is important in reaching physical activity–related goals when it is combined with a SMARTER goal-setting approach.

The concept of using workplace physical activity to develop team cohesion amongst employees and effect positive behaviour changes – for example, productivity – was explored in the United Kingdom by Evans in 2002. This study, using both quantitative and qualitative research methods, examined the effectiveness of a 5 km running event in Liverpool for employees in the voluntary, public, and private sectors. In the intervention design, social support was a key psychosocial determinant of physical activity behaviour by encouraging team entry (four employees per team) into the race. Team cohesion was developed through task and social constructs during training and in the competition itself. Many participants reported on the benefits of team-based physical activity interventions and also cited taking part because a colleague had asked them to do so. Findings suggested that this 5 km corporate event was successful in attracting and sustaining running behaviour in previously inactive employees, particularly women. The social aspect of training and competing as a team emerged as one of the main motives for participating in the event.

7.5   Effectiveness of workplace interventions on psychosocial factors and physical activity

A systematic review by Dugdill and colleagues (2008) aimed to identify which types of workplace intervention were effective in changing physical activity or other psychosocial outcomes for different workforce sectors and

workplace types. They identified 33 articles that met the inclusion criterion of being a workplace intervention to increase physical activity in adults
where the intervention was initiated or endorsed by the employer and physical activity was an outcome measure. The studies were grouped into five
intervention types: stair walking, walking, active travel, other (including
physical activity counselling, motivational interviewing, health checks,
screening, led activity sessions, health-promotion messages or information),
and multicomponent. Fourteen of these studies were graded as high quality or good by the authors. Seven assessed the effectiveness of decisional
prompts on workplace stair walking where health signs or messages promoted cues to action for employees. Review findings were that there was
limited evidence for the effectiveness of stair walking workplace physical
activity interventions with minimal long-term behaviour change evident;
all studies but one used behavioural observation as the assessment method.
Included in the review were four studies examining workplace-based walking interventions. Dugdill and colleagues concluded that workplace walking interventions using pedometers as a motivational and monitoring tool
could increase daily step count if accompanied by facilitated goal setting,
self-monitoring, self-report diaries, and good-quality walking routes in the
vicinity. The authors also found strong evidence of effectiveness for four
studies that used physical activity counselling in the workplace, yet psychosocial factors that could have mediated this positive effect of counselling on physical activity were not assessed. Overall, the majority of research
was limited to larger companies, with physical activity and other physical
characteristics as the main outcome measures. There is a need to examine
in greater detail the social processes and psychosocial factors that could
mediate changed physical activity behaviour in the workplace as a result of
interventions. This focus is currently missing from the literature.

Eleven Well@Work projects were established across nine regions in
England in 2007 to focus on three key lifestyle behaviours in the workplace: increased physical activity, healthy eating, and smoking cessation.
Bull and colleagues (2008) provided the final evaluation report of the Well@
Work initiative and testified that different approaches were used according to the needs, interests, and resources of each workplace and its employees. Initiatives to increase physical activity behaviour included team-based
events, competitions, and 'come and try' events. Activities were conducted
during the workday, usually on site, were free of charge, and involved low
levels of time commitment. Employers and employees reported barriers to
implementing workplace physical activity initiatives; these included lack
of suitable site space both to conduct events and for suitable shower and
changing facilities. Of the 11 projects, 9 showed a significant increase (more
evident in female employees) in sport and physical activity participation.
The proportion of employees meeting the physical activity guidelines for

health significantly increased as a result of the Well@Work initiative in 5 of 11 projects. Finally, approximately two-thirds of employees reported improvements to health and well-being. Overall, the report suggested that the Well@Work initiative had a positive impact on the lifestyle behaviours of employers and employees in the workplace.

The most recent meta-analysis of the effectiveness of workplace physical activity interventions was conducted by Conn and colleagues (2009), who aimed to address three research questions: (1) What are the overall effects of physical activity interventions on physical activity behaviour, health, well-being, and work-related outcomes? (2) Do the interventions' effect on outcomes vary depending on workplace characteristics? (3) Are there treatment effects on participants before versus after the intervention? They reported data on 38,231 participants in the 344 sources reviewed (papers, unpublished reports, small-sample studies, pre-experimental research) and found a small effect size (0.21) for physical activity behaviour and a moderate effect size (0.57) for fitness (VO_2 max). The authors reported that the findings were unclear as to whether these effects were sufficient to raise physical activity to recommended guidelines. In relation to their second question, the authors concluded that neither a company's size nor whether it was a profit or non-profit organisation was a significant moderator of the reported mean effect sizes on physical activity or fitness. Finally, in relation to the physical activity intervention on work-related outcomes, the effect size was small-to-moderate (0.33) for job stress and small for job satisfaction (0.20) and absenteeism (0.19). They also identified difficulties in reporting on the effectiveness of workplace interventions; for example, the number of studies with sufficient data to calculate effect sizes. Cautious interpretation of the findings was recommended due to significant heterogeneity in relation to measures used to assess physical activity, workplace characteristics, and population sample characteristics across the studies. This meta-analysis shows the need for further research to assess the effectiveness of physical activity interventions where cross-study heterogeneity is significantly reduced. Furthermore, a focus on potential psychosocial factors that could moderate the impact of interventions on physical activity, as well as other work-related outcomes, is needed to develop specific and tailored workplace programmes.

Malik, Blake, and Suggs (2013) conducted a systematic review of workplace health promotion interventions for increasing physical activity. Of the 58 studies included, the majority utilised health-promotion initiatives. There were 8 physical activity or exercise interventions, 13 counselling or support interventions, and 39 health promotion messages or information interventions. However, the review identified only 6 studies that included an actual workplace physical exercise component (e.g., aerobic classes or walking groups). In relation to the characteristics of the intervention

programmes, the review found the majority of studies utilised psychological or behavioural strategies to change people's physical activity behaviour.
Almost half of the 58 studies were designed to target multiple health behaviours, and the mode and delivery of intervention also varied considerably
across the studies, ranging from face-to-face communication, posters, logging of activities, emails, and group exercise. Findings from the review also
pointed towards conflicting evidence for the recommendation of tailored
intervention programmes. Some studies suggested tailoring was beneficial, whilst others found them no more effective in changing behaviour
than generic interventions. The authors suggested that in a workplace setting, social influences may play a greater role in health behaviour choices
than individual factors. This needs further consideration when targeting
intervention components in the design phase of workplace intervention
programmes.

7.6   Practical applications for workplace physical activity programmes

7.6.1   Workplace champions and social media

As highlighted earlier, the most effective method of ensuring your workplace intervention is relevant, feasible, and targeted to employees' needs is to
consult with them at the inception stage. Making employees a central part
of the intervention development process fosters feelings of being included,
informed, and valued. One of the key findings of the Well@Work initiative
concerned the importance of developing workplace 'champions' to help plan,
implement, and advocate a workplace physical activity programme. This
allows employees to develop a sense of autonomy and engagement with the
programme. Developing more than one champion will increase the capacity
for social support and social processes to spread amongst employees in relation to physical activity behaviour.

There has been some suggestion that social and competitive interaction via
social networking sites could be channelled to motivate behaviour change
in its users. In this sense, social media could be an innovative and current medium for workplace champions to create and foster a virtual social
environment to facilitate behaviour change. This tool could be used by
workplace champions to disseminate physical activity-related information,
share ideas and issues related to their own behaviour with colleagues, and
develop amongst them a sense of cohesion and relatedness. As discussed
earlier, social media and its role in physical activity and health promotion is
in its infancy in the research literature. In a study by Foster and colleagues
(2010), a Facebook application, StepMatron, was used to provide a social

and competitive context for daily pedometer use in a working environment. Ten nurses working in a UK hospital used the application in two conditions over the study's course. In the socially enabled condition, participants could view, compare, and comment upon each other's step data. In the non-social condition, participants could view only their own step data. Findings of a significant increase in step activity in the socially enabled condition highlight the potential of social media for generating positive physical activity behaviour change.

7.6.2   Stage-matched interventions

Research has shown that workplace physical activity programmes tend to recruit only 20% of an organisation's employees (Wanzel 1994) and volunteers for the programmes are generally already physically active or value that lifestyle. Therefore, 'hard-to-reach' individuals, who are typically in the pre-contemplation and contemplation stages of the TTM (Prochaska and Velicer 1997), should be a priority for workplace intervention recruitment. Yet it is important to bear in mind that employees differ in motivational readiness to engage in physical activity; this needs to be acknowledged and valued by the employer. Marcus and Forsyth (2009) note the need to consider the target audience when developing a workplace intervention and to match each intervention component to a specific stage of change in the TTM.

Individuals in the pre-contemplation and contemplation stages need to be reinforced in the concept that *anyone* can be physically active and all individuals can be made to reflect on how their current inactivity may impact on themselves and those important to them. This can be achieved using the specific processes of change (Prochaska et al. 1988) outlined in the TTM: the strategies and techniques that help individuals modify their behaviour and allow them to move through the stages of change. There are five cognitive processes of change; they involve modifying an individual's cognitions and attitudes and increasing the awareness of physical activity. The five behavioural processes of change focus on actioning cognitions and engaging in behaviour. For those who are in the pre-contemplation and contemplation stages of change, these cognitive processes – increasing knowledge of physical activity, awareness of the risks of continuing physical inactivity, caring about the consequences for others of being inactive; comprehending the benefits of being active, and increasing opportunities for PA – have been effective in eliciting behaviour change. For those in the preparation, action, and maintenance stages, the behavioural processes – substituting sedentary behaviours for physical activities, enlisting social support, rewarding oneself for being active, publicly displaying commitment to being physically active, reminding oneself, and using cues to be physically active – have been effective in eliciting behaviour change. Marcus and Forsyth (2009, 138–145) offer stage-specific strategies for workplace physical activity interventions.

7.6.2.1   Pre-contemplators

For those employees not thinking about changing their physical activity behaviour, the key is to 'plant the seed' regarding physical activity. Adopting a holistic approach focusing on lifestyle changes rather than physical activity may allow employers to gain more 'buy-in' from sedentary individuals. Conducting an online survey to gain understanding of employees' motives and the barriers to health behaviours, including physical activity, could allow employers to tailor future workplace activities. Use workshops on other lifestyle behaviours – for example, smoking and weight management – to promote physical activity. Use incentives to deliver tailored physical activity messages regarding common misconceptions surrounding becoming active to increase the sense of relatedness (i.e., I thought that walking wouldn't make a difference to my health). Host a health fair in the workplace where employees can get a free health check on site and relate their results to physical activity.

7.6.2.2   Contemplators

For employees who are thinking about becoming more active, focus on increasing awareness of how they can use the workplace to help them become more physically active. Use decisional prompts to cue desired actions; for example, using the stairs instead of the lift. Encourage ten-minute walking breaks for all employees at lunchtime, and provide incentives to those who reach weekly targets. Organise workshops on creating a physical activity plan to become more active in the workplace, and promote a buddy system where contemplators are paired with those in the action or maintenance stages of change.

7.6.2.3   Preparers

Those in the preparation stage of the TTM are moving towards being physically active on a regular basis. These individuals will be receptive to workplace programmes yet need support to increase their physical activity levels. Encouraging them to monitor physical activity levels both in the workplace and outside it will develop a sense of autonomy and control over physical activity behaviours. Using this information to provide incentives to employees who are pro-active in increasing their workplace physical activity could also help with behaviour change. Support them with regular workshops and messages, delivered via email or social media, containing useful tips on increasing physical activity and reducing sedentary behaviour at work.

7.6.2.4   Action and maintenance

Employees in these stages are regularly active and meeting the guidelines for health. Those in the action stage have been at this level only for the prior six months, whereas this has been a regular behaviour for over six months for those in the maintenance stage. These employees see that using the social networks to facilitate, support, and encourage physical activity is important for enhancing team cohesion and other work-related outcomes (e.g., productivity, job satisfaction). Walking and running groups that are active during the workday should be promoted in the workplace, with participating employees allowed extra time for lunch and showering. Employers could also liaise with local gyms to negotiate a reduced membership rate for their employees if an on-site facility is not feasible. Offering information on local physical activity events and bringing in external companies and guest speakers to introduce new physical activity initiatives is also recommended to maintain motivation and enthusiasm for a physically active lifestyle and to provide new opportunities for employees to consider.

7.6.3   NICE guidelines

The majority of the stage-matched strategies are advocated in the NICE guidelines on how to encourage employees to be physically active in UK workplace settings. Taking a top-down approach, the guidelines suggest that employers develop an organisation-wide plan that encourages and supports employees in being more active both at and outside the workplace. The guidelines also recommend employers consult with employees prior to implementing any plan to ensure maximum buy-in, to give employees a sense of their value to the employer, and to create ownership over the process. Once a programme has been developed, it is the employer's responsibility to implement and monitor it; doing so can be facilitated by using workplace champions. The guidelines offer several avenues for encouraging physical activity in the workplace: (1) flexible working policies and incentives for being physical active; (2) policies to encourage walking and cycling; (3) tailored information dissemination through appropriate communication channels on how to be more physically active; (4) advice and support networks to help employees increase their physical activity; and (5) independent health checks in the workplace for all employees. The guidelines also provide suggestions for implementing specific components of a physical activity programme; for example, working with employees to develop an active travel plan, encouraging employees to have walking meetings, using decisional prompts in the workplace to encourage cues to action, and using goal setting in relation to walking and cycling behaviours to motivate and monitor progress.

The NICE guidelines were developed by the Public Health Interventions Advisory Committee (PHIAC) which consists of public health practitioners, clinicians (both specialists and generalists), local authority employees, representatives of the public, patients or carers, academics, and technical experts. PHIAC reviewed the evidence, conducted an economic appraisal, considered stakeholder comments, and conducted fieldwork in developing these guidelines, which are for small, medium, and large organisations that have a direct or indirect role in and responsibility for improving health in the workplace. PHIAC also advised that employers should not assume that a one-off intervention would suffice to ensure long-term behaviour change in the workplace. Ongoing support, development, and evaluation of interventions is critical for sustained behaviour change. Finally, the importance of creating a workplace ethos and the need for employers to lead and galvanise efforts to promote and support initiatives to increase physical activity in the workplace were stressed.

7.7 Summary

Employers, employees, local partners, and the government all contribute to the social processes involved in encouraging physical activity in the workplace. This starts with a top-down approach to developing a physically active workforce, whereby the employer creates an ethos where being physically active is valued and embedded into organisational policies and procedures. Goal setting, companionship support, team cohesion, self-efficacy, verbal encouragement, and similar processes enable employees to increase physical activity, which could lead to positive work-related outcomes. The case study discusses specific strategies for employers to utilise to help their employees change their physical activity behaviour at work.

7.8 Case study

7.8.1 Setting the scene

A small, independent business in the United Kingdom called 360 Managment employs 250 people, 116 males and 124 females, aged between 22 and 64. The company is located in an urban business park; its limited access to local transport is compensated by ample car parking. There are three departments in the organisation, each with approximately 80 employees and a head of department who has overall responsibility. Each department has five sections of approximately 20 employees and a section leader who is responsible for their day-to-day organisational management. The majority of employees in all departments spend their working day at a desk; their daily activity is very limited. This sedentary pattern is consistent throughout the company. Recently the company was audited by the awarding body, Investors in People, to gain accreditation as a business that values its employees. Findings from the audit indicated high levels of absenteeism and presenteeism and low levels of productivity in all departments. In addition, staff were asked to complete a health-and-well-being survey; its results pointed to high levels of stress, anxiety, and poor physical and mental well-being. Investors in People advised the director of 360 Management to consult the NICE guidelines on workplace health promotion to encourage employees to become more physically active.

How can the director of 360 Management encourage the workforce to become more active, with a view to increasing psychosocial attributes and work-related outcomes?

7.8.2 Assessing the situation

The key socialising agent in this situation is the employer, which needs to acknowledge its role as the leader in developing a workplace ethos that promotes a healthy lifestyle. A change in working cultural norms is clearly required if the company is to become a happier, healthier, and more productive organisation. The NICE guidelines advocate a top-down approach that makes changes in cultural norms at all levels as the most effective method of ensuring long-term behaviour change. Demonstrating full endorsement of and commitment to a workplace physical activity programme is essential; explaining the benefits of increasing physical and mental well-being through physical activity to employees constitutes time and effort well spent. Anecdotally, the director is aware that individuals in the workplace have a range of attitudes and values towards being physically active and varying levels of physical activity; so there is a need to target multiple levels of motivational readiness.

The director of 360 Management needs to start this process with an initial consultation with the employees to ascertain their interest in a workplace physical activity programme, identify employees who would benefit most from such an intervention, and assess the work-related barriers to implementation. This can be done via several methods. An online survey, sent to the whole workforce and completed in work time, could help the director understand the employees' interest level and assess the perceived barriers to becoming more active. Second, the director needs to be aware of the employees' motivational readiness to become physically active. This can be done using the questionnaire developed by Marcus and colleagues (1992; see Table 7.1); it is quick to complete and can be administered electronically during work time. Once it is known which employees and how many are in the five stages of change, the director can develop stage-matched interventions for all, utilising the naturally occurring teams and social networks in place in the three departments and five sections.

7.8.3 Specific strategies to be implemented in the workplace

The following strategies could be used by the employer, the director of 360 Management, to ensure the ethos and environment in the organisation centre on being healthier and happier through physical activity.

Table 7.1 *Motivational readiness questionnaire*

For each of the following questions, please circle Yes or No. Be sure to follow the instructions carefully

Physical activity or exercise includes activities such as walking briskly, jogging, bicycling, swimming, and any other activity in which the exertion is at least as intense as these activities.

	No	Yes
I am currently physically active.	0	1
I intend to become more physically active in the next six months.	0	1

For activity to be *regular*, it must add up to a *total* of 30 minutes or more per day and be done on at least five days per week. For example, you could take one 30-minute walk or three 10-minute walks for a total of 30 minutes.

	No	Yes
I currently engage in *regular* physical activity.	0	1
I have been *regularly* physically active for the past six months.	0	1

SCORING

If question 1 = 0 and question 2 = 0, then you are at stage 1 (pre-contemplation).
If question 1 = 0 and question 2 = 1, then you are at stage 2 (contemplation).
If question 1 = 1 and question 3 = 0, then you are at stage 3 (preparation).
If question 1 = 1, question 3 = 1, and question 4 = 0, then you are at stage 4 (decision/action).
If question 1 = 1, question 3 = 1, and question 4 = 1, then you are at stage 5 (maintenance).

Source: From Marcus, B., Rossi, J. S., Selby, V. C., Niaura, R. S., and Abrams, D. B. (1992). The stages and processes of exercise adoption and maintenance in a workplace sample. Health Psychology, 11, 386–395. Reprinted with permission from the American Psychological Association.

- In the three departments, appoint workplace champions to advocate, promote, support, and implement all physical activity strategies in the organisation and act as a point of contact for both employer and employees. This will also add buy-in from other employees, who will have a role model in their department in relation to physical activity behaviour.
- Consider the impact of the company's location and physical environment on workplace psychosocial factors. Develop a travel policy in the organisation which encourages active travel (e.g., enrol in the tax-free bike scheme paid through employees' monthly salary and funded by the UK government's green transport initiative), whilst ensuring the presence of sufficient cycle sheds and showering facilities. The director could also consider incentivising employees active travel to increase motivation and long-term adherence. *This strategy would target employees in the action and maintenance stages of change.*

- Place decisional prompts throughout the building to spur employees to change behaviour instantaneously (e.g., have posters encouraging employees to use the stairs instead of the lift; link employer's computers to printers all around the building to encourage regular activity breaks). *This type of strategy would target those employees in the contemplation and preparation stages of change.*
- Use external professionals to hold work-time workshops for employees; they should be free and incentivised and tailored to different stages of motivational readiness (e.g., hold a workshop titled 'What does being healthy matter to me?' for those in the pre-contemplation and contemplation stages; hold a workshop titled 'Why can't I fit more activity in my day?' for those in the preparation and action stages). *This type of strategy would target employees in every stage of change.*
- Use internal communication channels and social media to deliver stage-matched physical activity messages to all employees on a weekly basis. This can be facilitated by the workplace champions in each department. *This type of strategy would target employees in every stage of change.*
- Use individual and team physical activity goal setting in the sectional teams in each department to develop a sense of team cohesion. These goals should be linked to the organisational strategies developed in relation to physical activity (e.g., steps recorded in walking meetings, steps recorded through using the stairs, walking to remote printers, etc.).

7.9   Further study and recommended reading

The following literature is recommended for further reading on key concepts addressed in this chapter.

- Biddle, S. J., and Mutrie, N. (2008). *Psychology of Physical Activity: Determinants, Well-Being and Interventions*, 2nd ed. London: Routledge. 325–328.
- Dugdill, L., and Coffey, M. (2009). Developing physically active workplaces. In L. Dugdill, D. Crone, and R. Murphy (eds), *Physical Activity and Health Promotion: Evidence-Based Approaches to Practice*. Chichester: Wiley Blackwell.
- Kelly, M., Huntley, J., Carmona, C., Crombie, H., Jagroo, J., and Naidoo, B. (2008). Workplace health promotion: how to encourage employers to be physically active. In National Institute of Clinical Excellence (ed.). London: Department of Health.
- Marcus, B., and Forsyth, L. (2009). *Motivating People to Be Physically Active*, 2nd ed., ch. 9. Champaign, IL: Human Kinetics.

8 Gyms and Leisure Centres

8.1 Learning objectives

The purpose of this chapter is to examine the social context of the leisure setting and its importance in relation to volitional exercise enjoyment and long-term adherence. The key learning objectives are:

- to explore the role of exercise leaders, who have the potential to influence the psychosocial environment via their attitudes and behaviours in an exercise class. Links to models of leadership and leadership styles will be discussed in relation to individual and group motivation and long-term adherence;
- to consider the importance of perceptions of competence, social anxiety, and self-presentational issues of individuals in a gym environment. Links to characteristics of the exercise environment and self-presentational issues are discussed in relation to their impact on exercise choices and behaviours;
- to examine the role of group exercise and psychosocial processes involved in group behaviours; for example, social facilitation, social loafing, social and task cohesion, and collective efficacy. Links to Carron and colleagues' model of group cohesion are used to understand the relative importance of group cohesion for exercise adherence;
- to discuss the practical implications of the research so that exercise leaders, personal trainers, and gym and leisure centre managers can create an optimal social context for increased motivation, enjoyment, and long-term exercise adherence, with specific strategies outlined.

8.2 Introduction to the context

According to the recent 'Gyms and Fitness Centres Market Research Report' (IBIS 2013), this industry has expanded strongly since 2005, particularly since 2010. In 1996, the fitness market was worth £682 million, increasing to

147

£1.6 billion in 2001, and it was recently estimated to be worth over £2.5 billion (Mintel 2010). In the United Kingdom, the 8.7 million adults who have membership in a gym or leisure centre equate to some 17% of the adult population. Yet research by the online accounting firm crunch.co.uk estimates that UK adults waste £37 million per year on unused gym memberships and sport equipment. This highlights the key issue, long-term adherence, in this volitional exercise setting: individuals who choose to exercise in a gym environment and commit to membership often discontinue participation after a time. This could be due to lack of motivation and interest, the gym's psychosocial environment, or other personal barriers (lack of time, cost). Despite high levels of discontinuation, UK gyms and leisure centres that assist, advise, and motivate individuals to participate in exercise in a social context have become more prevalent and employ roughly 26,000 staff members. These exercise professionals play a significant role in the enjoyment, motivation, and long-term behaviours of individuals who exercise in a gym environment, yet there has been limited research on their effectiveness.

In a gym, the interaction between the individual and the social environment can be influential in determining exercise choices and behaviours. A growing body of literature has examined the role of the exercise leader as an agent of social influence, one who is able to foster positive behaviours in individuals in exercise classes (Beauchamp, Welch, and Hulley 2007). Exercise leaders (i.e., exercise class instructors, personal trainers) can facilitate the psychosocial environment of their sessions through their own attitudes and behaviours, which in turn may influence the behaviours of the participants. Furthermore, exercisers may see their instructors as role models and replicate their attitudes and behaviours. Consequently, the exercise leader can have a significant influence not only on the actual exercise behaviours of individuals but on the psychosocial processes related to group exercise, the quality and enjoyment of the exercise experience, and the likelihood of future exercise intentions.

The decision to exercise in a public setting (e.g., gym, local park) or a private setting (e.g., at home) may be influenced not only by accessibility or facilities but by an individual's self-presentational concerns. Self-presentational concerns are one of the key psychosocial processes involved in group-based exercise. As exercise participation occurs in social contexts, it is possible that self-presentational strategies may have an impact on exercise behaviours. Self-presentation has been described as the selective presentation and omission of aspects of the self to create a desired impression and avoid undesired impressions on specific people in a social encounter (Hart, Leary, and Rejeski 1989; Leary 1992). For example, individuals may avoid exercising in front of others in the gym because they feel they are not good enough and do not want to be judged by other gym users. Self-presentational concerns might be associated with an increased motivation to exercise or, conversely, might result in demotivation (Leary 1992). Consequently, consideration of the social environment (i.e., exercise group, exercise leader) and its potential influence on self-presentational concerns can be important in relation to long-term exercise adherence in a gym.

The majority of structured, volitional exercise takes place in a social context. Group cohesion and collective efficacy in an exercise setting can be key to understanding individual adherence via the psychosocial processes in an exercise class. The research examining group cohesion in a team-sport setting has been extensive; however, it has yet to be fully translated into examination of group cohesion in an exercise setting. Unlike group cohesion in a sport setting, in exercise classes group cohesion may not be an inevitable by-product of group processes, structure, or task outcomes (Carron and Spink 1993).

Two group factors are regarded as important for individuals to adhere to exercise: group cohesion and social support (Courneya and McAuley 1995). Further examination of the interaction of the exercise leader, the exercise group, and the individual is needed to understand the psychosocial processes influencing choices and behaviours in the leisure setting, where a large proportion of UK adults choose to participate in regular exercise.

8.3 The role of the exercise leader

The role of the exercise leader is central to understanding the volitional exercise behaviours of individuals in a group exercise class and the psychosocial processes involved to ensure long-term exercise adherence. The exercise leader can also provide companionship and instrumental support for individuals on a one-to-one basis through the use of a personal trainer, yet the research examining this dyad is limited.

8.3.1 Definitions and models of leadership

There are numerous definitions available to understand the concept of leadership. Chemers (2000) defined leadership as 'a process of social influence in which one person is able to enlist the aid and support of others in the accomplishment of a common task' (27). With respect to exercise and physical activity settings, leadership is considered a prescribed rather than an emergent role; however, in the exercise group itself, individuals may emerge as leaders in relation to certain group tasks. Although several models of leadership in a sporting context have been developed, to date there are no leadership models specific to an exercise setting. Chelladurai's (1990) multidimensional model, developed to understand leadership in sport-specific contexts, is based on the concept that leadership effectiveness depends on the situation's constraints and characteristics and the athletes. According to the model, leader behaviours are influenced by three antecedents: situational, leader, and member characteristics. As a result of these antecedents, the preferred leader behaviour (i.e., what is preferred by the members of the group) and required leader behaviour (i.e., the behaviour required by the affiliated organisation's cultural norms) will dictate *actual* behaviour. This will, in turn, influence group performance and group members' satisfaction, the two key consequences of leadership behaviours. In an exercise setting, the situational characteristics could relate to the size and composition of the exercise class, the leader characteristics to the leader's teaching style, and the member characteristics to the social interaction of other group members with both the leader and each other. However, performance as an outcome of actual leader behaviour is perhaps not as appropriate in an exercise setting as in a sport setting. Yet what could be considered salient is long-term adherence in addition to member satisfaction, as they are inextricably linked.

Chemers (2000) proposed a multidimensional framework of leadership, which was considered in an exercise context by Estabrooks and colleagues (2004). Chemers identified three major functions of successful leadership. The first function, termed image management, is based on the assumption that 'a leader must build credibility in the legitimacy of his or her authority by projecting an image that arouses feelings of trust in followers' (37). It could be argued that in an exercise setting a successful leader would successfully demonstrate the exercise behaviour or skill to the class members. The leader should communicate values and beliefs about engaging in a physically active lifestyle to the group and portray its benefits via physical appearance and fitness levels. The second function, relationship development, is based on the assumption that 'a leader must develop relationships with subordinates that enable those subordinates to move toward individual and collective goal attainment' (37). In an exercise setting research has shown that a supportive relationship between the class leader and class participants is effective in attainment of class enjoyment, motivation, and adherence (Annesi 1999; Estabrooks et al. 2004; Loughead, Colman, and Carron 2001). Resource deployment, the third function, is based on the assumption that 'leaders must effectively use the knowledge, skills, and material resources present within their group to accomplish the group's mission' (37). In an exercise setting it is essential that the leader understand the group capabilities and strive to maximise them in order to attain the individual's and group's main goals. The individual's are likely to be related to fitness, enjoyment, and appearance, yet the group's could be related to social interaction, group cohesion, and long-term adherence.

8.3.2   Leadership styles and characteristics

Exercise leaders are key socialising agents who can exert significant social influence on an individual class participant and the exercise group as a whole. Research has indicated that participants' perceptions of group cohesion, attitudinal and emotional responses to the class (Carron and Spink

1993; Turner, Rejeski, and Brawley 1997), and future exercise intentions (Spink 1999) can all be influenced by the exercise leader. Based on this, it can be suggested that the exercise leader's leadership style can have an impact on the individual's psychosocial responses to exercise in a social environment. A study demonstrated that a socially enriched leadership style, characterised by reinforcement of positive behaviours in the exercise class, encouragement, and social interaction, resulted in more positive feeling states and increased exercise self-efficacy among young females (Turner et al. 1997). This was compared to a bland leadership style, characterised by verbal punishment of negative behaviours and no verbal encouragement or social interaction. The findings emphasised how a supportive, enriched leadership style could enhance positive psychological responses to exercise.

Martin and Fox (2001) studied the effect of leadership style and group environment on a negative psychological response to exercise – social anxiety – during a single aerobics class. 'Social anxiety' describes the affective consequences individuals may experience when they doubt their ability to make a desired impression on others (Schlenker and Leary 1982). Participants in the study were 48 male and 42 female undergraduate students from a health course who were randomly assigned to one of four groups (socially enriched leadership style/socially enriched group environment; socially enriched leadership style/bland group environment; bland leadership style/ socially enriched group environment; bland leadership style/bland group environment). The leadership style was manipulated by the exercise leader of the aerobics class. The group environment was manipulated using student confederates who helped to create a socially enriched group environment by interacting with other class members at the start of the class, complying with the exercise leader, and providing verbal encouragement to the group during the class. Alternatively, they created a bland group environment, where certain behaviours were implemented or omitted so as to create a neutral, non-interactive social environment. Detailed verbal and behavioural scripts were written for the leadership style and group environment manipulations and taught to the leader and confederates prior to the aerobics class. Social anxiety and class members' perceptions of the exercise leader and the exercise group were assessed. Contrary to the authors' hypothesis, a socially enriched group environment produced greater levels of social anxiety among class members than the bland group environment. However, a socially enriched leadership style seemed to reduce the social anxiety experienced, meaning that class members were less likely to worry about making a desirable impression on others. These findings emphasise the importance of a supportive exercise leader in reducing negative psychological responses, particularly if the group environment results in increased levels of social anxiety.

Research conducted to identify the leadership styles needed to support positive psychological responses to exercise has been predominantly conducted with young population samples; older adults and their preferences for exercise leaders have received less attention. To address this, Estabrooks and colleagues (2004) used a qualitative approach to understand the perceptions of older adults regarding their exercise group leader. Twenty-three older adults (mean age = 78.5 years) considered healthy enough to engage in regular exercise were asked their thoughts on important characteristics of an exercise group leader. Findings were based on the three major functions of leadership outlined by Chemers (2000): image management, relationship development, and resource deployment. Key themes linked to image management included the leader's personality characteristics (e.g., charismatic, energetic, outgoing, positive attitude, positive disposition), professionalism (businesslike, prepared, committed), and qualifications (good presentation, appropriate skills, knowledgeable, certified). Key themes linked to relationship development were guidance (providing assistance, demonstration, encouragement, explanation, instruction) and individual attention (understanding participants' capabilities and expectations, making eye contact, interacting, recognising names, showing concern, providing individual support). Finally, key themes linked to resource deployment were environment (appropriate music, a clear voice) and group processes (group goals, member relationships, social integration). From this study, it is apparent that a leader is required to exhibit a vast range of positive characteristics during an exercise session, which often lasts for less than an hour; exercise class members demand much of their leader during this time. Developing these characteristics and translating them into practice can be a challenge.

Beauchamp and colleagues (2007) examined two types of leadership styles, transactional and transformational, typically used in other settings (business, military, education) in an exercise setting. According to Bass (1985) transactional leadership exerts influence by setting goals, providing feedback, and exchanging rewards for achievement. Transformational leadership exerts influence by elevating members' goals and giving them the confidence to go beyond minimally accepted standards. As outlined by Bass (1998), transformational leadership acts to augment the effects of transactional leadership to increase self-efficacy beliefs. Beauchamp and colleagues examined whether transactional leadership is related to exercisers' self-efficacy beliefs and whether transformational leadership augments the effects of transactional leadership in relation to exercise-related self-efficacy. Female participants at university (N = 164), enrolled in a 10-week exercise class, were classified as either 'experienced exercisers' (N = 78) or 'initiate exercisers' (N = 86). A modified version of the multifactor leadership questionnaire (MLQ; Bass and Avolio 1995) was used to assess transactional and transformational leadership after each class from week 3 onwards. Three measures of self-efficacy were also examined: in-class self-efficacy (i.e., confidence in completing important tasks in the exercise class), barrier self-efficacy (confidence to overcome barriers to exercise), and scheduling self-efficacy (confidence to complete specific behaviours required to attend their scheduled exercise class). As expected, findings indicated that initiate exercisers reported significantly lower levels of all three types of self-efficacy compared to experienced exercisers. For exercise initiates, the transactional leadership dimension of contingent-reward behaviours (positive reinforcement and reward when an identified goal is achieved) explained the variance in barrier self-efficacy and scheduling self-efficacy, yet no leadership behaviours were related to the self-efficacy of experienced exercisers. Findings also indicated that none of the transformational leadership behaviours outlined by Bass (1985) were related to exercise-related self-efficacy. The authors suggested that transformational leadership may not augment transactional leadership in a structured exercise class in the same way it does in other organisational settings due to the limited amount of contact time between the exercise leader and the class participants.

A socially enriched, supportive leadership style emphasising social interaction and positive reinforcement has been shown to have an impact on the positive psychological responses to exercise for class participants. The influence of the exercise leader's attitudes and motives for exercise might also translate to class members, particularly those who have enhanced negative psychological responses such as social anxiety and social physique anxiety. A study conducted by Raedeke, Focht, and Scales (2007) examined the extent to which exercise leaders create a health- or appearance-related class atmosphere for socially anxious females. It was hypothesised that instructors who wear form-fitting attire and make appearance-oriented comments may create class atmospheres that emphasise physique. Conversely, wearing more casual clothes and making health-oriented comments may foster more of a health orientation and lessen attention on appearance-related issues. Females aged 18 to 27 (N = 99) with high levels of social physique anxiety participated in the study. Social physique anxiety is a subtype of social anxiety that originates in self-presentational concerns about appearance. Individuals with high social physique anxiety experience apprehension and fear of negative social evaluation in situations where they perceive their appearance is being evaluated by others (Hart et al. 1989). The study also examined the influence of the presence of mirrors on levels of social physique anxiety (see Section 8.4.3). Participants were randomly assigned to one of four groups (appearance-focused leadership style / mirrors; appearance-focused leadership style / no mirrors; health-focused leadership style / mirrors; health-focused leadership style / no mirrors) To accentuate an appearance-focused style, the instructor wore tight-fitting aerobics attire and made appearance-related comments all through the exercise session; for example, 'stand tall, you'll look five pounds lighter' and 'work it, let's get your legs toned so they look good'. To minimise evaluated threat associated with physique issues, the instructor attempted to create a health-focused leadership style by making health-oriented comments and creating a more casual atmosphere by wearing gym shorts and a T-shirt. For each cue in the appearance-focused condition, the instructor had a health-oriented counter cue: 'shoulders back for good posture'; 'work it, let's get fit and healthy'. Positive affect, enjoyment, task self-efficacy, and future intentions to exercise were assessed pre- and post-exercise class. Findings suggested that a leadership style with a health-focused approach influenced the quality of an acute bout of exercise in females with high levels of social physique anxiety; they reported more positive affect and greater enjoyment and were more likely to exercise in the future.

Overall, it is clear that the exercise leader is a significant socialising agent in the gym environment and can influence a range of class members' psychosocial behaviours, including self-efficacy, enjoyment, positive affect, and future intentions to exercise. The leader can also contribute to the development of group cohesion in the exercise class, which in turn, can increase long-term exercise adherence (see Section 8.5). The leadership style adopted and the exercise leaders' physical appearance can also influence participants' negative psychosocial processes (e.g., social physique anxiety) and impact on the decision to engage in or avoid group exercise situations. Qualitative findings have identified numerous characteristics exercise leaders need to be considered effective by class participants. These range from displaying positive personality traits and being prepared and professional to more complex qualities such as managing and encouraging social interaction and gauging individual goals and group capabilities. The high expectations of an exercise leader can be difficult to deliver with the limited contact time in a typical exercise class; they may develop only over time in an exercise group consisting of regular attendees.

8.4   Self-presentational issues in a gym setting

The gym setting is a social context; therefore, the presence of others whilst an individual exercises is inevitable. For an individual, exercising in the presence of others can elicit a range of psychological responses that may enhance exercise participation and provide a supportive network or may discourage exercise participation due to worry and concern about others' social approval. Prior to the discussion of self-presentational issues in a gym setting, key terms in this area need to be defined.

8.4.1   Definitions and key terms related to self-presentation

As outlined earlier, self-presentation is the selective presentation and omission of aspects of the self to create a desired impression and avoid undesired impressions with specific people in a social encounter, such as exercising in a gym environment (Hart et al. 1989; Leary 1992). It has been suggested that self-presentational concerns can affect an individual's exercise cognitions, attitudes, and behaviours. These concerns can be associated with an increased motivation to exercise to improve or maintain physical appearance or construct a social identity as an exerciser. Conversely, self-presentational concerns can cause demotivation to engage in exercise when an individual feels incapable of creating a desired impression and fears others' negative evaluation (Leary 1992). The individual's level of certainty about being able to make a derisible impression (i.e., how certain an individual is of creating a good impression in a certain context) has been conceptualised as self-presentational efficacy, a concept based on the integration of the self-efficacy and self-presentation theories of social anxiety (Maddux, Norton, and Leary 1988). In an exercise setting self-presentational efficacy may be related more to concerns about appearance and physique; perceptions of physical competence, coordination, and fitness levels may also be relevant. All of these can influence how confident an individual feels in their ability to create a desirable impression in these areas, and these in turn may impact exercise choices and behaviours in the gym environment.

'Social anxiety' refers to the negative consequences that may be experienced when an individual doubts their ability to make a desired impression on others (Schlenker and Leary 1982). In relation to an exercise setting, Hart and colleagues (1989) developed a measure of social anxiety specific to the physique, social physique anxiety. Defined as the anxiety experienced by those who perceive that their physique will be negatively evaluated by others, it was originally considered a personality trait. Since it results from the perception that others may evaluate one's body, situations which emphasise both physique and evaluation (e.g., exercise classes) could temporarily increase social physique anxiety.

8.4.2   Social physique anxiety and exercise behaviour

There has been extensive research examining the relationship between social physique anxiety and exercise behaviour, particularly in females, who typically exhibit higher levels of the anxiety than males (Haase, Prapavessis, and Glynn Owens 2002; Motl and Conroy 2000). Lantz, Hardy, and Ainsworth (1997) examined social physique anxiety and perceived exercise behaviour in 120 males and 180 females between 18 and 60. Findings indicated a negative relationship between social physique anxiety and exercise behaviour, with individuals with high levels of social physique anxiety engaging in less exercise. Furthermore, this finding, moderated by gender and age, showed that exercise behaviour was lowest in older female adults with high levels of social physique anxiety. Yet findings from an intervention study by Treasure, Lox, and Lawton (1998) examining adherence of obese females

(N = 31) to a 12-week walking programme highlighted that for younger obese females, social physique anxiety had a greater effect on walking adherence than older obese females. In this study, social physique anxiety decreased with age; its influence on walking adherence consequently decreased.

The link between social physique anxiety and exercise behaviour in females was further examined by Ransdell and colleagues (1998) in post-menopausal women. Findings indicated that social physique anxiety was higher in women who engaged in low-to-moderate levels of physical activity compared to those who engaged in high-to-vigorous levels of physical activity, independent of percentage of body fat. This suggests that the link between social physique anxiety and exercising to improve appearance is not necessarily attributable to an objective need to reduce body fat. In addition, it should not be assumed that only overweight or obese individuals will have high levels of social physique anxiety. Social physique anxiety and self-presentational concerns have also been linked to risk-taking behaviours in gym settings, particularly in male exercisers. Martin, Leary, and O'Brien (2001) found that 28% of male university students surveyed, compared to 3% of females, reported lifting excessive weights at the gym for self-presentational reasons and in some cases reported taking anabolic steroids to create a desirable impression on others in a gym setting. Overall, research consistently shows self-presentational concerns, social physique anxiety, and exercise behaviours to be inextricably linked; however the complexity of the relationship is influenced by factors related to the psychosocial environment where the exercise takes place. Discussing these factors will aid in understanding the links between self-presentational concerns, social physique anxiety, and exercise behaviour in a gym setting.

8.4.3   The psychosocial exercise environment and self-presentational concerns

As discussed earlier, Martin and Fox (2001) examined the effect of leadership style and group environment on social anxiety, a negative psychological response to exercise, during a single aerobics class. Manipulation of the group environment was deliberate; it created a socially enriched exercise group using confederates for one condition and a bland group environment for the other. Social anxiety and class members' perceptions of the exercise leader and group were assessed. Contrary to the authors' hypothesis, a socially enriched group environment produced higher levels of social anxiety than the bland one among the class members. In this instance, the social attention by the confederates to the class participants may have provoked social anxiety as they attempted to present favourable impressions of themselves. Therefore, emphasising social interaction to make class members feel welcome and comfortable in the exercise environment may not necessarily reduce feelings of social anxiety and could, for some, increase feelings of social anxiety.

Research by Crawford and Eklund (1994) examined the exercise environment and self-presentational concerns in 104 female university students aged 18 to 25, with a specific focus on attire's influence on various self-presentational outcomes during an aerobics class. The participants were shown two videotapes of a class. In one, participants wore aerobics fashion attire (e.g., lycra); in the other, they wore shorts and T-shirts. Prior to watching the videos, participants completed measures of social physique anxiety, body size satisfaction, exercise motives, and self-report exercise behaviour. Afterwards, participants had to rate their attitudes towards the exercise settings of the two exercise videos. Findings suggested that social physique anxiety was negatively associated with the setting that emphasised physique (i.e., aerobics attire) and positively related to the setting that minimised its salience (i.e., shorts and T-shirt attire). This study was one of the first to highlight the importance of the social environment to self-presentational concerns for individuals in an exercise class. A follow-up study, conducted by Eklund and Crawford (1994) to examine similar self-presentational concerns related to exercise environment attire, attempted to control for body composition. Contrary to the first study, there was no significant relationship between social physique anxiety and attitudes towards attire in the setting. However, the authors commented that the participants recruited for this study were physical education undergraduate students and therefore a biased population sample with a lower body mass than the participants used in the Crawford and Eklund (1994) study had. More recently, Brewer and colleagues (2004) examined two forms of self-presentational behaviour in 86 female participants attending an aerobics class at a university fitness centre. They examined the relationship between social physique anxiety and proximity to the exercise instructor during a class and the wearing of concealing exercise attire. In support of Crawford and Eklund (1994), findings highlighted that social physique anxiety was positively related to clothing concealment (r = 0.25) and proximity to the exercise instructor (r = 0.31), suggesting that for female exercisers, having a choice over one's standing position in an exercise class – further from the instructor – could reduce self-presentational concerns. The study increases support for the importance of choice of attire in reducing self-presentational concerns in an exercise class setting.

In addition to shaping self-presentational concerns, Gammage, Martin Ginis, and Hall (2004) suggested that situational factors in the exercise environment (e.g., revealing clothing) can affect an individual's self-presentational efficacy due to increased self-awareness. They argued that this self-evaluative process leads to an increased awareness of shortcomings and a reduced self-efficacy for completing the task. The aim of their study was to manipulate self-presentational efficacy in an exercise context through a range of situational factors and to determine the effects of the manipulation on manifestations of social anxiety. Regular female exercisers were recruited for the study (N = 68) and randomly assigned to either a low or high self-presentational efficacy group. Manipulation of low self-presentational efficacy involved ensuring that all mirrors and windows in the exercise environment were uncovered and looked out onto a public hallway. A video camera was set up at the front of the class, and a male individual, with a second video camera, walked around during the class. All clothing, a cropped lycra top and lycra shorts, was provided for the participants, and they were instructed to wear name badges throughout the exercise class. Manipulation of high self-presentational efficacy involved ensuring that all mirrors and windows were covered, that no video cameras present, and that they were provided loose T-shirts and shorts to wear. The above descriptions of the dance studio where the exercise class was to take place were given to the participants, who were told they would be moving to the classroom to complete several questionnaires and then would be supplied clothing for the class in the changing room before returning to the dance studio to start the class. Assessments of impression motivation, self-presentational efficacy, task self-efficacy, state social anxiety in an exercise class, social physique anxiety, and physical appearance anxiety were conducted. At this point, the participants were informed they would not be required to do the class and were fully debriefed on the study. Despite not actually having to participate in the class, findings indicated that those women in the low self-presentational efficacy group scored higher on exercise-related state social anxiety, physical appearance anxiety, and social physique anxiety than those in the high self-presentational efficacy group. Furthermore, participants in the former group reported looking forward to taking part in the class significantly less than those in the latter group. This study was one of the first to highlight that *perceptions* of an exercise environment associated with low levels of self-presentational efficacy can impact self-presentational concerns and future intentions to exercise even prior to participating in the session.

The presence of others whilst exercising is a central component of self-presentational concerns. Previous research (Carron et al. 1999) has shown that in a social scenario where the physique is emphasised, self-presentational anxiety in females was less pronounced among female friends or a mixed group of male and female friends than when alone or in a group of male friends. This suggests that a group's gender composition can have an impact on the levels of self-presentational anxiety females experience. The group gender composition in an exercise class in relation to self-presentational concerns was examined by Kruisselbrink and colleagues (2004). Study participants consisted of 51 males and 80 females who completed the 9-item scale (Hart et al. 1989) assessing situational social physique anxiety and indicated their immediate exercise intention for three exercise-setting scenarios. For each scenario the instructions were, 'Imagine that you are going to an exercise workout. Clad in your usual exercise attire, you enter the exercise area. When you look around you notice that everyone in the room is…' The statement's completions were (a) female, (b) male, (c) an even mix of females and males. The order of presentation of the scenarios was counterbalanced. Findings demonstrated that the exercise group's gender composition had no influence on situational social physique anxiety and exercise intentions in males. Yet females reported highest levels of situational social physique anxiety to an all-male exercise class scenario. The authors, concluding that females have reduced levels of social physique anxiety and are less likely to shorten their workout in an all-female class, emphasised the importance of the class's gender composition in relation to self-presentational concerns experienced by female exercisers.

Further research that has examined the presence of co-exercisers, coupled with the presence of mirrors in the exercise environment, was conducted by Martin Ginis, Burke, and Gauvin (2007). In their study, 92 sedentary females aged 20 performed 20 minutes of moderate-intensity exercise in one of four conditions: (1) exercising alone in a mirrored studio; (2) exercising with others in a mirrored studio; (3) exercising alone with no mirror; (4) exercising with others with no mirrors. Exercise-induced feeling state was assessed pre-, mid- and five minutes post-exercise, and self-consciousness and perceived social evaluation and comparison were assessed post-exercise. Multilevel modelling analysis demonstrated that participants in the group exercising with others in a mirrored studio reported increased physical exhaustion, higher levels of self-consciousness, and increased perceptions of social evaluation and comparison. Thus, for inactive females, exercising in the presence of others in a mirrored environment may not be conducive to positive psychological well-being and minimising self-presentational concerns.

Research has demonstrated that the exercise environment itself is central to understanding self-presentational concerns of exercisers and their potential impact on exercise choices, behaviours, and long-term adherence. Situational factors, such as the presence of mirrors, can also exacerbate feelings of self-presentational efficacy and self-consciousness. Although exercisers use mirrors in a gym environment to correct technique and monitor behaviour, for some they can be a deterrent to exercise. As the attire worn to an exercise class has been shown to negatively impact on self-presentational efficacy and social physique anxiety, the importance of allowing exercisers control over choice of clothing for group exercise sessions is underlined. That the group's gender composition can also change the degree to which female exercisers experience social anxiety and social physique anxiety suggests that female-only sessions could minimise self-presentational concerns and maximise the likelihood of future exercise intentions and long-term exercise adherence. Finally, the psychosocial environment created by both exercise leader and group members can encourage social interaction and integration. This has been shown to both increase social anxiety levels through the desire to create a positive impression on others and reduce social anxiety through feelings of relatedness to other class members. Further research is needed to clarify whether a socially enriched environment in an exercise class is optimal for reducing feelings of social anxiety and increasing exercise intentions and to establish whether the social support's source (i.e., the class leader or group members) can have a different effect on the positive outcomes.

8.5   Group cohesion and social processes in an exercise class setting

Group cohesion and collective efficacy in an exercise setting are central to understanding individual adherence through the social processes developed in an exercise class. Discussion of the links between group cohesion and exercise adherence follow a definition of what a group is and how it can be cohesive so as to understand group cohesion in an exercise context.

8.5.1   Definitions and key terms related to group cohesion

Early theoretical concepts of a group, as outlined by Zander (1982), suggest that 'a body of people is not a group if the members are primarily interested in individual accomplishments, are not concerned with the activities of other members...and are often absent' (1–2). This explanation suggests that for exercise groups composed of individuals with separate goals and interests, interest in the activities of other class members is needed for the group to be conceptually defined. This echoes the sentiments of Carron, Brawley, and Widmeyer (1998), who previously defined 'group cohesion' as 'a dynamic process reflected in the tendency of a group to stick together and remain united in the pursuit of its instrumental objectives and/or for the satisfaction of member affective needs' (213). They developed a conceptual model of group cohesion in sport, dividing cohesion into four distinct dimensions across two specific levels: an individual versus group level and a task versus social aspect of cohesion.

At the individual level, attraction to the group (ATG) reflects the individual's perceptions about personal motivations acting to attract and retain the individual in the group. This is related to both a task (ATG-T) and social aspect (ATG-S). At the group level, group integration (GI) reflects the individual's perceptions of closeness, similarity, and bonding in the group. This is also related to both a task (GI-T) and social aspect (GI-S). In relation to their conceptual model in an exercise context, Brawley, Carron, and Widmeyer (1987) suggest that attraction to the group task (ATG-T) is the most salient predictor of exercise adherence, with group integration to the task (GI-T) the next most important predictor. Once the group has become efficient at the task, attraction to the group's social aspects (ATG-S) should develop and become predictive. Finally, once the group integrates around these social interactions, group integration socially (GI-S) will become a predictor of exercise adherence.

8.5.2   Developing group cohesion in an exercise context

It is apparent that group cohesion leads to long-term exercise adherence behaviours. However, during an exercise class, cohesion is not an inevitable by-product of group processes, structure, or outcomes, as it can be in a sports team. Consequently, research examining the relationship between group cohesion and exercise adherence has centred on using exercise class strategies such as team building and goal setting to enhance the cohesiveness of the group in an effort to influence long-term exercise adherence. Research by Carron and Spink (1993) determined whether a team-building programme would increase perceptions of cohesion in a fitness class (N = 94) compared to a control group (N = 101). All participants were female, between 18 and 25, and involved in aerobics and aqua fitness classes three times a week for 13 weeks. In the experimental group, exercise leaders received instructions on how group cohesion and the benefits of exercise enjoyment and adherence could be increased. The leaders became active agents in developing strategies for the team-building programme based around positions, norms, sacrifices, distinctiveness, interaction, and communication. The team-building programme was implemented in the experimental group for the 13-week programme. The control group received standard exercise leader protocol during this time; cohesiveness was assessed in both groups at week 8. Findings highlighted significant group differences in the ATG-T dimension, with the experimental group reporting higher levels than the control group. In addition, higher levels of satisfaction and lower levels of dropout were also reported in the experimental group, emphasising the potential positive influence of team-building strategies on exercise class cohesion and subsequent long-term adherence. Carron and Spink (1995) extended these finding to examine how a team-building intervention would influence cohesiveness in small (<20) and large (<40) exercise classes. Findings suggested that an exercise leader's team-building strategies can offset the potential negative impact of class size on group cohesion. Team-building strategies can be useful in small- and large-group exercise contexts for developing cohesion and exercise adherence.

The efficacy of team-building strategies in increasing cohesion in exercise groups has also been evidenced in older adults. Estabrooks and Carron (1999) examined group cohesion and exercise participation in 75 older adults at 1, 6, and 12 months of an exercise programme of aerobic fitness and strength and flexibility training (study 1). They also examined the effectiveness of a team-building intervention based on developing class cohesion for improving class attendance at weeks 6 and 10 in a subsample of 33 older adults (study 2). Findings of study 1 suggested that cohesion predicted exercise attendance at 1 month, 6 months, and 12 months after an exercise programme. Findings of study 2 supported the use of a team-building intervention for immediate and long-term effect on exercise attendance. Overall the authors concluded that short-term participation was associated with the social aspect of group cohesion but long-term participation was associated with the task aspect. This suggests that for older adults, the social aspect of group exercise may be more salient for developing group cohesion than the activity itself, contrary to the early findings by Carron, Widmeyer, and Brawley (1985) and Brawley and colleagues (1987).

Tailoring group-cohesion strategies for the group an exercise leader is working with was further emphasised by Annesi (1999), who stated that private and public gyms and leisure centres may require different cohesion-promotion methods. This study examined group cohesion in new exercisers (those exercising for six months or less) in a private fitness centre. Participants were randomly assigned to a control or treatment condition. Treatment participants differed from controls in that an exercise professional led them in small groups for a five-minute warm-up and cool-down before and after they completed the prescribed exercise programme alone. Group cohesion was assessed at weeks 1, 5, 10, and 15 for participants in both conditions. Findings indicated that ATG-T increased between weeks 1 and 5, with higher attendance and decreased dropout in the treatment group. This showed that placing participants under minimal supervision in surroundings that might promote independent social interaction can increase aspects of group cohesion and attendance and reduce dropout in a private leisure centre setting.

More recently, Christensen and colleagues (2006) examined the formation of group cohesion and social support among a group of sedentary adults. The intervention consisted of 32 weekly exercise sessions of approximately 90 minutes, where social activities were incorporated into each session to develop group cohesion among participants (e.g., scheduled coffee breaks before and after class, encouragement of group discussion during the cool-downs, and participant-led choice of group exercise activities during class). Findings indicated social relations in the class had a significant effect on future exercise intentions, yet the intervention had no effect on self-reported loneliness. A subsample of the participants (N = 18) were interviewed on their past experiences with exercise, their exercise experience during the intervention, barriers to participation, and the dynamic processes in the group during the intervention period. Findings suggested that none of the exercise class groups had experienced similar social processes and that the initial meeting phase was decisive in the developing group processes and establishing cohesion. It was apparent that integrated groups were characterised by feelings of acceptance, solidarity, and mutual respect among the participants. In relation to the four dimensions of group cohesion, the participants discussed their attraction to the group in relation to the social aspect and their integration with the group in relation to both the group's tasks and social aspect. The findings provide further support for the conceptual model of group cohesion in an exercise setting and also suggest that for sedentary individuals, both task and social aspects of cohesion are needed to enhance overall cohesion in an exercise class setting.

Although research has shown that team-building strategies in an exercise class setting can be efficacious in enhancing group cohesion and consequently exercise adherence, research on use of group goal setting as a specific strategy to develop cohesiveness has been limited. In 2010 Burke and colleagues looked to examine group goal setting and performance in a physical activity context, where individuals predominantly focus on personal rather than collective outcomes (e.g., increase fitness, develop competence, lose weight), even when engaging in group exercise. The study's main aim was to examine the relationship between group goal setting and group performance in 1,325 walking groups. A secondary aim was to examine factors that might influence the magnitude of the group's goal setting and performance relationship – specifically task cohesion, prior levels of physical activity, and self-efficacy. The eight-week walking programme was part of a community-based project in Kansas involving 6,356 adults in self-selected walking groups of three to six individuals, with a designated walk leader for each group. Findings revealed a positive, significant relationship between group goal setting and group performance. Task cohesion was not a significant moderator of this relationship, yet prior levels of physical activity and self-efficacy were. There was also evidence of conjunctive moderation effects on this relationship, where high levels of prior physical activity and high levels of self-efficacy were more influential than a combination of medium or low levels of prior physical activity and self-efficacy. Overall this study supports the use of group goal setting as a strategy to increase group performance in a walking group, with the importance of self-efficacy further emphasised. Additional research is needed to examine whether group goal setting in a group exercise class can enhance long-term exercise adherence, as group performance is not directly relevant in this context.

8.6   Exercise leaders and group cohesion

Exercise leaders have been shown to influence the psychosocial processes of an individual involved in group exercise, yet they can also act as socialising agents to develop group cohesion in an exercise class. The relationship of the exercise leader, group cohesion, and exercise adherence was examined by Loughead and colleagues (2001). The purpose of their study was to determine whether cohesion serves as a mediator between exercise leader behaviours and exercise adherence in older adults. Participants were 117 older adults (aged 67) who regularly participated in exercise classes. Cohesion was assessed using the physical activity group environment questionnaire (Estabrooks and Carron 2000), and leadership behaviours were assessed on a nine-point Likert scale pertaining to participants' perceptions of the leaders' enthusiasm, ability to motivate class members, availability outside class, and ability to provide personal information. Findings demonstrated that the leader behaviours of enthusiasm, motivation, and availability were positively related to ATG-T and GI-T. For older adults, these behaviours may create an optimal psychosocial environment that promotes exercise adherence by making the task more attractive to the class members and increasing perceived value of the exercise class based on common goals. Further support for the potential influence of the exercise class leader on developing group cohesion has been found in qualitative research in this area. Estabrooks and colleagues (2004) found that group processes relating to group goals – membership relationships and social integration – were factors of social and task cohesion identified by older adults as important characteristics of an exercise leader. Similar findings were reported by Christensen and colleagues (2006), where the teaching ability of the exercise leader influenced group cohesion and development in a group exercise class for previously sedentary adults.

In order to enhance group cohesion, Carron, Spink, and Prapavessis (1997) outlined a four-stage process of developing team-building in an exercise class:

1. Introductory stage – provide the exercise class leader with an overview of the benefits of developing group cohesion in relation to class member enjoyment, enthusiasm, and long-term adherence.
2. Conceptual stage – introduce a conceptual framework for team building, as developed by Carron and Spink (1993), to the exercise leader in a fitness class. This framework postulates that group cohesion is influenced by the group environment and group structure via group processes.
3. Practical stage – allow the exercise leader to become an active agent in the development of practical strategies, tailored to the leader's exercise group, for promoting group cohesion. The exercise leader's autonomy with the group will be enhanced and commitment to developing group cohesion increased.
4. Intervention stage – have the leader introduce specific team-building strategies to the exercise group and continue them in each session.

This four-stage process can be used by exercise leaders and practitioners aiming to develop group cohesion in a gym or leisure centre setting (see Section 8.8 for additional strategies for use at the practical stage).

8.7 Summary

Exercise leaders and co-exercisers contribute to the social processes involved in volitional exercise behaviour choices and adherence in the gym or leisure centre setting. Long-term exercise adherence can be ensured by developing a cohesive environment focused on group tasks and social interaction. For individual exercisers, certain self-presentational concerns (e.g., social physique anxiety, self-presentational efficacy) can contribute to negative psychological well-being; minimising this will ensure long-term exercise adherence. The case study discusses specific strategies that exercise leaders, personal trainers, and gym managers can use to create an optimal social environment for long-term adherence in their settings.

8.8 Case study

8.8.1 Setting the scene

Sarah is a 23-year-old female who experienced low levels of self-efficacy for sport at school and felt uncomfortable participating in sport in front of her classmates. Since leaving school, she did not engage in regular exercise until recently, when she decided join her local private gym. This decision was prompted by an increasingly stressful job; she hoped to use exercise to reduce stress levels and feel better about herself. She also wanted to improve her fitness and tone, make friends, and lose weight.

Sarah joins an aerobics exercise class in the gym, and during the session she finds other class members cliquey and unsociable. As it has been a while since Sarah was in a gym environment, she is wearing loose clothing for the class and prefers to stand at the back of the class, behind all other class members and away from the mirrors and the exercise leader. She finds the exercise class leader, who offers limited instruction and interaction with the group, unfriendly towards her. She continues to attend the same session for the next few weeks, yet her experience remains the same. This leads to a lack of enjoyment during the class and a reduced intention to go to the class in the future. Sarah is considering cancelling her gym membership at the end of the month.

How can the exercise class leader, co-exercisers, and gym manager change the exercise environment to increase Sarah's enjoyment in class and thus increase her future intentions and long-term exercise adherence?

8.8.2 Assessing the situation

The key socialising agent in this situation is the exercise class leader, who needs to acknowledge the importance of being a facilitator of each class

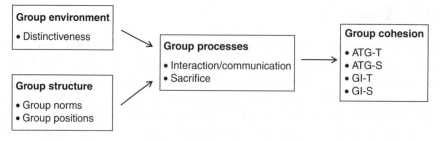

Figure 8.1   *Conceptual framework used as a basis for the implementation of a team-building program in fitness classes*

Source: Reprinted, with permission, from Carron, V. and Spink, K. S. (1993). Team building in an exercise setting, *Sport Psychologist*, 7(1), 8–18.

member's exercise experience. To increase the likelihood of future participation, that experience needs to be motivating, enjoyable, and fun. The class leader needs to be aware of the different levels in the class, not only in relation to physical abilities but with regard to levels of self-presentational efficacy, social physique anxiety, and confidence as an exerciser. The leader also needs to manage the social integration of the group to create a balance. In Sarah's case, she felt the group was too cliquey; it made her feel isolated in her first class. Equally, the exercise leader is not there to enforce social interaction. Doing this can exacerbate certain individuals' level of social anxiety in a new exercise setting. Encouraging social interaction in a natural and gradual manner is what is needed.

It is difficult for an exercise leader to 'assess' all class members in relation to their levels of social physique anxiety and self-presentational efficacy in each session; contact time (usually one hour) is limited, and frequency of contact irregular. The exercise leader thus has to attempt to gauge these self-presentational concerns by using cues during the session; for example, the distance that class members stand from the front of the class and from the mirrors (further away suggesting high social physique anxiety and low self-presentational efficacy) and the attire they wear during the session (i.e., loose clothing suggesting high social physique anxiety and low self-presentational efficacy). The exercise leader should gauge from Sarah's conduct that she is a new member of the class and may be experiencing high social physique anxiety and low self-presentational efficacy. Consequently the leader should ensure Sarah's first exercise experience is positive, motivating, and enjoyable.

8.8.3   Specific strategies

The following strategies could be used by both the gym manager and the exercise leader to ensure that the psychosocial environment in the sessions promotes increased enjoyment, exercise group cohesion, and motivation and consequently long-term exercise adherence behaviours. Using the conceptual framework (Figure 8.1) developed by Carron and Spink (1993), gym managers and exercise practitioners can promote and increase awareness in their exercise class instructors of the importance of enhancing group cohesion for long-term exercise adherence. The framework can be used, alongside the four-stage process, by exercise leaders and practitioners aiming to develop group cohesion in a gym or leisure centre setting (See Section 8.6).

Linked to Carron and Spink's (1993) framework, several strategies could be employed by the exercise leader to develop a more cohesive exercise class:

- Group environment (distinctiveness) – consider having group T-shirts, posters, and a group name.
- Group structure (individual positions) – allow members to choose their own spot for the class and encourage them to remain in it throughout the year.
- Group structure (group norms) – encourage class members to set up and tidy away each other's equipment. Create a goal for each session that is developed by the group.
- Group processes (individual sacrifices) – encourage regular attendees to buddy up with new class members.
- Group processes (interaction and communication) – encourage members to introduce themselves to each other. Develop activities during the class that encourage class members to work together.

As outlined, it is the exercise leader who needs to orchestrate these strategies to develop task and social cohesion in the class and also needs to display all the key characteristics of an efficacious leader on the basis of the class members' expectations (the characteristics are discussed in Section 8.3.2). Salient qualities include a health-focused and professional approach and a positive disposition and attitude, with energy and enthusiasm shown throughout the class. The exercise leader must also judge individual capabilities and provide the necessary support whilst managing social interaction. A key strategy that could help reduce self-presentational concerns of exercisers, particularly those new to the gym environment, might be establishing female-only sessions, with no mirrors or windows present, to reduce levels of social physique anxiety. The gym manager would be responsible for endorsing this class and integrating it into the class timetable.

8.9   Further study and recommended reading

The following literature is recommended for further reading on key concepts addressed in this chapter.

- Pridgeon, S., and Grogan, S. (2012). Understanding exercise adherence and dropout: an interpretative phenomenological analysis of men and women's accounts of gym attendance and non-attendance. *Qualitative Research in Sport, Health and Exercise*, 4(3), 382–399.
- Tenenbaum, G., Eklund, R. C., and Kamata, A. (2012). *Measurement in Sport and Exercise Psychology*, chs 22, 23, 35. Champaign, IL: Human Kinetics.

Additionally, reading in the following relevant areas is recommended. The materials address other social aspects of the gym and leisure centre setting that are not covered in this chapter but are important to both the exerciser and exercise professionals.

Exercise addiction and social physique anxiety in exercise professionals:

- Banbery, B., Groves, M., and Biscomb, K. (2012). The relationship between exercise dependence and identity reinforcement: a sociological examination of a gym-based environment in the United Kingdom. *Sport in Society: Cultures, Commerce, Media, Politics*, 15(9), 1242–1259.
- Landolfi, E. (2013). Exercise addiction. *Sports Medicine*, 43(2), 111–119.

Muscle dysmorphia:

- Murray, S. B., Rieger, E., Touyz, S. W., and De la Garza García, L. Y. (2010). Muscle dysmorphia and the DSM-V conundrum: where does it belong? A review paper. *International Journal of Eating Disorders*, 43(6), 483–491. doi: 10.1002/eat.20828.
- Olivardia, R. (2001). Mirror, mirror on the wall, who's the largest of them all? The features and phenomenology of muscle dysmorphia. *Harvard Review of Psychiatry*, 9(5), 254–259.

9 Primary Health Care

9.1 Learning objectives

The purpose of this chapter is to examine the social context of the primary health care setting and its importance to individuals who have been advised to exercise by a health care professional but whose motivational readiness for exercise is often limited. The key learning objectives are:

- to explore the role of health care professionals, particularly general practitioners (GPs), who, as the initial point of contact for the majority of individuals who need to change their physical activity behaviours, are key socialising agents of change. The recent shift in the level and type of social support for such behaviour change offered by GPs and health care professionals is debated;
- to discuss the impact of the consultation style adopted by health care professionals on their patients' physical activity behaviour change, with a specific focus on the use of motivational interviewing and brief advice approaches in the primary health care setting;
- to examine the role of exercise referral schemes as a structured social context to promote behaviour change, particularly in clinical populations. The positive psychosocial processes that can develop from exercise referral schemes – for example, collective efficacy, a sense of relatedness, and empathy – are considered, as are links to the self-determination theory (SDT) and the motivational readiness of these individuals;
- to discuss the practical implications of research for health care professionals to ensure compliance and adherence to the range of interventions offered in the primary health care setting, with specific focus on the relevant psychosocial processes required to achieve long-term physical activity behaviour change.

9.2 Introduction to the context

Since the 1990s, the integration of physical activity promotion across a range of sectors in the primary health care setting has increased, coinciding with the growing economic burden caused by the physical inactivity of the population. The annual estimated direct cost of inactivity to the National Health Service (NHS) in the United Kingdom is £1.06 billion (Department of Health 2011), with recent data from Scotland indicating the annual cost is approximately £94 million, equating to £18 per Scottish resident. From this report, Foster and Allender (2012) calculated that the cost of prescriptions related to physical inactivity diseases was £58 million and the cost of GP consultations related to physical inactivity diseases was £8.3 million. This suggests that in the primary health care setting, there is a clear economic rationale to promote physical activity to reduce the economic consequences of increasing prevalence of physical inactivity diseases. There are other reasons why the primary health care setting is commonly used to promote physical activity and is considered an appropriate context for encouraging behaviour change. According to the Health Education Authority, approximately 75% of the UK population visit their GP once a year, allowing a GP access to a large and diverse population sample. As individuals also engage with other health care professionals in the primary health care setting, it provides an ideal window of opportunity for discussing physical activity. In 2007/2008, an estimated 292.4 million consultations took place in primary health care settings, with the average patient receiving 5.3 consultations (QRESEARCH and the Health and Social Care Information Centre 2008). Furthermore, health care professionals are considered credible sources and can be important socialising agents of behaviour change (Gidlow and Murphy 2009). That the majority of individuals in primary health care settings exercise because they are advised to by health care professionals has motivational connotations for long-term behaviour change. Individuals' extrinsic motivation may suffice to sustain short-term physical activity behaviour; however, once they leave the primary health care setting, long-term behaviour change is a fundamental concern for health care professionals. Consequently they need to ensure that the social context for exercise develops a sense of autonomy, enjoyment and competence to increase the likelihood of continued physical activity behaviour beyond the primary health care setting.

9.2.1   Understanding key terms

The primary health care setting utilises a number of strategies to get individuals to exercise. An examination of the literature evaluating their effectiveness indicates that various terms are used, often interchangeably, to describe the strategies. Outlining the terms will ensure clarity in this chapter, but readers should not expect consistency in terminology beyond it. Exercise referral schemes, the most commonly used primary health care strategy, generally involve collaboration between a health care professional, usually a GP or practice nurse, and a local exercise professional. As Fox et al. (1997) outline, there are many variations on the exercise referral model used in primary health care settings (see Section 9.5 for details of a typical process). The initial consultation relating to increasing physical activity behaviour, where current activity is discussed and goals are set, is often referred to as 'exercise on prescription' or 'brief advice'. Brief advice is defined by the National Institute for Health and Clinical Excellence (NICE 2013, 6) as 'verbal advice, discussion, negotiation or encouragement, with or without written or follow-up. It can vary from basic advice to a more extended, individually focused discussion.' In 2006, the NICE guidelines on brief advice for health care professionals, recommended that, whenever possible, they should identify inactive adults and advise them to aim for 30 minutes of moderate activity five days a week. NICE also suggested that they reinforce brief advice with written information about the benefits of activity and local opportunities to be active and follow up at appropriate intervals over a three- to 6-month period. A recent update on brief advice (NICE 2013) supported these guidelines yet suggested that health care professionals' judgement regarding inactive or at-risk individuals and the amount or length of brief advice given might need to be reconsidered. The report also found that supportive written materials health care professionals gave was at times of questionable quality, thereby reducing the potential effectiveness of brief advice.

Once an individual is referred to an exercise professional, additional consultations can occur. In the literature and applied practice, these consultations vary with regard to content delivered, length of delivery, frequency of consultations, and delivery strategies used. It is also difficult to ascertain from the evidence base the delivery style practitioners adopt, yet the style can have significant social influence on the individual's behaviour. In the United States, though exercise consultations are often referred to as physical activity counselling, elements of counselling practice are not necessarily involved. Furthermore, some US and UK research and evidence-based practice in primary health care settings report that a motivational interviewing style in exercise consultations is adopted. In the early 1990s, Miller and Rollnick (1991) defined motivational interviewing as 'a directive, client-centred counselling style for eliciting behaviour change by helping clients to explore and resolve ambivalence'. More recently, Miller and Rollnick (2009) modified this definition to 'a collaborative, person-centred form of guiding to elicit and strengthen motivation for change' (137). (Consultation style and its impact on behaviour change is discussed in detail in Section 9.4.3.)

The distinction between freely choosing exercise and being prescribed exercise by a health care professional has been considered by Brawley and Culos-Reed (2000) in terms of adherence and compliance. They argue that these terms point to key motivational differences: 'adherence' suggests that individuals choose to engage in behaviours, whereas 'compliance' implies that they engage in them only because they are following the advice or prescription of health care professionals. Despite this distinction, these terms are used interchangeably in the literature, with a tendency to focus more on individuals' adherence to an exercise referral scheme than on their compliance.

9.3   Role of health care professionals in physical activity behaviour change

As noted, health care professionals are salient socialising agents for most individuals who encounter the primary health care setting. There has been a shift in the level and type of social support for behaviour change expected of GPs, with provision of basic informational support expanded to include tailored informational support, emotional support with follow-up, and validation support through sharing of case examples to motivate individuals via a sense of relatedness. Despite the benefits of using health care professionals to promote physical activity, they face several challenges: lack of time due to workload pressures, inadequate training and knowledge, and possible conflict with their own beliefs and attitudes. A detailed examination of these and other barriers to delivery of brief advice interventions appeared in the 2013 NICE report. Structural factors identified included conflicting priorities, lack of time and support, and lack of incentives to incorporate brief advice into consultations. Practitioner factors identified were concern whether it was part of their remit (role), doubts as to their own physical activity levels, lack of confidence in their knowledge of physical activity, and lack of belief in the effectiveness of brief advice on physical activity. Patient factors identified as barriers to delivery included the likely uptake of physical activity advice, access and quality of local physical activity provision, and the level of rapport developed.

The barriers outlined find support in the literature. Early UK research by McKenna, Naylor, and McDowell (1998) examining barriers to physical activity promotion by GPs and practice nurses found that GPs' own physical activity levels influenced how likely they were to advocate increased physical activity. GPs in the highest stages of change (i.e., action or maintenance) were three times as likely to regularly promote physical activity. This supports the view that in a professional-patient dyad, health care professionals consider themselves role models for certain behaviours, including physical activity. According to Bandura (1986), the more the role model and the observer (i.e., the patient) are alike, the more that modelling is likely to facilitate the latter's behaviour and self-efficacy in executing that behaviour. In addition, GPs and practice nurses that cited lack of time and incentives as barriers to physical activity promotion were less likely to promote physical activity on a regular basis.

It is evident that health care professionals perceive barriers to incorporating physical activity promotion into daily practice; to date, there is no robust evidence to indicate what proportion of health care professionals, particularly GPs and practice nurses, regularly promote physical activity. McKenna and Vernon (2004) explored how 234 GPs from one health authority in the south of England promoted lifestyle advice. Findings demonstrated that 47.1% regularly and actively promoted the physical activity message; these GPs had more knowledge of their patients' physical activity levels. GPs adopted three key roles in relation to physical activity promotion: arranging follow-ups for patients whom they deemed pre-contemplators, referring patients in the contemplation stage to exercise referral schemes, and asking relapsed patients about their physical activity.

A key priority outlined in Scotland's physical activity strategy is to ensure all adults who come into contact with primary health care staff are offered an assessment of health risks associated with their inactivity and an individualised programme to help increase their future physical activity. In 2013, the Scottish government commissioned a pilot scheme in six health boards where GPs actively engaged in brief interventions during routine consultations with patients. This involved asking patients about their physical activity levels and offering advice and follow-up support if appropriate (Scottish Government 2013). Previous research evidence consistently showed that a GP can be a key socialising agent of behaviour change relating to physical activity via brief advice, exercise on prescription, and exercise referral schemes. As Swinburn et al. (1998) noted, prescriptions represent a well-understood interaction between patient and GP. They examined the impact on sedentary patients (N = 491) of written versus verbal physical activity advice randomly offered by a GP over six weeks. Findings supported the role of the GP as a socialising agent of change: both groups increased weekly levels of physical activity to exceed one hour, but the written advice, exercise on prescription, was more effective than verbal advice alone. The visual reminder of an exercise prescription was an effective yet simple method for a GP to increase physical activity in sedentary patients.

The concept of an exercise prescription delivered in a consultation has been extended in the literature to include a combination of GP verbal and written advice, leaflets and newsletters, and follow-up telephone counselling. A randomised control trial examining the effectiveness of counselling patients on physical activity in general practice was conducted by Elley et al. (2003). Participants (N = 878) eligible for the study were screened to ensure low levels of physical activity and were randomly assigned to either the intervention or the control group. Those in the intervention group discussed their physical activity with either the GP or practice nurse and were prescribed appropriate physical activity goals. The prescription was given to the patient to keep as a record and also passed on to exercise professionals at a local fitness centre; they made three follow-up telephone calls to support the patients in their prescribed activity goals. Energy expenditure, self-reported physical activity, quality of life, and blood pressure were assessed at baseline and 12 months later. Results indicated that for every 10 prescriptions written, one patient achieved and sustained 150 minutes of moderate-to-vigorous physical activity per week after 12 months. Compared to the results in the control group, these patients' self-rated aspects of quality of life significantly increased, and patients prescribed physical activity showed a trend towards decreased blood pressure.

However, subsequent research examining GPs' effectiveness at increasing physical activity among inactive patients found that prescribed brief advice did not influence quality of life yet increased self-reported physical activity (Grandes et al. 2009). A sample of 4,317 participants who did not meet recommended levels of physical activity were recruited and randomly assigned to either the intervention group (N = 2248) or control group (N = 2069). The intervention consisted of the GP providing brief advice and educational materials to all patients, who then were offered an additional 15-minute appointment to devise an individualised physical activity plan. Only a third of the intervention group booked an additional appointment. Overall, the proportion of the sample achieving minimal physical activity recommendations was 3.9% higher in the intervention group; this provides additional support for the GP's key social role for physical activity behaviour change in the primary health care setting. More support came in a systematic review of exercise on prescription in general practice conducted by Sorenson, Skovgaard, and Puggaard (2006). Of the 12 studies included in the review, 50% found that exercise prescribed by the health care professional significantly increased patients' physical activity levels. In three studies, aerobic fitness was also assessed, with two studies demonstrating a 14% increase in maximal aerobic fitness in patients prescribed physical activity compared to a 3% increase in the control group patients. Overall the authors of the review concluded that exercise on prescription had a moderately positive effect on physical activity in approximately 10% of patients. This suggests that during a routine consultation, a GP has an instrumental role in influencing change in the physical activity of their patients in a relatively short time frame.

9.4   Impact of the consultation style on physical activity behaviour change

9.4.1   Characteristics of motivational interviewing

It is apparent that a health care professional has a degree of social influence on a patient's physical activity choices and behaviours. In general, patients do not engage in regular physical activity without being advised to by a GP or another external source; consequently their motivation to comply may be reduced. It is important that the health care professional delivering the advice adopt the most appropriate consultation style to increase the likelihood of long-term compliance. The literature has paid increased attention to the use of motivational interviewing as a consultation approach to physical activity behaviour change in the primary health care setting. Motivational interviewing, first developed in the early 1990s by Miller and Rollnick (1991), is considered a patient-centred approach to behaviour change, as it adopts a guiding consultation style. Characteristics of motivational interviewing outlined by Miller and Rollnick (1991) include the following:

- Motivational interviewing is considered a set of techniques and a counselling style.
- It is directive: a client-centred counselling approach to understanding and eliciting behaviour change.
- It relies upon identifying and mobilising the patient's intrinsic values and goals to stimulate behaviour change.
- Motivation to change is elicited from the patients themselves, not by the external source.
- Motivational interviewing attempts to elicit, clarify, and resolve ambivalence through discussion of costs and benefits associated with change.
- Resistance and denial are common; they are signals to modify motivational strategies used by the health care professional.
- Eliciting and reinforcing patients' belief in their ability to succeed in achieving a specific goal is fundamental for long-term behaviour change.

Motivational interviewing strategies are considered more persuasive than coercive, more supportive than argumentative; their overall goal is increasing a patient's intrinsic motivation. Motivation to change needs to originate from within rather than be imposed by external sources.

9.4.2   Self-determination theory and motivational interviewing

Characteristics of motivational interviewing are closely aligned with aspects of the self-determination theory (SDT) developed by Deci and Ryan (1985), where motivation moves away from a dichotomised view of intrinsic versus extrinsic motivation to being viewed on a continuum. The four main types of extrinsic motivation are external, introjected, identified, and integrated regulation (see Figure 9.1). External regulation is where an individual is motivated to engage in behaviour to avoid punishment or gain reward. In an exercise context, a woman might exercise because the GP has told her to; otherwise her blood pressure will become dangerously high (i.e., she exercises to avoid the 'punishment' of high blood pressure). Introjected regulation is where an individual is motivated to engage in a behaviour to avoid feelings of guilt or a sense of obligation or to seek others' approval for the behaviour. In an exercise context, a man might exercise because he feels guilty or feels his GP would be annoyed if he didn't comply with his exercise programme. The third type, identified regulation, is where an individual acts to achieve a goal; feelings are characterised by 'want to' rather than 'ought to'. In an exercise context, a man might exercise to lose weight, prevent ill health, or increase fitness levels. The last type of extrinsic motivation, integrated regulation, is the most self-determined form. Though integrated into an individual's sense of identity, the behaviour is still extrinsic, as it is instrumental in achieving personalised goals. In an exercise context, this could be where an individual considers herself an exerciser. Exercising is part of who she is, but she does not exercise for its intrinsic pleasure. Engaging in a behaviour for the pure joy of the activity is known as intrinsic motivation. It has three main facets: to learn, to accomplish tasks, and to experience sensations such as enjoyment and fun. Both identified and integrated regulations are autonomous and are associated with enhanced maintenance and transfer of behaviour change. Moving towards more intrinsic, integrated, and identified forms of behavioural regulation increases the likelihood an individual will become more self-determined and accomplish long-term behaviour change. Motivation to change through motivation interviewing strategies emphasises a need to shift behavioural regulation from the professional to the patient and links to the SDT's preferred shift along the continuum from external regulation to identified, integrated, and intrinsic forms of behavioural regulation.

According to Deci and Ryan (1985), an individual's behavioural regulation can be modified to become more self-determined by ensuring that three basic needs are fulfilled. These are developing a sense of autonomy, competence, and relatedness. Autonomy is the desire to have self-regulation of a behaviour. If a sense of autonomy is present, intrinsic motivation is

	Extrinsic motivation				
Amotivation	External regulation	Introjected regulation	Identified regulation	Integrated regulation	Intrinsic motivation
Limited motivation to engage in the behaviour	Motivated by gaining reward or avoiding punishment	Motivated by a sense of obligation, guilt or seeking approval	Motivated by personal goals	Motivated by confirmation of sense of self and identity	Motivated by learning, a sense of accomplishment and experiencing stimulation
– ⟵ Self-determination ⟶ +					

Figure 9.1 *A continuum of self-determination in terms of different types of motivation*

Source: Adapted with permission from Biddle, S. J. and Mutrie, N. (2008). *Psychology of Physical Activity: Determinants, Well-Being and Interventions*, 2nd ed., figure 4.3 (86). London: Routledge.

facilitated. Competence is the desire to be able to perform a particular behaviour. If an activity provides a sense of competence, intrinsic motivation is facilitated. Finally, relatedness is the desire for social interaction. If relatedness is perceived to be present, intrinsic motivation is facilitated. All three needs are consistent with the philosophy and delivery of motivational interviewing (Resnicow and McMaster 2012). Developing a sense of competence for a specific behaviour is central to the motivational interviewing approach; it can be achieved by creating appropriate goals and providing positive feedback. A sense of relatedness is achieved through building a meaningful social connection with the practitioner via expression of empathy and non-judgemental discussion and via the patient's wider social network. Finally, autonomy support is central to the practice of motivational interviewing through eliciting behaviour change from the patient in a guided manner.

9.4.3   Guided vs. directing consultation style

The links between motivational interviewing and SDT were first established by Markland et al. (2005), who suggested that both assume that humans have an innate tendency for personal growth toward psychological integration and that motivational interviewing provides the social-environmental facilitating factors suggested by SDT to promote this tendency. The social-environmental facilitators for behaviour change originate from the practitioner delivering the consultation; thus, consultation style can strongly influence the likelihood of behaviour change occurring. Generally when a health care professional discusses behaviour change with patients, the default consultation style is to inform and direct them as to what to do and why they should do it. Perceived lack of time is a common reason professionals give for the almost reflex use of a directing style when trying to change behaviour.

A discussion on the consultation style that health care professionals can adopt in the primary health care setting was offered by Rollnick and colleagues (2005). Comparing a directing consultation style with a guided style, which aligns more closely with motivational interviewing delivery, they suggested that the directing style regularly manifests in a rigid routine of closed questions – 'How much exercise do you do per week?' and the like – before the advice to try increasing weekly exercise is delivered. This results in patients being told what they already know (or considered, tried, and rejected) and offered a single, apparently simple solution. Resistance is a common reaction. As this dysfunctional interaction can leave professionals blaming patients for lacking motivation or being in denial, the likelihood of behaviour change is reduced. A guided style allows the health care professional to move from using coercion to simply informing the patient, giving encouragement and exploring through patient-led discussions. The interactional dyad of professional and patient can facilitate exploration of ambivalence, where the key aim for the professional is to get the patient to identify his or her own reasons and motivations for change.

The use of a guiding style aligned with motivational interviewing principles has been examined in the research literature from the practitioners' viewpoint and for its feasibility for consultation in a practical setting. Miller and Beech (2009) conducted focus groups with 33 health care professionals who provided care to African American women with type II diabetes. In relation to their own practices, 55% reported limited or no physical activity counselling to these patients due to lack of knowledge of the guidelines and to individual challenges relating to their own activity levels. During the focus groups, the professionals were shown two video clips of a patient–health care professional consultation, one with motivational interviewing principles incorporated into the consultation delivery style and one without. Perceived advantages of the former delivery style from the professionals' viewpoint included positive communication between patient and practitioner, positive disposition of both parties, a relaxed consultation environment, and an emphasis on patient autonomy. The perceived disadvantages were that using motivational interviewing, a consultation took too much time, and there were concerns over the limited input the health care professional had on the consultation's outcome.

Several recent studies examining the effectiveness of motivational interviewing in changing physical activity behaviour in a primary health care setting have had encouraging results. Sjoling and colleagues (2011) recruited 33 patients with mild to moderate hypertension and low physical activity levels to participate in four motivational interviewing sessions with the practice nurse at baseline, 3, 6, 9, and 15 months alongside the use of exercise diaries and a prescribed physical activity programme. Findings indicated that the combined intervention succeeded in encouraging patients to increase leisure time physical activity from less than 60 to approximately 300 minutes per week. Positive changes were also seen in blood pressure, waist circumference, body mass index (BMI), total cholesterol, and maximal oxygen uptake. Although encouraging, the findings were unclear as to how much the motivational interviewing sessions influenced behaviour change on their own.

Use of motivational interviewing as a stand-alone intervention component to elicit behaviour change in a disadvantaged community was examined by Hardcastle, Blake, and Hagger (2012). Although the intervention was not delivered by a GP or practice nurse, eligible patients not meeting the recommended physical activity levels were referred for a lifestyle change facilitation service, which was delivered by lifestyle change facilitators who participated in two motivational interviewing courses delivered by an accredited motivational interviewing network of trainers (MINT) trainer. The first was a two-day introduction; the second, a four-day advanced course. Both events focused on the principles of motivational interviewing and emphasised the key underlying spirit: ensuring a patient-centred approach to behaviour change. Lifestyle change facilitators were also required to conduct an audiotaped consultation session and have it assessed by the independent MINT trainer. Hardcastle and colleagues' article is one of very few that offer a detailed description of the motivational interviewing strategies used by the lifestyle change facilitators, which included exploring ambivalence, eliciting self-directed change talk, setting self-determined goals, and using the confidence ruler technique (Rollnick 1997). Outcomes measures, assessed at baseline and six months, included self-reported physical activity, stage of change, self-efficacy, behavioural regulation in exercise, attitudes towards exercise, perceived behavioural control, and perceived social support. Findings demonstrated a significant increase in self-reported physical activity after six months. There was also evidence of a dose-response relationship, where more than two motivational interviewing sessions over six months elicited larger increases in physical activity behaviour change, with the optimum number being four to five hours of motivational interviewing sessions. Perceptions of social support, stage of change, and self-efficacy significantly increased as a result of the lifestyle change facilitation service. This suggests that motivational interviewing has an impact on key psychosocial factors which play a central role in relation to physical activity behaviour change.

9.4.4   Clinical populations and exercise consultations

Evidence for the effectiveness of utilising exercise referrals and exercise consultations for clinical populations has been shown in a range of clinical populations, including type II diabetes and cardiac rehabilitation patients. Kirk and colleagues (2001) found that a one-to-one exercise consultation lasting 30 minutes (compared to a standard leaflet on type II diabetes and exercise) significantly increased objective physical activity levels after five weeks in a sample of sedentary type II diabetes patients. These findings were extended in 2004 by Kirk and colleagues (2004) to examine the effectiveness of an exercise consultation on long-term physical activity behaviour change in sedentary type II diabetes patients. Participants were randomly assigned to either an exercise consultation group or a group that received a standard leaflet. The exercise consultation group received one-to-one exercise consultations lasting 30 minutes at baseline and at six months, with support telephone calls at one and three months. The standard-leaflet group received the leaflet at baseline and telephone calls at one and three months, yet these were unrelated to the discussion of physical activity behaviour. Outcome measures were assessed at baseline and 6 and 12 months, with findings demonstrating significant improvements in the exercise consultation group in self-reported physical activity and stage of change but not in objectively measured activity. Furthermore, findings indicated that participants who had received the exercise consultations utilised significantly more processes of change than those in the standard-leaflet group. Overall the study highlighted that engagement with a health care professional in an exercise consultation can be influential on perceptions of physical activity and the strategies used to engage in behaviour change. The social context of a one-to-one dyadic relationship with a health care professional, where informational, emotional, and validation support occurs, can elicit behaviour change that standard-leaflet support alone fails to achieve.

Exercise consultations have also been used to maintain physical activity behaviour after a patient's released from an exercise programme. Hughes, Mutrie, and MacIntyre (2006) compared the longer-term effects of a consultation with standard exercise information on maintaining physical activity and cardiorespiratory fitness after completion of a supervised exercise programme for phase III cardiac rehabilitation. Seventy cardiac patients recruited from the programme were randomly assigned to a control group or the exercise consultation group. Consultations involved a 30-minute one-to-one discussion with a trained researcher, where strategies included discussion of current physical activity levels, pros and cons of being active, problem-solving barriers, social support, activity options, setting realistic activity goals (for one, three, and six months), and preventing relapse. These consultations occurred at baseline and six months later, with telephone support at three months. The findings supported the use of exercise consultations to maintain self-reported physical activity 12 months after cardiac patients completed the phase III cardiac rehabilitation exercise programme. However, findings suggested that the consultations did not influence peak oxygen uptake, quality of life, or levels of depression in cardiac patients, suggesting that they may have a stronger influence on perceptions of physical activity levels and attitudes and cognitions towards physical activity than on specific physiological fitness outcomes.

9.4.5   Practical considerations for health care professionals' consultation styles

Overall the evidence supports adoption of a guiding style for health care professionals in a primary health care setting, yet the feasibility of consistently delivering this style whilst working with economic and time constraints is still questionable. Many professionals may feel they require training in motivational interviewing principles to effectively offer this style, but training could be hindered by barriers of cost and time. In addition, the shift to a patient-led consultation style may not be deemed appropriate for all patients or the health care professional may not be comfortable assuming a more passive role. However, this can be altered accordingly depending on the situation; for example, if a patient responds with resistance to a guiding style, it might be a signal for the practitioner to modify the approach.

Brief advice interventions might be found more suitable in certain primary health care settings where time constraints, limited specialist knowledge in motivational interviewing, or the need to tailor consultation style to the patient are a concern. As detailed by NICE (2013), brief advice consists of verbal advice, discussion, negotiation, or encouragement, with or without written follow-up or other support. Brief advice might be opportunistic and take less than a minute or as much as 20 minutes. It could be very basic or be an extended, individually focused discussion. It might be delivered in a GP surgery, health centre, or other primary care setting or be delivered by health care professionals in other settings (e.g., a residential home). People who might give this advice include community nurses, GPs, health visitors, pharmacists, physiotherapists, exercise professionals, and health trainers. A social encounter involving a patient and a professional in any primary health care setting allows the latter to provide brief advice on physical activity, if deemed appropriate. It would be unrealistic to expect all professionals across the range of primary care settings to have specialist knowledge of the motivational interviewing principles required to elicit physical activity behaviour change in a limited time frame. Yet, as Rollnick and colleagues (2005) emphasised, the goal for health care professionals is to adjust their routine and default approach to talking about behaviour change and engage the patient in decision making via simple and subtle strategies. It may be that in-depth and extensive motivational interviewing interventions in the primary health care setting should come from exercise and health care professionals with specialist knowledge and training in motivational interviewing principles; this would align well with exercise referral schemes in primary settings. The end goal is to increase the patient's physical activity, and there is no prescriptive method of achieving this. Practitioners should be encouraged to choose an approach that suits the patient to facilitate a positive outcome.

9.5   Exercise referral schemes and physical activity behaviour change

Exercise referral schemes have been defined by Pavey and colleagues (2011, 2) as 'schemes in which a general practitioner (or another member of the primary care team) identifies and refers a sedentary individual with evidence of at least one cardiovascular risk factor to a third party service (often a sports centre or leisure facility). This service then prescribes and monitors an exercise programme tailored to the individual needs of the patient.' Exercise referral schemes provide a structured social context where behaviour change can occur via several psychosocial processes. Since the integration of exercise referral schemes in primary health care settings in the early 1990s, such schemes have significantly increased in the United Kingdom and are now considered among the main avenues to increase physical activity behaviour in individuals, particularly those with clinical conditions. As outlined by Fox and colleagues (1997), there are several variations on the exercise referral model used in primary health care settings. A typical process, involving several health care professionals as key socialising agents of change, consists of numerous stages where dropout can occur. The process starts with an initial referral of the patient to an exercise specialist (usually a GP or a practice nurse). The referral decision usually has a mutual basis: regarding the patient's physical activity levels and health issue(s), patient and practitioner agree that an exercise programme would be beneficial. At this point, most referral schemes require the patient to consent to having their details – height, weight, blood pressure, BMI – passed on to the exercise specialist. If consent is not provided at this stage, the exercise referral cannot continue, and patient dropout from the scheme will occur. Research has shown that GPs and health care professionals are more likely to offer advice on physical activity and refer a patient if they see that the patient contemplates behaviour change (i.e., initiates the discussion on being more active with the GP; Ackermann, Deyo, and LoGerfo 2005; Elley et al. 2003). Furthermore, patients who were pro-active in identifying that their inactivity was related to health were more likely to embrace a multicomponent exercise intervention programme (Elley et al. 2003). More recent evidence has demonstrated that health care professionals saw their advice as a weaker determinant of activity adherence than the patient's self-determined decision to seek help (Moore, Moore, and Murphy 2011). These findings support the guiding consultation style of motivational interviewing where patient and health care professional work together to adopt a 'meet in the middle' approach to physical activity behaviour change rather than have it directed and dictated solely by the health care professional.

Once the patient has agreed to attend an initial consultation with the exercise specialist, subsequent interaction between the patient and the exercise specialist can influence the likelihood of adoption and compliance to the proposed programme. Building rapport through positive psychosocial processes is fundamental to ensuring patient participation. Communication skills (e.g., reflective listening, open body language, paraphrasing), empathy, and non-judgemental discussions can all be used to reassure patients that the exercise programme will be beneficial and that they will be able to engage with the programme on a regular basis. If the exercise specialist fails to establish a rapport with the patient, the likelihood that the patient will not commit to the scheduled programme after the initial consultation increases. At this stage, the exercise specialist plays a central social role in the uptake to the programme. Duda and colleagues (2014) conducted an exploratory cluster randomised controlled trial examining the effects of a standard provision exercise referral scheme compared to an autonomy-supportive scheme based on SDT. Findings indicated that in both types of referral provision, moderate-to-vigorous physical activity significantly increased at three and six months; there were no significant differences in moderate-to-vigorous activity between the groups. Contrary to the previous discussion, these findings suggest that developing autonomy-supportive strategies in exercise referral schemes may not be necessary to elicit behaviour change. Furthermore, the two groups' perceptions of the autonomy support provided by the health and fitness professionals did not differ. However, it is important to note that physical activity behaviour was assessed by self-report, and there was no reported monitoring of the strategies used by the health and fitness professionals in the delivery exercise referral schemes.

The majority of exercise referrals are gym-based at a local leisure centre to minimise cost for both the NHS and the patient (programmes tend to be subsidised or free of charge). Alternatively, exercise referral schemes involving post-surgery patients have a hospital setting and form part of the palliative care provided. If the patient decides to continue with the programme, typically lasting 8 to 12 weeks with 2 or 3 sessions per week, the social influence of other referral patients comes into play. The majority of referral schemes offer a combination of one-to-one sessions with the exercise specialist, particularly during the first few weeks of the programme, alongside group exercise sessions. The social relationships that naturally develop in group exercise sessions can impact upon programme compliance and long-term physical activity behaviours. These relationships can be markedly intense in clinical populations where patients suffering from a shared illness (e.g., type II diabetes) can relate to one another through empathy, collective efficacy, modelling, distraction, and self-presentational issues. (See Section 9.5.2 for further discussion of the positive psychosocial processes that can emerge through group exercise in referral schemes.)

Moreover, assimilation into an exercising environment and an unfamiliar social context can be daunting for the majority of patients who don't engage in regular physical activity and can create a sense of social anxiety. Therefore, the exercise leader can play a key role in minimising these concerns at the start of the programme by manipulating the social environment to ensure a sense of autonomy, competence, and relatedness amongst exercisers. On completion of the scheduled programme, the focus is usually on assessing changes in physiological outcomes it has produced (e.g., maximal oxygen uptake, self-reported levels of physical activity, height, weight, BMI, blood pressure). Gidlow and Murphy (2009) emphasise the need to assess individuals' positive psychosocial outcomes; for example, enhanced mental well-being, social interaction, and improved quality of life. In addition to changes in physiological outcomes, a referral scheme's success is also based on the number of patients who complete the referral process (i.e., quantity), with little attention given to the quality of the patient experience using a more holistic approach. Generally speaking, once patients have completed a scheme where exercise behaviour has been supervised, guided, and supported for up to three months, they are left to maintain the behaviour on their own with no additional follow-up support. At this point, long-term physical activity behaviour change may be jeopardised if the social networks created during the referral scheme with health care professionals and fellow exercisers have not fostered a sense of autonomy, competence, and relatedness for habitual physical activity beyond the scheme.

9.5.1 Facilitating compliance and adherence in exercise referral schemes

In recent years attention has been given to evaluating referral schemes, using a qualitative approach, from the perspective of the professionals offering the programmes and the patients themselves. On this basis, a wide range of factors affecting compliance and adherence to the schemes have been established, yet the one consistently reported in the literature is the role of social support from all of the key socialising agents in the process. Wormald and Ingle (2004) conducted focus groups with 30 patients referred to an exercise scheme by their GP. Findings showed that a positive approach from the exercise specialist was important to the overall patient experience, along with social support from exercise instructors, family, and fellow exercisers, who act as powerful motivators for some individuals. Focus group findings of participants involved in UK referral schemes (Milton 2008) highlighted key social processes that positively impacted on the patient experience. Participants emphasised the importance of the social aspects of the group exercise class and the sense of peer support that developed. They also reported that the sessions could have been improved had the class leader used the buddy system and initial meetings for new referrals to encourage greater social interaction.

The perspectives of professionals involved in the delivering these schemes have also been examined; qualitative findings show the importance of the social climate created in the programme. In a study by Moore and colleagues (2011), 38 exercise professionals took part in semistructured telephone interviews to gain insight into their experiences of the national exercise referral scheme in Wales. They saw themselves as valued components of the patients' social networks, even for guidance on other health concerns than physical activity. Whilst some participants stated that this was part of the role they had in the exercise referral scheme and were happy to provide the added counselling, others stated that these discussions detracted from the programme's main purpose, which was to increase the physical activity of the patients. They also commented on the success of patient-only classes as opposed to generic group classes offered at local facilities in relation to patient adherence and enjoyment of the programme. All of the exercise professionals commented on the role of peer support in relation to adherence: patients provided realistic role models for one another. They deemed this particularly pertinent for new referrals to the programme. The exercise professionals felt that participants in the sessions, sharing a sense of empathy, were able to remove all social stigmas attached to their illness. Finally, some of the exercise professionals recommended making explicit efforts to foster the emergence of social networks, to last beyond the typical 12-week programme, to maximise the likelihood of long-term behaviour change in patients. There has also been a suggestion to move from the typical facility-based referrals that often occur in a gym environment, where other exercisers' motivational readiness differs from that of those involved in exercise referral schemes, to alternative referrals (e.g., walking schemes, cycling schemes). This could help minimise social anxiety concerns that patients experience when encountering a gym environment and increase the likelihood of future engagement with the referral scheme. As there is limited research evidence to date examining the effectiveness of alternative exercise referral schemes, they are an important avenue for future research.

9.5.2   Clinical populations and exercise referrals

Consideration of exercise groups in a clinical setting where individuals have been referred to an exercise scheme due to a clinical issue is important for a number of reasons. Levels of compliance and adherence may be increased by group members having a sense of relatedness and by developing task and social cohesion. The role of social support and group cohesion in exercise compliance in a clinical population was examined by Fraser and Spink (2002). Female participants were referred to an exercise scheme for clinical issues including diabetes, osteoporosis, hypertension, and obesity. The programme lasted 12 weeks, with three sessions per week, and participant levels of cohesion, social support, and compliance were assessed at weeks 4, 8, and 12. Findings were similar to those in non-clinical group exercise settings where attraction to the group-task aspect of group cohesion was positively associated with increased compliance. This suggests that encouraging members to focus on a group task could increase compliance through a sense of responsibility and ownership toward the task. The importance of social support was also evident in a clinical exercise group, where individuals reporting higher levels of social support were less likely to drop out of the referral scheme.

The importance of the social context of schemes involving clinical populations has been further emphasised in qualitative research where patients' experience of group cohesion in an exercise setting has been explored. Midtgaard and colleagues (2006) conducted semistructured interviews with 55 cancer patients receiving chemotherapy treatment. These patients had just completed a six-week (four sessions per week) exercise programme involving physical training, body awareness, relaxation, and massage. Working as a group with a shared illness appeared to have a significant impact on the motivation to exercise, on levels of competence, and on their capabilities. Being part of the group motivated individuals to pursue personal efforts beyond perceived physical limitations. This created a healthy level of competition amongst the patients, yet they reported using each other as role models when they experienced down periods during the programme, often while experiencing the side effects of chemotherapy. A collective identity emerged, one reflected in their use of 'we' when describing their individual experiences – again highlighting the potential for a referral scheme to develop a strong sense of social and task cohesion in clinical populations. The patients commented on the group fighting the same opponent (viz., cancer) and they were united in this task. This sense of collective identity and efficacy closely aligns with the sense of relatedness that is often needed to increase motivation to exercise (Deci and Ryan 1985) – a sense that this study, where motives became more self-determined, reinforced. Finally, participating in the exercise scheme distracted patients from their illness; many of them called it a chance to escape from the role of victim that they were experiencing in other social networks – for example, when spending time with their family. Being part of the group allowed them to re-create their identity, to extend its sense beyond that of 'the cancer victim'.

Many of the positive psychosocial factors that emerged from their experiences of group exercise as a clinical population have been reported elsewhere. Emslie and colleagues (2007) examined the experiences of women with breast cancer who were involved in a 12-week scheme. Thirty-six women participated in seven focus groups, with findings clearly emphasising the salience of the social context of the exercise scheme as a critical aspect of their experiences. Self-presentational concerns (Leary 1992; Schlenker and Leary 1982) can be intensified amongst clinical population groups for several reasons, including post-surgery changes and weight fluctuations caused by medication. Women suffering from breast cancer may be particularly sensitive to gender identity and self-presentational concerns and worries. The latter appeared to be significantly reduced for the women, who strongly emphasised the importance of exercising in a group with other women who had breast cancer: they didn't have to explain themselves to anyone. This shared understanding of the physical issues connected with having breast cancer and its associated self-presentational concerns were frequently discussed by the women. They valued the empathy they received from other exercise group members and reported their feelings moved from isolation to acceptance. Consonant with the findings of Midtgaard and colleagues (2006), these women motivated each other via a sense of relatedness. The sessions also gave them achievement and purpose; they found this particularly important as they were not then in full-time employment. Discussion of a sense of control during the sessions also supports the theoretical links to SDT as a key framework for understanding the

psychosocial processes that develop in group exercise for clinical populations. This was echoed in a study by Balneaves and colleagues (2014), where
breast cancer survivors participated in a 24-month diet and physical activity intervention. Focus groups findings suggested that the women appreci-
ated and valued the intervention's group-based delivery. Women remarked
that exercising with other survivors in a supportive environment surpassed
the experience of exercising independently in a gym. The research clearly
highlights that the sense of autonomy, competence, and relatedness that
developed during the exercise schemes and interventions caused patients
to become more self-determined and more intrinsically motivated in their
exercise behaviours.

Overall the evidence for the effectiveness of exercise referral schemes as
a social context to increase physical activity behaviour in a primary health
care setting is building. The majority of studies still emphasise physical
health outcomes, with few studies examining psychosocial outcomes and
patients' experiences, which are often more influential in determining
long-term behaviour change. However, it is apparent that exercise referral
schemes allow clinical patients the opportunity to develop self-confidence
through shared experiences, social support for physical activity, and a sense
of relatedness, all of which may make them more likely to translate these
behaviours to an everyday context in the future.

9.6   Summary

Health care professionals and co-exercisers contribute to the psychosocial
processes involved in prescribed exercise behaviour in the primary health
care setting. Understanding the motivational orientation of the individual
who is being referred is essential to ensure adoption of the appropriate consultation style. Ensuring compliance with an exercise prescription is essential for individuals, their physical and mental health, and the economy of
the NHS. Compliance can be achieved using a guiding consultation style
to ensure the decision to engage in physical activity is self-determined
and patient-led. This in itself creates challenges for health care professionals, yet small changes to consultation style can be made to achieve it.
Exercise referral schemes are also critical social contexts where a sense
of autonomy, competence, and relatedness can be fostered in individuals
who share an illness; the illness can impact positively on physical activity choices and motives. The case study discusses specific strategies that
health care professionals and exercise specialists can utilise to develop
an appropriate social environment in the primary health care setting for
short-term compliance for prescribed exercise and long-term adherence for
habitual physical activity.

9.7   Case study

9.7.1   Setting the scene

Dave, a 57-year-old sedentary male, has made an appointment with his GP for a routine check-up. The GP assesses Dave's height, weight, and blood pressure during the consultation. Dave's blood pressure is 145/95 mm Hg, indicating he is at stage 1 hypertension. The GP informs Dave of the results as follows: 'Your test result show that your blood pressure is dangerously high. This means you really need to start to exercise much more and watch your diet carefully. How active are you, Dave?' Dave's response is limited: 'Not very.' The GP then asks whether his diet is balanced; Dave's response is again brief: 'I try to eat healthily, but I am in the car a lot with work, so I tend to grab convenience food when I'm on the go.' The GP then repeats that Dave needs to change these behaviours immediately to reduce his blood pressure and gives him a leaflet on managing hypertension through diet and exercise. He also asks if he can refer Dave to an exercise specialist at the local leisure centre who will contact Dave in the next few days. This is to arrange an initial consultation at the leisure centre to start a 12-week exercise programme with others who have hypertension. Dave agrees, takes the leaflet, and leaves. Four weeks later, Dave has yet to respond to the letter from the exercise specialist requesting a date and time for his initial exercise consultation.

How can the GP adapt his consultation style to ensure Dave is more likely to comply with his prescribed exercise through the exercise referral scheme and increase the likelihood of long-term physical activity adherence?

9.7.2   Assessing the situation

The key socialising agent in this situation is the GP. Adopting the default consultation style of directing, he informs Dave of his issue (increased hypertension) and then tells him to address the issue by improving his diet and increasing his physical activity levels. There is no development of rapport, no discussion between the GP and Dave at this stage. Dave's motivational orientation would be classed as external regulation: he feels obliged to exercise because his GP tells him to, and he is motivated to avoid the punishment of increased blood pressure. His self-determination will be relatively low at this point; his three basic needs of autonomy, competence, and relatedness were not addressed by his GP. The exercise specialist has not yet had the opportunity to engage with Dave. This is because the initial socialising agent of change in the exercise referral process, his GP, failed to elicit any form of patient-led behaviour change. Therefore, it is expected that Dave will not respond to the letter from the exercise specialist due to his extrinsic motivation to start the exercise programme; his lack of perceived competence to carry out exercise in a local leisure centre; his lack of choice and control over the referral decision, and his feeling that he is alone, with no support to engage in an exercise programme.

9.7.3   Specific strategies

Motivation to change needs to originate with the patient rather than be imposed by external sources. The GP needs to adapt his consultation style to allow Dave to lead the discussion, through exploration of ambivalence, as to how to address his high blood pressure. On first diagnosing the hypertension, the GP could have used the following sentence, which requires a more open-ended response from Dave and offers opportunity for discussion. 'Your test result shows that your blood pressure is dangerously high. I was wondering why you think this might be?' By combining 'informing' with 'asking' the patient as opposed to simply 'informing', the discussion's emphasis is shifted to Dave, who needs to consider and take responsibility for his behaviours. It is then more likely that Dave will start to 'think aloud' in the consultation as to why his blood pressure is high, to explore possible reasons by himself, with appropriate and timely prompts from his GP. The GP could also use communication techniques to build rapport with Dave; for example, using reflective listening. By reflecting back to a patient what he or she has stated, it reiterates that the GP has actively listened and has accurately understood the content. For example, the GP might respond to Dave with, 'OK; so what you have told me is that you think that sitting in your car all day is causing you to have high blood pressure because you feel you don't have the opportunity to get any exercise and you tend to buy convenience food whilst on the go. Is that about right?' The GP could follow this up with another open-ended question to prompt Dave to explore solutions to these barriers and the pro and cons of implementing them.

The social interaction between Dave and his GP is critical in determining Dave's future intentions and behaviours in relation to exercise. Rollnick and colleagues (2005) have provided guidance on techniques, closely aligned with motivational interviewing principles, which can be used by practitioners to change behaviour in a patient-led manner.

- Use open-ended questions to allow discussions to take place between practitioner and patient.
- Use a combination of 'informing' and 'asking' to shift the focus of the consultation onto the patient.
- Use reflective listening, open body language, and paraphrasing to develop a rapport with the patient.
- Guide, prompt, and nudge the patient into exploring solutions to the issue.

- Allow the patient to investigate ambivalence regarding physical activity behaviours. This is a key part of the process to allow the patient to become more self-determined.
- Roll with resistance from the patient. Patient-led behaviour change may not happen instantaneously, and the practitioner needs to accept that resistance may be an integral part of the consultation.

Once Dave has recognised that his sedentary lifestyle and lack of exercise is a key contributor to his high blood pressure, it is more likely he will decide to change his activity behaviours and engage fully with the referral scheme. It is then the responsibility of the exercise specialist to create an appropriate social climate in the scheme to encourage and support Dave in his attempts to change his behaviour. As noted earlier, developing exercise schemes specific to clinical populations, such as hypertension groups, where all members of the group have a shared experience, aids the process. This approach is more likely to foster a sense of autonomy, competence, and relatedness amongst group members. Group cohesion and social support are key determinants of adherence, compliance, and intrinsic motivation and could translate to long-term habitual physical activity for Dave in the future.

9.8　Further study and recommended reading

The following literature is recommended for further reading on key concepts addressed in this chapter.

- Gidlow, C., and Murphy, R. (2009). Physical activity promotion in primary care. In L. Dugdill, D. Crone, and R. Murphy (eds), *Physical Activity and Health Promotion: Evidence-Based Approaches to Practice*. Chichester: Wiley-Blackwell.
- National Institute for Health and Clinical Excellence. (2006). *Brief Interventions and Referral for Smoking Cessation in Primary Care and Other Settings*.
- National Institute for Health and Clinical Excellence. (2013). *Physical Activity: Brief Advice for Adults in Primary Care*.

10 The Outdoors

10.1 Learning objectives

The purpose of this chapter is to examine the social context of exercising outdoors, its importance in developing social networks, and its restorative effects on physical and mental health and well-being. The key objectives are:

- to understand the benefits of exercising in the outdoor environment for a range of populations. Discussion focuses on the physical, psychological and social benefits for individuals and groups;
- to discuss the proposed mechanisms underlying the green space effect;
- to consider the range of activities that can be undertaken in the outdoor environment, with emphasis on the social attributes developed through participation;
- to discuss the green space effect on physical, psychological, and social well-being, with consideration of the type and intensity of the exercise itself and the salient characteristics of the outdoor environment;
- to discuss the practical implications of the research for physical activity practitioners, policymakers, and urban planners for creating an optimal social and environmental context for the green space effect in an outdoor setting.

10.2 Introduction to the context

The outdoor setting provides spaces and opportunities for a range of individuals to engage in various activities (e.g., walking, cycling, gardening) that appeal to all age groups. The outdoor setting is a positive physical environment where social aspects (e.g., cohesion, relatedness, mastery) can be developed through participation in physical activity, with additional benefits to psychological well-being via exposure to the natural environment. Such exposure has been shown to result in positive psychological well-being and reduce symptoms of depression and anxiety (Hartig et al. 2003; Pretty et al. 2003). Barton and Pretty (2010) called upon health practitioners to recognise the potential positive contribution of natural ecosystems to human population health, particularly in addressing issues related to physical inactivity, obesity, and mental health. Historically, large, publicly funded city parks were created to provide places for recreation and encourage social interaction. In 2014 the United Kingdom had approximately 27,000 urban parks; it is estimated that in England 33 million people annually make in excess of 2.5 billion visits to parks. This suggests that access and usage of parks and green spaces is prevalent yet the extent to which this impacts on physical, psychological, and social well-being has not been fully established. Exposure to nature has been shown to influence physiological markers, including decreased resting heart rate, blood pressure, and adrenaline, noradrenaline, and cortisol levels (Gladwell et al. 2012). Access to green space has been shown to be important for mental health and improved quality of life, particularly in aging populations (Thompson Coon et al. 2011). The social benefits of green environments have also been highlighted by Sugiyama and colleagues (2008), who associated a green environment with recreational walking and social cohesion and interaction. The overall positive influence of the outdoor environment, in particular green space, on physical, psychological, and social well-being is known as the 'green space effect'.

Performing physical activity in green spaces and other natural environments may have additional benefits above and beyond the well-documented physical and psychological ones experienced when exercising indoors. Combined, physical activity and natural environments appear to offer potentially greater benefits to physical, psychological, and social well-being than either one in isolation. Since the year 2000, research evidence has become abundant for the concept of 'green exercise', which has been defined by Pretty and colleagues (2005) as physical activities undertaken whilst exposed to natural environments. It has been linked to positive physical, psychological, and social outcomes – including improvements in social networking, companionship, social connectedness, and escape from modern life – and has been shown to help individuals accrue ecological knowledge, gain a sense of mastery, and influence other health-behaviour choices (Kawachi et al. 1997). In the research literature self-esteem and mood regularly appear as the primary outcome measures to ascertain the effects of green exercise (e.g., walking, cycling, golf) and nature-based interventions (e.g., social and therapeutic horticulture, wilderness therapy, green gyms); the majority of findings support the green exercise effect on psychological well-being. Green exercise has been advocated by mental health services practitioners, as being physically active in green environments can play a pivotal role in reducing social isolation (Richardson et al. 2005), and recommended as a viable treatment option for individuals with depression who do not want to rely solely on anti-depressants (Barton, Griffin, and Pretty 2012). The importance of access to green space for physical and mental health benefits has had increased exposure, with many now advocating its economic benefit to the United Kingdom. In 2013, the Woodland Trust chief executive, Sue Holden, stated that increasing individuals' access to green space could save the National Health Service an estimated £2.1 billion per year (*BBC News* 2013).

10.3 Proposed mechanisms underlying the green space effect

Psychologically, natural environments have been shown to have restorative effects, which are defined by Hartig (2004, 273) as 'the process of renewing, recovering, or re-establishing physical, psychological and social resources or capabilities diminished in ongoing efforts to meet adaptive demands'. According to Pretty (2004) there are three levels of engagement with nature that can create a restorative effect. The first is viewing nature, as through a window, in a book, on television, or in a painting. The second is being in nature's presence incidental to another activity, such as walking or cycling to work, reading on a garden seat, or talking to friends in a park. The third is active participation and involvement with nature, such as gardening, farming, trekking, or running. Pretty (2004) suggests that each level plays a pivotal role in understanding the effect of green space and green exercise on physical, psychological, and social well-being.

Two major theories have been proposed to explain restorative environments' positive effect on physical, psychological, and social well-being. These are the psychophysiological stress recovery theory and the attention restoration theory. The former theory, proposed by Ulrich and colleagues (1991), is based on patterns of affective and aesthetic responses to the visual stimuli an environment presents. The theory postulates that restoration can occur when a scene elicits feelings of mild to moderate interest, pleasantness, and calm. These positive feelings of affect replace negative feelings of affect, resulting in a reduced physiological arousal. Ulrich and colleagues have suggested that natural environments offer a restorative advantage over artificial environments due to their more favourable visual stimuli.

The attention restoration theory (Kaplan 1995; Kaplan and Kaplan 1989) is primarily concerned with restoration from attentional fatigue. As a person's direct attention mechanism is largely under voluntary and effortful control, it can become fatigued. It is proposed that restorative environments (e.g., natural ones) facilitate recovery from directed attentional fatigue when an individual experiences fascination, conceptualised by Kaplan and Kaplan (1989) as a mode of attention that has an involuntary quality, does not require effort, and does not have capacity limitations. When someone relies on fascination in an ongoing activity, demands on the central inhibitory capacity are relaxed, and a capacity for directing attention can be renewed.

According to Kaplan and Kaplan (1989), there are four progressive stages of restoration. The first stage, 'clearing the head', refers to an individual allowing random thoughts to wander through the mind and eventually fade away. The second stage is known as 'recharging directed attention capacity', a consequence of stage 1 of restoration. Stage 3 involves an individual's ability to tune into unbidden thoughts or matters on the mind due to reduced internal noise and enhanced cognitive quiet, which are facilitated by soft fascination. The final and deepest stage involves 'reflections on one's life, on one's priorities and possibilities, on one's actions and one's goals' (197). Kaplan and Kaplan suggested that attention restoration is enhanced when exploration of the environment and aesthetic features in it engage what they refer to as 'effortless attention or fascination'. This is aligned to stages 3 and 4 of progressive restoration, where soft fascination and deep reflection are evoked more readily by natural environments compared to other environments. In summary, the restorative effects of the natural environment have been shown to have a positive effect on physical, psychological, and social well-being. This can be achieved by replacing negative affect and cognitions with positive affect and cognitions via favourable visual stimuli presented in the natural environment. Alternatively, the natural environment can allow an individual to recharge directed attentional capacity through four progressive stages of restoration.

10.4 Outdoor activities and psychosocial development

Individuals and groups can participate in a wide range of outdoor activities, the most common being walking and cycling. Walking, frequently reported as the most popular recreational activity in the United Kingdom, is considered the most accessible form of exercise for all individuals: it is free, low impact, and requires no specialist equipment or training. Data from the Sport England (2009) survey found that 9.1 million adults in England, or 22% of the population, walked recreationally for at least 30 minutes in a four-week period. This was almost twice as many as reported swimming (5.6 million, 13.4%) and more than twice those that reported going to the gym (4.5 million, 10.7%). Data from the Scottish Household Survey (Scottish Government 2013) are similar: walking was the most popular form of exercise for adults. Overall, 59% reported walking for 30 minutes for recreational purposes in a four-week period, while 10% reported cycling during the same period.

Walking addresses many of the reported barriers to being more active: lack of time, money, poor health and well-being and physical limitations. It is also accessible to people from groups that could most benefit from being more active; for example, older adults and adults from poorer areas. Walking is associated with increased social interaction, reduced crime and fear of crime, increased perceptions of safety, social capital development, and an enhanced network of interactions between individuals and their communities. Walking as part of an organised group is often recommended as a way of enhancing mental health and well-being, and exercise referral schemes have started to incorporate walking programmes in their service provision (see Ch. 9). Walking as part of a group has the additional benefit of providing an opportunity for social interaction, communication, a sense of relatedness, and cohesion with other walking group members. The United Kingdom now has thousands of programmes and initiatives to encourage individuals to walk for health and well-being.

According to the cited survey data, cycling is the UK's second most popular outdoor activity. Since the success of professional cyclists on the Tour de France and in the 2012 London Olympic Games, the number of those cycling for recreational purposes is estimated to have increased. Between October 2011 and October 2012 in England, the number of individuals cycling once a week increased by 200,000, with an estimated 1.9 million people cycling once a week (Sport England 2012). The annual distance cycled has also increased by 20% since 1998, from 4 billion to 5 billion kilometres in 2011 (www.ctc.org.uk). As with walking, cycling as part of a group has the additional benefit of providing the opportunity for social interaction, communication, a sense of relatedness, and cohesion with other cycling group members. Since 2010, the number of cycling groups that individuals of varied abilities and ages can join has increased.

Aside from walking and cycling, outdoor activities that can develop social attributes include gardening, golf, rock climbing, skiing and other snow sports, horse riding, canoeing, and sailing. Of these, the one to which the literature has accorded notable interest regarding exercise's green space effect is gardening. Gardens are important for the psychological processes of self-esteem, self-efficacy, and personal identity (Bernardini and Irvine 2007). Gardening can give an individual a sense of achievement and mastery. In a report for the UK National Association for Mental Health (MIND) examining the mental health benefits of green activities and green care, gardening was the most popular outdoor activity in programmes across the United Kingdom (Peacock, Hine, and Pretty 2007). Overall, 52% of the participants engaged in gardening and allotment activities, 37% participated in regular walking, 3% ran, and 1% cycled regularly. A key focus of the report was on understanding participants' perceptions of the benefits of participating in green exercise. In addition to the physical benefits, the participants identified numerous psychosocial ones. The opportunity to be part of a group, have companionship, and be with like-minded people was an important aspect of exercising in green spaces. The majority of participants reported that green activities inspired new friendships to develop. The sense of achievement and mastery was another psychosocial benefit of green space exercise, one that was particularly relevant for participants who engaged in gardening and allotment activities. Feeling relaxed, reduced stress levels, and increased coping were also cited as important benefits; participants reported feeling good about themselves through a heightened sense of self-worth, self-confidence, and self-esteem. Overall, exercising outdoors alone or as part of a group can elicit a wide range of psychosocial benefits, including laying the ground for social interaction and social capital, developing a sense of relatedness, gaining a sense of mastery and achievement, reducing levels of stress and anxiety, and enhancing self-worth and self-confidence by being outdoors. The next section examines whether these benefits of exercise are augmented by engaging with the outdoor environment compared to exercising indoors.

10.5   The green space effect of exercise on psychosocial well-being

Exercising in an outdoor setting, particularly one with green space, may have benefits above and beyond those experienced exercising indoors. This concept, debated in the literature since the early 2000s, has become a key aspect of the political agenda. The 'Be Active, Be Healthy' report (Department of Health 2009) has emphasised the need for provision of and access to high-quality green spaces to further promotion of physical activity. The impact of green space and the wider neighbourhood's physical environment on health and well-being in Scotland were recognised in the 'Equally Well' report (Scottish Government 2008). The literature has supplied evidence of the positive impact of exposure to natural environments on mental well-being, with green exercise linked to social networking and feelings of connectivity and companionship, increased appreciation of nature, improved self-esteem, and a means of escape from modern life (Thompson Coon et al. 2011). Anecdotal evidence suggests that long-term adherence to exercise programmes conducted in outdoor natural environments or urban green spaces may be superior to exercising in an indoor environment, but no empirical evidence to support this concept has yet been published.

10.5.1   Indoor vs. outdoor exercise: is there a green space effect?

One of the earliest studies comparing the effects of indoor and outdoor exercising was conducted by McMurray and colleagues (1988). They found that running for 10 miles, either indoors on a treadmill or outdoors, had no significant effect on self-reported well-being in eight male participants. As the men were competitive runners, generalising the findings to the majority of the population is difficult, as they do not examine the green space effect on the most popular mode of outdoor activity, walking. Several other research studies have compared the effects of walking indoors and walking outdoors in relation to various outcome measures. To further understand the three levels of engagement with nature proposed by Pretty (2004), Plante and colleagues (2006) created three experimental conditions where 102 participants completed (1) a 20-minute brisk walk outside, (2) a 20-minute brisk walk on the treadmill whilst looking at a visual reality video of the outdoors, or (3) simply watched the visual reality video for 20 minutes. Findings provided partial support for the three levels of engagement (Pretty 2004), where greater energy was experienced whilst walking outside, whereas less energy was reported when viewing the virtual reality walk with no exercise. The findings suggest that individuals who engage in an exercise (walking) outdoors rather than indoors are more energised via the active participation and involvement with nature. This is comparable to the third level of engagement with nature, the one that can create a restorative effect, which in this instance was increased energisation.

Researchers suggest that the novel stimuli in outdoor environments provide a pleasant distraction from feelings of exertion, thus leading to greater enjoyment and more positive affect than indoor exercise. This concept was examined by Focht (2009), who compared a brief 10-minute outdoor walk to a treadmill in a laboratory environment for affective responses, enjoyment, and intention to walk for exercise. Findings showed that both walking conditions resulted in enhanced affective responses, and participants reported pleasant affective states, enjoyment, and intention to walk in future. However, as the findings also suggested that affective responses were related to enjoyment only when walking in the outdoor environment, the green space effect on exercise received partial support. Yet it is important to note that the study participants were self-reported active women; therefore, the generalisation of the findings to the majority of the population that can engage in walking outdoors is limited. Thompson Coon and colleagues (2011) attempted to explore the green space effect concept comparing indoor versus outdoor exercise. They published a systematic review of exercise participation in outdoor natural environments compared with exercise indoors for the effect of each on physical and mental well-being. In their review, only 11 studies met the relevant inclusion criteria, and these included 833 adults, the majority being young adults. A total of 13 different outcome measures were used to evaluate the effects of exercise on mental well-being, and four outcome measures were used to assess attitude to exercise. No studies assessed and compared exercise adherence indoors and outdoors. Based on their review, Thompson Coon and colleagues concluded that outdoor exercise may elicit positive effects on measures of psychological well-being that are not in evidence when similar exercise is done indoors. Yet all of the studies included in the review examined a single bout of either walking or running; therefore, the chronic effects of outdoor versus indoor exercise are yet to be investigated. Thompson Coon and colleagues also stressed that their review highlighted the paucity of high-quality evidence on which recommendations for green exercise could be based. There is a clear need for further research in this area.

10.5.2   Characteristics of greenness and proximity of green space

To ensure a positive effect of green space on psychosocial well-being, the environmental aspects that support restoration and well-being need to be identified and included in the design of urban outdoor environments. This is particularly salient in today's society, where access to natural green space is decreasing due to the increase in urban settlements. The characteristics of green space and its impact on psychosocial well-being has been explored to some extent in the literature in relation to greenness and other specific aspects of the outdoor environment (e.g., wild vs tended forests) and the proximity of access to green space. In a study by Mackay and Neill (2010), the greenness of the outdoor environment was assessed in relation to state anxiety in 101 participants before and after they engaged in pre-existing outdoor activities. Consistent with previous research on green exercise, moderate short-term anxiety was reduced, yet interestingly the reduction was more marked in participants who perceived themselves to be exercising in more natural, green environments. Furthermore, greenness of the outdoor environment accounted for 5% of the reduction in anxiety, after controlling for pre-anxiety levels. This provides some evidence that the greenness of the outdoor environment could potentially influence an individual's psychosocial well-being.

The importance of the characteristics of the outdoor environment on enhancing psychosocial well-being was addressed by Pretty and colleagues (2005). In their study, 100 individuals ran for 20 minutes at light intensity on a treadmill. Whilst running, they were shown photos of rural outdoor scenes that were made to look 'pleasant' and 'unpleasant' and urban photos of outdoor scenes that were similarly manipulated. The control condition was running on the treadmill without the visual prompts. Exercising whilst viewing both rural and urban pleasant scenes resulted in a significantly greater rise in self-esteem in comparison to exercising with no visual prompts. Viewing unpleasant scenes reduced the positive effect of exercise on self-esteem. Though this provides further support for green exercise, it also demonstrates that the outdoor environment's characteristics need to be considered pleasant in order to enhance self-esteem. More recently, Martens, Gutscher, and Bauer (2011) explored the influence of environmental characteristics on psychosocial well-being whilst walking in two conditions. Participants were randomly assigned to walking in either a wild or tended forest condition for 30 minutes in the morning and afternoon. The tended forest condition caused a stronger increase in positive affect relative to enhanced mood and calmness and a greater decrease in depression, anger, and lethargy levels before and after the walk. Overall, the study showed that ensuring tended forests (e.g., by creating accessible natural conditions with moderate density and low amounts of deadwood) could enhance positive affect and reduce negative affect for individuals walking in a natural environment.

A final consideration for urban planners aiming to ensure the outdoor environment is designed appropriately is the proximity of access to green space for individuals. Van den Berg and colleagues (2010) found that Dutch residents with a large amount of green space in a 3 km radius were less affected by stressful life events than those with a lower amount. Mitchell and Popham (2007) used UK census data for England to determine the association between the percentage of green space in an area and the standardised rating of self-reported 'not good' health. Findings showed that a higher proportion of green space in an area was associated with better health and well-being, yet the association depended upon the area's degree of urbanity and level of income deprivation. The authors also reported that the quality as well as quantity of green space may be significant in determining health benefits. This links to earlier discussions of salient outdoor characteristics that can enhance psychosocial well-being. Mitchell (2013) also found evidence of an association between access to green space to exercise and mental well-being in the Scottish population. Based on data from the Scottish Health Survey (2008), it was evident that risk of poor mental health was 50% less for regular users of woods and forests to exercise than for non-users. Recent findings have also shown individuals to be happier when living in urban areas with larger amounts of green space (White et al. 2014). In summary, access to green space can also impact on physical activity behaviours, with evidence suggesting that adults with better access to parks and other green environments tend to walk more (Giles-Corti et al. 2005; Li et al. 2005). Proximity, access, aesthetic pleasantness, and greenness could all help to create an optimal natural outdoor environment to enhance psychosocial well-being during physical activity.

10.5.3   Social interaction and the green space effect

As noted earlier, the outdoor environment provides a social context for developing a variety of psychosocial attributes through engaging with others, either informally, by sharing the green space itself (e.g., walking, running, gardening in a shared allotment), or in more formal group activities (walking, cycling, mountain climbing). Evidence also suggests that green features in neighbourhoods can enhance social connections and an individual's sense of belonging to a community. However, the relative influence of different types of exercise and social interaction on the green space effect needs further consideration. The association of perceived greenness of local areas with perceived physical and mental health was examined by Sugiyama and colleagues (2008), with a secondary focus on determining whether the association was influenced by the quantity of walking and social factors (social coherence and social interaction). Participants (N = 1,895) completed a mailed survey assessing physical and mental health, perceived neighbourhood greenness, amount of walking for recreation and transport, social coherence, local social interaction, and sociodemographic variables. Findings indicated that individuals who saw their local area as highly green had significantly greater odds of enhanced physical and mental health compared to those who did not perceive high greenness levels. Perceived greenness was also correlated with recreational walking and social factors. Walking for recreation seemed to explain the association between greenness and physical health, whereas such walking and social coherence only partly accounted for the relationship of greenness and mental health. Sugiyama and colleagues suggested that the restorative effects of natural environments may be involved in the residual association of the latter relationship. Overall, this study supported the concept that green environments that encourage people to walk for both recreation and transport could enhance physical and mental health. The authors recommended that to promote community health through enhancement of the environment, the planning and design of neighbourhood open spaces should place emphasis on the importance of 'walkable' green spaces.

In the majority of research examining the relationship between physical activity and social support, social support emerges as a strong positive correlate (Trost et al. 2002). Consideration of the importance of social support in green environments whilst exercising needs to be examined. Staats and Hartig (2004) proposed that the company of a friend could enable and enhance restoration to different degrees in different environments. They suggested that this could be done by making time in the environment more enjoyable, drawing attention away from everyday demands, either via the social interaction itself or through mutual exploration of the environment. The influence of social interaction on psychosocial well-being whilst exercising outdoors is a relatively limited research area. In order to address this research gap, Johansson, Hartig, and Staats (2011) examined the psychological benefits of walking, moderated by the presence of company and the outdoor environment. Their findings identified that when one walked in a park, feelings of revitalisation increased more when walking was done alone rather than with a friend. Yet when walking along urban streets, feelings of revitalisation increased only when walking with a friend; they showed no change when walking alone. Interestingly, in either condition feelings of exhaustion increased whilst walking alone, yet feelings of exhaustion did not increase with a friend present. Overall, the authors concluded that certain psychological benefits of a brisk walk vary with the influence of the immediate social context (i.e., walking with a friend) and features of the outdoor urban environment, including such natural features as greenery and water. This supports the data noting the importance of key characteristics and features in the outdoor environment in enhancing psychosocial well-being. Yet it also provides partial support for the unique role of social interaction whilst engaging in green exercise.

The impact of social interaction alongside exercise in a natural environment was further explored in an intervention study conducted by Barton and colleagues (2012). All participants involved in the study (N = 53), were between 21 and 83 and experienced a range of mental health conditions. The study evaluated three existing group-based health promotion initiatives: a social club (indoor activity, no exercise, social component), a swimming group (indoor activity, exercise, no social component), and a walking group (outdoor activity, exercise, social component). Self-esteem and mood were assessed before and after each session, and participants attended one session per week for six weeks. Participants in all three groups experienced improved self-esteem and mood after a single session, yet over the six weeks, the change in self-esteem was significantly greater in the walking group than in the swimming and social club groups. This supports the concept that social interaction whilst exercising in the outdoors, in green space, could benefit psychosocial well-being. However, the fact that no group in this study exercised alone in an outdoor environment limits the conclusions that can be drawn in relation to the independent contribution of social interaction and connectedness and the natural environment on psychosocial well-being.

Research examining social integration and interaction of communities through green space exercise is relatively limited. In their conceptual model of the role of parks in public health, Bedimo-Rung, Mowen, and Cohen (2005) outlined the antecedents, behaviours, and outcomes of park usage. In this model, psychological and social benefits of both being physically active in parks and park visitation were emphasised, alongside physical health, economic, and environmental benefits. Yet it is very difficult to measure the psychological and social benefits to be gained from being in green space whilst being physically active. In addition, the experiences of individuals who may access green spaces independently yet socially interact there due to the outdoor environment – for example, dog walkers – needs further exploration. In their review of dog ownership, physical activity, and health, Cutt and colleagues (2007) found that dogs provide an important type of social support (viz., companionship) that encourages individuals to walk regularly. Dogs are also a catalyst for social interaction (McNicholas and

Collis 2000). However, to our knowledge there is no research examining social interactions amongst groups of dog walkers.

10.5.4　Intensity, frequency, and type of green exercise

With the majority of the literature suggesting that there is a green space effect on psychosocial well-being, particularly when participating in green exercise, there has been a focus on ascertaining the optimal amount of green exercise needed to gain these established benefits. This concept was explored by Pretty and colleagues (2007), who looked at ten green exercise case studies in the United Kingdom where 253 individuals engaged in green exercise activities (walking, cycling, horse riding, fishing, canal boating, conservation activities). Self-esteem (Rosenberg 1965) and total mood disturbance using the profile of mood states measure (McNair, Lorr, and Droppleman 1992) were assessed before and after the individuals engaged in activity. In relation to all types of green exercise, both self-esteem and mood significantly improved following participation, yet the enhancements were not influenced by the type of green exercise activity undertaken and were comparable for all types of green exercise activity. This provided initial evidence that green exercise activity brings mental health benefits regardless of the level of intensity, duration, or type of green activity undertaken.

More recently Barton and Pretty (2010) further explored this concept. They conducted a meta-analysis to examine the 'dose of green exercise', a term they defined as representing the linked relationship between duration of exposure, intensity of activity, and type of green space. In total, ten studies (N = 1,252) were included in their meta-analysis; all used the same measures of psychosocial well-being, Rosenberg's self-esteem scale (1965) and the profile of mood states (McNair et al. 1992). Their results showed that acute short-term exposures to facilitated green exercise improved both self-esteem and mood, irrespective of duration, intensity, location, gender, age, and health status. The dose-response relationship between duration in green exercise and self-esteem and mood displayed distinct U-shapes (see Figure 10.1). The greatest change in both was seen in the initial five minutes of exercise, suggesting that it has an immediate effect on psychosocial well-being. Relative to the intensity needed to elicit maximum psychosocial benefits during green exercise, light intensity seems to benefit self-esteem the most. It was also shown that as exercise intensity increased, self-esteem increased to a lesser extent. Conversely, the dose-response relationship between mood and intensity followed a U-shape curve, where improvements in mood were greatest for light and vigorous activity. Again, both findings provide evidence that physical activity of light intensity is sufficient to elicit psychosocial benefits, which is important to consider when explaining the green space effect of walking to those who are less inclined to exercise due to its perceived intense nature. Barton and Pretty

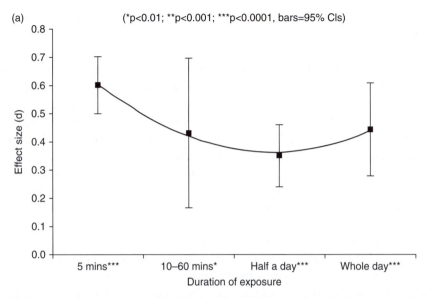

Figure 10.1a   *Dose-response data for the effect of exposure duration in green exercise on self-esteem*

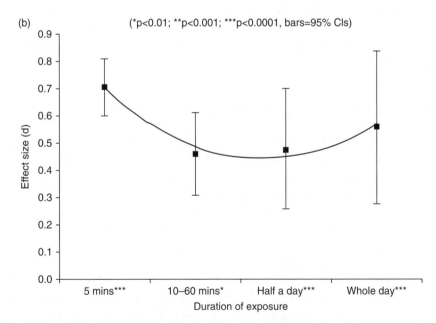

Figure 10.1b   *Dose-response data for the effect of exposure duration in green exercise on total mood disturbance.*

Source: Reprinted with permission from Barton, J. and Pretty, J. (2010). What is the best dose of nature and green exercise for improving mental health? A multi-study analysis, *Environmental Science and Technology*, 44(10), 3947–3955. Copyright © 2014, American Chemical Society.

(2010) also wanted to explore the influence of the characteristics and features of the outdoor environment on psychosocial well-being. Their findings showed that green spaces with water (beaches, rivers) brought larger improvements in self-esteem and mood than other green spaces categorised (urban green space, countryside, wilderness, woodlands). This adds to the research on the importance of key features of the outdoor environment in enhancing psychosocial well-being, an area that urban planners need to be aware of when designing new outdoor settings to expand social capital and engagement and enhance health and well-being.

Overall, there does appear to be some support for the green space effect of exercise on psychosocial well-being, in particular enhanced self-esteem and mood. Exercising outdoors in natural environments rather than indoors could add the benefits of increased social interaction, restoration, and enhanced affective states. However, in order to maximise these added benefits, salient features of the outdoor environment are needed, including greenness, pleasantness, tidiness, presence of water, and having a green space in close proximity to access. As for the amount of green exercise needed to enhance psychosocial well-being, it appears that short, acute bouts of light-intensity green exercise are sufficient. As the type of green exercise activity has no effect on psychosocial well-being, it should be determined by personal preference. These are key considerations for physical activity practitioners utilising the outdoors in their physical activity programmes and initiatives.

10.6   The green space effect in action

Since the mid-2000s, use of green space whilst exercising has increased, with exercise programmes focusing on the green space effect implemented in both the public and private sectors. These programmes, often termed 'green gyms', aim to support individuals who garden or improve the local environment while providing opportunities for physical activity and social interaction. In 2004 the Department for Health's policy document on public health urged communities to use green gyms. In 2008 Yerrell evaluated 52 UK green gym projects commissioned by the British Trust for Conservation Volunteers; 703 participants in green gym programmes completed an introductory questionnaire assessing motives for joining the programme, perceptions of health-related quality of life, and self-reported levels of physical activity. A continuation questionnaire was provided three months later, and 194 participants completed it within three to six months of joining the green gym programme. Contribution to the environment, health, confidence, skills, and training were the most commonly cited benefits of green gyms in the community. This supports anecdotal evidence on the positive psychosocial aspects of green exercise; specifically, an increased sense of mastery and confidence. There was also evidence of increased self-reported physical activity in those participants who completed the follow-up questionnaire after three months. Despite not being statistically significant, this increase provides partial evidence that green gym programmes contribute to increased physical activity and provide a range of psychosocial benefits

In 2014 in Scotland, Dr Ruth Jepson, at the University of Stirling, was engaged in conducting a year-long study comparing indoor and outdoor exercise habits through GP-referral schemes. The research was commissioned and undertaken by the Scottish Collaboration for Public Health Research and Policy, located in the University of Edinburgh, and the University of Stirling's Centre for Population Health and Public Health Research. The study has aimed to recruit 100 participants; half would be referred to indoor activities, such as swimming, gym sessions, and classes, and half to outdoor exercise, such as gardening (green gym), walking, or golf. Adherence levels, self-reported physical activity, enjoyment, and psychosocial benefits were to be assessed in the different activity types. At time of writing, the study was ongoing but expected to end in 2015. As the first of its kind in Scotland, it was hoped that the project would help councils and leisure trusts plan future health programmes and facilities, including new outdoor spaces, green gym environmental programmes, and walking routes.

Researchers at the European Centre for Environment and Human Health at the University of Exeter (www.ecehh.org/research/#!blue-gym) have been examining the psychological and physical health benefits of exercising while exposed to a natural water environment, termed a 'blue gym'. As of late 2014, they were conducting a range of studies focusing on the blue gyms' psychological and physical health benefits; one study, examining the importance of water for restorativeness (White et al. 2010), used 120 photographs of natural and built scenes, half of which contained 'aquatic' elements. Proportions of 'aquatic/green/built' environments in each scene (e.g., 1/3, 2/3) were also standardised. Preferences, affect, and perceived restorativeness ratings for the photographs were assessed. Findings suggested that both natural and built scenes containing water were associated with higher preferences, greater positive affect, and higher perceived restorativeness than those without water. Findings also suggested that images of built environments containing water were generally rated just as positively as natural green space. This provides preliminary evidence that exercising in or near natural water may have additive benefits for psychosocial and physical health compared to exercising in green spaces. At time of writing, the concept was being explored further by Dr White and colleagues in a controlled study focusing on the psychophysiological responses to indoor cycling in different environments. Participants were asked to cycle indoors for 15 minutes whilst viewing images and sounds of one of four outdoor environments (coast, countryside, town, blank wall as control). All participants were to cycle in each of the four environments for four weeks whilst their heart rate, blood pressure, mood, and arousal levels were monitored pre- and post-exercise.

10.7   Summary

The outdoor environment is an important social setting where a variety of psychosocial benefits can occur through exercise and physical activity. The outdoor environment, characterised by natural green space, is particularly salient for population groups often labelled 'hard to reach' (i.e., low-activity adults, older adults, adults from socio-economically poorer areas), as it offers the opportunity to exercise with few perceived barriers. The psychosocial benefits to be gained by exercising outdoors in a range of activities (walking, gardening, cycling) include restorative effects and improved mood, development of social networks and of a sense of relatedness, and an increased sense of mastery. Urban planners in the private and public sectors need to consider the key features of outdoor environment for which additive benefits for physical and psychosocial health and well-being, as well as social capital, have been documented. The green space effect of exercise and the impact of green gyms and blue gyms on physical and mental well-being are relatively new areas of research, yet there is a growing body of research evidence that individuals should be advised to move outdoors to gain the benefits of nature whilst engaging in regular physical activity.

10.8   Case study

10.8.1   Setting the scene

John, a 73-year-old male, is retired and lives alone in an area of town categorised as having low socio-economic status. He had a relatively active lifestyle in the past and enjoyed both indoor (e.g., squash) and outdoor activities (e.g., cycling), yet due to mobility issues in recent years, he has become relatively inactive save for his daily walk to the shops. John has felt lonely and isolated over the past few months, in a recent visit to his GP, he was diagnosed with mild clinical depression. The GP offered John several treatment options adjunctive to his medication, one of which was to consider joining a local GP-referral programme. He advised John that interacting with others through exercise could provide distraction from his low moods and also help his mobility issues if the exercise was relatively moderate in nature. The GP provided John with information on the types of programmes available, including both indoor activities and outdoor activities.

How can John engage in appropriate outdoor activities to help alleviate his depression and increase his physical activity and social interaction?

10.8.2   Assessing the situation

This situation has no specific socialising agent. The nature of the outdoor environment itself is what could contribute to enhancing John's psychosocial well-being through green exercise. The GP plays a key role in the programme's initial stages by helping increase John's awareness of the positive physical and psychosocial benefits to be gained by exercising outdoors and to also help John lower barriers to engaging in physical activity. John's barriers include cost, mobility issues, and low levels of self-efficacy for certain types of activities. In John's case, activity of low intensity would be most appropriate; for example, joining a walking group or a green gym programme of gardening activities.

10.8.3   Important role of the outdoor environment in behaviour change

As outlined by Pretty (2004) in his levels of engagement, in order to maximise the restorative benefits of being physically active in the natural environment outdoors, active participation and involvement with nature (e.g., walking or gardening) should be recommended to John. Joining a walking group could elicit for him a range of physical and psychosocial benefits, including increased social interaction and a sense of relatedness with others in the GP-referral walking group. Walking could also increase his perceptions of safety in his local community and also make him feel more connected to it. In addition, participating in a green gym gardening programme could give John a sense of mastery, accomplishment, and achievement. As both of these low-intensity activities can be undertaken outdoors and will allow John to become more active and independent, they could enhance his psychosocial well-being. They might also help to treat his mild depression via the combined benefits of restoration in a natural environment and green exercise.

10.8.4   Specific strategies for key socialising agents

Urban planners and environmental policymakers need to consider the following specific recommendations when designing and developing outdoor environments for engagement with nature on all three levels (viewing nature, being in nature's presence, active participation in exercise in a natural environment) so as to enhance physical and psychosocial well-being.

- Natural environments need to be in close proximity to urban areas to ensure ease of access and maximum usage.
- Natural environments need to have several key features: greenness, pleasantness, tidiness, and water.

The following specific strategies need to be considered by physical activity practitioners when implementing green exercise programmes in local communities to enhance physical and psychosocial well-being.

- Based on the recommendations above, wherever possible, physical activity practitioners should develop programmes incorporating outdoor environments in close proximity to urban settlements (e.g., towns, cities), where the majority of potential participants in green exercise programmes will reside.
- They should offer a range of outdoor activities, as evidence shows that all green exercise programmes have similar physical and psychosocial benefits.
- They should emphasise to all potential programme participants that even short, acute bouts of light-intensity green exercise enhance psychosocial well-being.

10.9   Further study and recommended reading

The following literature is recommended for further reading on key concepts addressed in this chapter.

- Peacock, J., Hine, R., and Pretty, J. (2007). The mental health benefits of green exercise activities and green care. *Mind Week Report.*
- Yerrell, P. (2008). *National Evaluation of TCV's Green Gym.* Oxford: School of Health and Social Care, Oxford Brookes University.

Additionally, reading in the following relevant areas is recommended. The materials address other aspects of the outdoor environment that are not covered in this chapter but are central to understanding the green space effect of exercise.

- Eden, S., and Barratt, P. (2010). Outdoors versus indoors? Angling ponds, climbing walls and changing expectations of environmental leisure. *Area*, 42(4), 487–493.
- Cavill, N., and Davis, A. (2007). *Cycling and Health – What's the Evidence?* Wokingham, UK: Transport Research Laboratory/Cycling England.

References

Acitelli, L. K., Kenny, D. A., and Weiner, D. (2001). The importance of similarity of partners' marital ideal to relationship satisfaction. *Personal Relationships* 8, 167–185.

Ackermann, R. T., Deyo, R. A., and LoGerfo, J. P. (2005). Prompting primary providers to increase community exercise referrals for older adults: A randomized trial. *Journal of the American Geriatrics Society* 53 (2), 283–289.

Agassi, A. (2010). *Open: An Autobiography*. New York: HarperCollins.

Agnew, G. A., and Carron, A. V. (1994). Crowd effects and the home advantage. *International Journal of Sport Psychology* 25, 53–62.

Ajzen, I. (1991). The theory of planned behaviour. *Organisational Behaviour and Human Decision Processes* 50, 179–211.

Allender, S., Cowburn, G., and Foster, C. (2006). Understanding participation in sport and physical activity among children and adults: A review of qualitative studies. *Health Education Research* 21, 826–835.

Ames, C. (1992a). Achievement goals, motivational climate, and motivational processes. In G. C. Roberts (ed.), *Motivation in Sport and Exercise* (161–176). Champaign, IL: Human Kinetics.

Ames, C. (1992b). Classrooms: Goals, structures, and motivation. *Journal of Educational Psychology* 84, 261–271.

Anderson, K. A., and Cavallaro, D. (2002). Parents or pop culture? Children's heroes and role models. *Childhood Education* 78 (3), 161–168.

Anderson, M. A., Wolfson, S., Neave, N., and Moss, M. (2012). Perspectives on the home advantage: A comparison of football players, fans and referees. *Psychology of Sport and Exercise* 13 (3), 311–316.

Annesi, J. J. (1999). Effects of minimal group promotion on cohesion and exercise adherence. *Small Group Research* 30 (5), 542–557.

Antonini Philippe, R. A., and Seiler, R. (2006). Closeness, co-orientation and complementarity in coach-athlete relationships: What male swimmers say about their male coaches. *Psychology of Sport and Exercise* 7, 159–171.

Appleton, P. R., Hall, H. K., and Hill, A. P. (2011). Examining the influence of the parent-initiated and coach-created motivational climate upon athletes' perfectionistic cognitions. *Journal of Sports Sciences* 7, 661–671.

Argyle, M. (1994). *The Psychology of Interpersonal Behaviour*, 5th edn. New York: Penguin.

Arthur-Banning, S. G., Wells, M. S., Baker, B. L., and Hegreness, R. (2009). Parents behaving badly? The relationship between the sportsmanship behaviors of adults and athletes in youth basketball games. *Journal of Sport Behavior* 32 (1), 3–18.

Atkins, M. R., Johnson, D. M., Force, E. C., and Petrie, T. A. (2012). 'Do I still want to play?' Parents' and peers' influences on girls' continuation in sport. *Journal of Sport Behavior* 36 (40), 329–345.

Babkes, M. L., and Weiss, M. R. (1999). Parental influence on cognitive and affective responses in children's competitive soccer participation. *Pediatric Exercise Science* 11, 44–62.

Balmer, N. J., Nevill, A. M., and Williams, A. M. (2003). Modelling home advantage in the Summer Olympic Games. *Journal of Sports Sciences* 21 (6), 469–478.

Balneaves, L. G., Van Patten, C., Truant, T. L., Kelly, M. T., Neil, S. E., and Campbell, K. L. (2014). Breast cancer survivors' perspectives on a weight loss and physical activity lifestyle intervention. *Supportive Care in Cancer* 22, 2057–2065.

Banbery, B., Groves, M., and Biscomb, K. (2012). The relationship between exercise dependence and identity reinforcement: A sociological examination of a gym-based environment in the United Kingdom. *Sport in Society: Cultures, Commerce, Media, Politics* 15 (9), 1242–1259.

Bandura, A. (1977). *Social Learning Theory*. Englewood Cliffs, NJ: Prentice-Hall.

Bandura, A. (1986). *Social Foundations of Thought and Action: A Social Cognitive Theory*. Englewood Cliffs, NJ: Prentice-Hall.

Bandura, A. (1997). *Self-efficacy: The Exercise of Control*. New York: Freeman.

Bandura, A. (1998). Health promotion from the perspective of social cognitive theory. *Psychological Health* 13, 623–649.

Barki, H., and Hartwick, J. (2004). Conceptualizing the construct of interpersonal conflict. *International Journal of Conflict Management* 15, 216–244.

Baron, R. S. (1986). Distraction-conflict theory. In L. Berkowitz (ed.), *Advances in Experimental Social Psychology* (1–39). Orlando, FL: Academic Press.

Barton, J., Griffin, M., and Pretty, J. (2012). Exercise-, nature- and socially interactive–based initiatives improve mood and self-esteem in the clinical population. *Perspectives in Public Health* 132 (2), 89–96.

Barton, J., and Pretty, J. (2010). What is the best dose of nature and green exercise for improving mental health? A multi-study analysis. *Environmental Science and Technology* 44 (10), 3947–3955. doi: 10.1021/es903183r.

Bass, B. M. (1985). *Leadership and Performance beyond Expectations*. New York: Free Press.

Bass, B. M. (1998). *Transformational Leadership: Industry, Military, and Educational Impact*. Mahwah, NJ: Erlbaum.

Bass, B. M., and Avolio, B. J. (1995). *MLQ Multifactor Leadership Questionnaire*, 2nd edn. Redwood City, CA: Mind Garden.

Batt, M. E. (2009). Physical activity interventions in the workplace: The rationale and future direction for workplace wellness. *British Journal of Sports Medicine* 43, 47–48.

Bauman, A. E., Reis, R. S., Sallis, J. F., Wells, J. C., Loos, R. J., Martin, B. W., and Lancet Physical Activity Series Working Group (2012). Correlates of physical activity: Why are some people physically active and others not? *Lancet* 380 (9838), 258–271. doi: 10.1016/S0140–6736(12)60735–1.

Baumeister, R. F. (1984). Choking under pressure: Self-consciousness and paradoxical effects of incentives on skillful performance. *Journal of Personality and Social Psychology* 46, 610–620.

Baumeister, R. F., and Showers, C. J. (1986). A review of paradoxical performance effects: Choking under pressure in sports and mental tests. *European Journal of Social Psychology* 16, 361–383.

Baumiester, R. F., and Steinhilber, A. (1984). Paradoxical effects of supportive audiences on performance under pressure: The home field disadvantage in sports championships. *Journal of Personality and Social Psychology* 47, 85–93.

BBC News. (2013). Green spaces 'can save NHS billions'. Retrieved 11 November 2013, www.bbc.co.uk/news/science-environment-24806994.

Beauchamp, M. R., Welch, A. S., and Hulley, A. J. (2007). Transformational and transactional leadership and exercise-related self-efficacy: An exploratory study. *Journal of Health Psychology* 12 (1), 83–88. doi: 10.1177/1359105307071742.

Bedimo-Rung, A. L., Mowen, A. J., and Cohen, D. A. (2005). The significance of parks to physical activity and public health: A conceptual model. *American Journal of Preventive Medicine* 28 (2 Suppl 2), 159–168. doi: http://dx.doi.org/10.1016/j.amepre.2004.10.024.

Bernardini, C., and Irvine, K. N. (2007). The 'nature' of urban sustainability: Private or public greenspaces? *Sustainable Development and Planning* III (102), 661–674.

Berscheid, E., Snyder, M., and Omoto, A. M. (1989). Issues in studying close relationships: Conceptualising and measuring closeness. In C. Hendric (ed.), *Close Relationships*. Newbury Park, CA: Sage.

Biddle, S. J., and Mutrie, N. (2008). *Psychology of Physical Activity: Determinants, Well-Being and Interventions*, 2nd edn. London: Routledge.

Blascovich, J., and Mendes, W. B. (2000). Challenge and threat appraisal: The role of affective cues. In J. Forgas (ed.), *Feeling and Thinking: The Role of Affect in Social Cognition* (59–82). Cambridge: Cambridge University Press.

Blascovich, J., Mendes, W. B., Hunter, S. B., and Salomon, K. (1999). Social 'facilitation' as challenge and threat. *Journal of Personality and Social Psychology* 77, 68–77.

Blascovich, J., Mendes, W. B., Tomaka, J., Salomon, K., and Seery, M. (2003). The robust nature of the biopsychosocial model challenge and threat: A reply to Wright and Kirby. *Personality and Social Psychology Review* 7 (3), 234–243.

Bloom, B. S. (1985). *Developing Talent in Young People*. New York: Ballantine.

Bloom, G. A., Loughead, T. E., and Newin, J. (2008). Team building for youth sports. *JOPERD: The Journal of Physical Education, Recreation and Dance* 79 (9), 44–47.

Bloom, G. A., Stevens, D. E., and Wickwire, T. L. (2003). Expert coaches' perceptions of team building. *Journal of Applied Sport Psychology* 15, 129–143.

Bois, J. E., Lalanne, J., and Delforge, C. (2009). The influence of parenting practices and parental presence on children's and adolescents' precompetitive anxiety. *Journal of Sports Sciences* 27, 995–1005.

Bois, J. E., Sarrazin, P. G., Brustad, R. J., Trouilloud, D. O., and Cury, F. (2005). Elementary school children's perceived competence and physical activity involvement: The influence of parents' role modelling behaviours and perceptions of their child's competence. *Psychology of Sport and Exercise* 6 (4), 381–397.

Borrego, C., Cid, L., and Silva, C. (2012). Relationship between group cohesion and anxiety in soccer. *Journal of Human Kinetics* 34, 119–127.

Bortoli, L., Bertollo, M., and Robazza, C. (2009). Dispositional goal orientations, motivational climate, and psychobiosocial states in youth sport. *Personality and Individual Differences* 47, 18–24.

Boyko, R. H., Boyko A. R., and Boyko, M. G. (2007). Referee bias contributes to home advantage in English Premiership football. *Journal of Sports Sciences* 25 (11), 1185–1194.

Braithwaite, R. A., Spray, C. M., and Warbuton, V. E. (2011). Motivational climate interventions in PE: A meta-analysis. *Psychology of Sport and Exercise* 12, 628–638.

Brawley, L. R., Carron, A. V., and Widmeyer, W. N. (1987). Assessing the cohesion of teams: Validity of the Group Environment Questionnaire. *Journal of Sport Psychology* 9, 275–294.

Brawley, L. R., and Culos-Reed, S. N. (2000). Studying adherence to therapeutic regimens: Overview, theories, recommendations. *Controlled Clinical Trials* 21, 156S–163S.

Brawley, L. R., and Paskevich, D. M. (1997). Conducting team building research in the context of sport and exercise. *Journal of Applied Sport Psychology* 9, 11–40.

Bray, C. D., and Whaley, D. E. (2001). Team cohesion, effort, and objective individual performance of high school basketball players. *Sport Psychologist* 15 (3), 260–275.

Bray, S. R. (1999). The home advantage from an individual team perspective. *Journal of Applied Sport Psychology* 11, 116–125.

Bray, S. R., and Widmeyer, W. N. (2000). Athletes' perceptions of the home advantage: An investigation of perceived causal factors. *Journal of Sport Behaviour* 23, 1–10.

Brewer, B. W., Diehl, N. S., Cornelius, A. E., Joshua, M. D., and Van Raalte, J. L. (2004). Exercising caution: Social physique anxiety and protective self-presentational behaviour. *Journal of Science and Medicine in Sport* 7 (1), 47–55.

Bronfenbrenner, U. (1993). The ecology of cognitive development: Research models and fugitive findings. In R. H. Wozniak and K. W. Fischer (eds), *Development in Context: Acting and Thinking in Specific Environments* (3–44). Hillsdale, NJ: Erlbaum.

Brown, B. A., Frankel, B. G., and Fennell, M. P. (1989). Hugs or shrugs: Parental and peer influence on continuity of involvement in sport by female adolescents. *Sex Roles* 20, 397–412.

Brustad, R. J. (1988). Affective outcomes in competitive youth sport: The influence of intrapersonal and socialization factors. *Journal of Sport and Exercise Psychology* 10, 307–321.

Brustad, R. J. (1992). Integrating socialization influences into the study of children's motivation in sport. *Journal of Sport and Exercise* 14, 59–77.

Bukowski, W. M., and Hoza, B. (1989). Popularity and friendship: Issues in theory, measurement and outcome. In T. J. Berndt and G. W. Ladd (eds), *Peer Relationships in Child Development*. New York: Wiley.

Bull, F. C., Adams, E., and Hooper, P. (2008). Well@Work: Promoting active and healthy workplaces: Final evaluation report: British Heart Foundation.

Bull, S. J., Albinson, J. G., and Shambrook, C. J. (1996). *The Mental Game Plan: Getting Psyched for Sport*. Eastbourne, UK: Sport Dynamics.

Bulter, J. L., and Baumiester, R. F. (1998). The trouble with friendly faces: Skilled performance with a supportive audience. *Journal of Personality and Social Psychology* 75, 1213–1230.

Burke, S., Shapcott, K., Carron, A. V., Bradshaw, M., and Estabrooks, P. A. (2010). Group goal setting and group performance in a physical activity context. *International Journal of Sport and Exercise Psychology* 8 (3), 245–261.

Burke, K. L. (2005). But coach doesn't understand: Dealing with team communication quagmires. In M. Andersen (ed.), *Sport Psychology in Practice*. Champaign, IL: Human Kinetics.

Callow, N., Smith, M., Hardy, L., Arthur, C. A., and Hardy, J. (2009). Measurement of transformational leadership and its relationship with team cohesion and performance level. *Journal of Applied Sport Psychology* 21, 395–412.

Camodeca, M., and Goossens, F. (2005). Aggression, social cognitions, anger and sadness in bullies and victims. *Journal of Child Psychology and Psychiatry* 46, 186–197.

Canary, D. J., Cunningham, E. M., and Cody, M. J. (1988). Goal types, gender, and locus of 7 control in managing interpersonal conflict. *Communication Research* 15, 426–446.

Canary, D. J., Stafford, L., and Semic, B. A. (2002). A panel study of the associations between maintenance strategies and relational characteristics. *Journal of Marriage and the Family* 64, 395–406.

Canary, D. J., and Zelley, E. D. (2000). Current research programmes in relational maintenance behaviors. In M. E. Roloff (ed.), *Communication Yearbook*. Thousand Oaks, CA: Sage.

Carr, S. (2006). An examination of multiple goals in children's physical education: Motivational effects of goal profiles and the role of perceived climate in multiple goal development. *Journal of Sport Sciences* 23 (3), 281–297.

Carron, A. V. (1982). Cohesiveness in sport groups: Interpretations and considerations. *Journal of Sport Psychology* 4 (2), 123–138.

Carron, A. V., Brawley, L. R., and Widmeyer, W. N. (1998). The measurement of cohesiveness in sport groups. In J. L. Duda (ed.), *Advancements in Sport and Exercise Psychology Measurement*. Morgantown, WV: Fitness Information Technology.

Carron, A. V., Colman, M. M., Wheeler, J., and Stevens, D. (2002). Cohesion and performance in sport: A meta-analysis. *Journal of Sport and Exercise Psychology* 24 (2), 168–188.

Carron, A. V., Estabrooks, P. A., Horton, H., and Prapavessis, H. (1999). Reductions in the social anxiety of women associated with group membership: Distraction, anonymity, security, or diffusion of evaluation? *Group Dynamics: Theory, Research, and Practice* 3 (2), 152–160.

Carron, A. V., Hausenblas, H. A., and Eys, M. A. (2005). *Group Dynamics in Sport*, 3rd edn. Morgantown, WV: Fitness Information Technology.

Carron, A. V., Loughead, T. M., and Bray, S. R. (2005). The home advantage in sports competitions: Courneya and Carron's (1992) conceptual framework a decade later. *Journal of Sports Sciences* 23, 395–407.

Carron, A. V., and Spink, K. S. (1993). Team building in an exercise setting. *Sport Psychologist* 7 (1), 8–18.

Carron, A. V., and Spink, K. S. (1995). The group size-cohesion relationship in minimal groups. *Small Group Research* 26, 86–105.

Carron, A. V., Spink, K. S., and Prapavessis, H. (1997). Team building and cohesiveness in the sport and exercise setting: Use of indirect interventions. *Journal of Applied Sport Psychology* 9 (1), 61–72.

Carron, A. V., Widmeyer, W. N., and Brawley, L. R. (1985). The development of an instrument to assess cohesion in sport teams: The Group Environment Questionnaire. *Journal of Sport Psychology* 7, 244–266.

Carver, C. S., and Scheier, M. F. (1981). The self-attention-induced feedback loop and social facilitation. *Journal of Experimental Social Psychology* 17, 545–568.

Casper, J. (2006). You can't be serious, that ball was in: An investigation of junior tennis cheating behavior. *Qualitative Report* 11 (1), 20–36.

Cavill, N., and Davis, A. (2007). *Cycling and Health – What's the Evidence?* Wokingham, UK: Transport Research Laboratory / Cycling England.

Cervelló, E., Escartí, A., and Guzmán, J. (2007). Youth sport dropout from the achievement goal theory. *Psicothema* 19, 65–71.

Chan, D. K., Lonsdale, C., and Fung, H. H. (2012). Influences of coaches, parents, and peers on the motivational patterns of child and adolescent athletes. *Scandinavian Journal of Medicine and Science in Sports* 22, 558–568.

Chanal, J. P., Marsh, H. A., Sarrazin, P. G., and Bois, J. E. (2005). Big-fish-little-pond effects on gymnastics self-concept: Social comparison processes in a physical setting. *Journal of Sport and Exercise Psychology* 27 (1), 53–70.

Chang, A., and Bordia, P. (2001). A multidimensional approach to the group cohesion–group performance relationship. *Small Group Research* 32 (4), 379–405.

Chelladurai, P. (1990). Leadership in sports: A review. *International Journal of Sport Psychology* 21, 328–354.

Chemers, M. M. (2000). Leadership research and theory: A functional integration. *Groups Dynamics: Theory, Research and Practice* 4 (1), 27–43.

Chen, L., Chen, M., Lin, M., Kee, Y., Kuo, C., and Shui, S. (2008). Implicit theory of athletic ability and self-handicapping in college students. *Psychological Reports* 103, 476–484.

Christensen, U., Schmidt, L., Budtz-Jorgensen, E., and Avlund, K. (2006). Group cohesion and social support in exercise classes: Results from a Danish intervention study. *Health Education and Behavior* 33 (5), 677–689. doi: 10.1177/1090198105277397.

Cleland, V. J., Timperio, A., Salmon, J., Hume, C., Telford, A., and Crawford, D. (2011). A longitudinal study of the family physical activity environment and physical activity among youth. *American Journal of Health Promotion* 25 (3), 159–167.

Collins, K., and Barber, H. (2005). Female athletes' perceptions of parental influences. *Journal of Sport Behavior* 28, 295–314.

Conn, V. S., Hafdahl, A. R., Cooper, P. S., Brown, L. M., and Lusk, S. L. (2009). Meta-analysis of workplace physical activity interventions. *American Journal of Preventive Medicine* 37 (4), 330–339.

Cooper, C., and Dewe, P. (2008). Well-being, absenteeism, presenteeism, costs and challenges. *Occupational Medicine* 58 (8), 522–524.

Côté, J. (1999). The influence of the family in the development of talent in sport. *Sport Psychologist* 13 (4), 395–417.

Côté, J., and Fraser-Thomas, J. (2011). Youth involvement and positive development in sport. In P. R. E. Crocker (ed.), *Sport Psychology: A Canadian Perspective*, 2nd edn (226–255). Toronto: Pearson Prentice Hall.

Cottingham, M., II, Blom, L. C., Hubble Burchell, S., and Johnson, J. T. (2010). Understanding the relationships among social cohesion, the coach-athlete relationship, and socioeconomic status of high school softball and baseball players. *Journal for the Study of Sports and Athletes in Education* 4 (1), 9–22.

Cottrell, N. B., Wack, D. L., Sekerak, G. J., and Rittle, R. H. (1968). Social facilitation of dominant responses by the presence of an audience and the mere presence of others. *Journal of Personality and Social Psychology* 35, 245–250.

Courneya, K. S., and Carron, A. V. (1992). The home advantage in sport competitions: A literature review. *Journal of Sport and Exercise Psychology* 14, 13–27.

Courneya, K. S., and McAuley, E. (1995). Cognitive mediators of the social influence–exercise adherence relationship: A test of the theory of planned behavior. *Journal of Behavioural Medicine* 18 (5), 499–515.

Cox, A., and Williams, L. (2008). The roles of perceived teacher support, motivational climate, and psychological need satisfaction in students' physical education motivation. *Journal of Sport and Exercise Psychology* 30 (2), 222–239.

Cox, T., Griffiths, A., and Rial-Gonzalez, E. (2000). Work-related stress. The European Agency for Safety and Health at Work, Brussels. Retrieved 2 April 2013, www.bvsde. paho.org/bvsast/i/fulltext/eustress/eustress.pdf.

Crawford, S., and Eklund, R. C. (1994). Social physique anxiety, reasons for exercise, and attitudes toward exercise settings. *Journal of Sport and Exercise Psychology* 16, 70–82.

Csikszentmihalyi, M., Rathunde, K., and Whalen, S. (1993). *Talented Teenagers: The Roots of Success and Failure.* New York: Cambridge University Press.

Cunningham, I., and Eys, M. A. (2007). Role ambiguity and intra-team communication in interdependent sport teams. *Journal of Applied Social Psychology* 37, 2220–2237.

Cutt, H., Giles-Corti, B., Knuiman, M., and Burke, V. (2007). Dog ownership, health and physical activity: A critical review of the literature. *Health and Place* 13 (1), 261–272. doi: http://dx.doi.org/10.1016/j.healthplace.2006.01.003.

Dainton, M., and Zelley, E. D. (2011). *Applying Communication Theory for Professional Life: A Practical Introduction.* London: Sage.

Daniel, M. (1981). The choke and what you can do about it. *Scholastic Coach* 13, 75–79.

Davis, N. W., and Meyer, B. B. (2008). When sibling becomes competitor: A qualitative analysis of same-sex sibling competition in elite sport. *Journal of Applied Sport Psychology* 20, 220–235.

Davison, K. K., Werder, J. L., and Lawson, C. T. (2008). Children's active commuting to school: Current knowledge and future directions. *Preventing Chronic Disease* 5 (3), A100.

Deci, E. L., and Ryan, R. M. (1985). *Intrinsic Motivation and Self-Determination in Human Behaviour.* New York: Plenum Press.

De Michele, P., Gansneder, B., and Solomon, G. (1998). Success and failure attributions of wrestlers: Further evidence of the self-serving bias. *Journal of Sport Behavior* 21, 242–255.

Department for Culture, Media and Sport (2012). *Creating a Sporting Habit for Life: A New Youth Sport Strategy.* London: Crown Copyright. Retrieved 22 October 2014, https://www.gov.uk/government/uploads/system/uploads/attachment_data/file/78318/creating_a_sporting_habit_for_life.pdf.

Department of Health. (2004). *Choosing Health: Making Healthier Choices Easier.* Crown Publishers

Department of Health. (2009). *Be Active, Be Healthy: A Plan for Getting the Nation Moving.* Crown Publishers.

Department of Health. (2011). *Start Active, Stay Active. A Report on Physical Activity for Health from the Four Home Counties' Chief Medical Officers.* Crown Publishers.

DeVito, J. A. (1986). *The Interpersonal Communication Book.* New York: Harper and Row.

DeVito, J. A. (1994). *Human Communication: The Basic Course.* New York. HarperCollins.

DiClemente, C. C., Prochaska, J. O., Fairhurst, S. K., Velicer, W. F., Rossi, J. J., and Velasquez, M. (1991). The process of smoking cessation: An analysis of precontemplation, contemplation and preparation stages of change. *Journal of Consulting and Clinical Psychology* 59, 295–304.

Dindia, K., and Canary, D. J. (1993). Definitions and theoretical perspectives on maintaining relationships. *Journal of Social and Personal Relationships* 10, 163–173.

Dionigi, R., Fraser-Thomas, J., and Logan, J. (2012). The nature of family influences on sport participation in master athletes. *Annals of Leisure Research* 15, 366–388.

Dishman, R. K., Dejoy, D. M., Wilson, M. G., and Vanderberg, R. J. (2009). Move to improve: A randomised workplace trial to increase physical activity. *American Journal of Preventive Medicine* 36 (2), 133–141.

Dishman, R. K., Vanderberg, R. J., Motl, R. W., Wilson, M. G., and DeJoy, D. M. (2010). Dose relations between goal-setting, theory-based correlates of goal setting and increases in physical activity during a workplace trial. *Health Education Research* 25 (4), 620–631.

Dixon, M. A., Warner, S. M., and Bruening, J. E. (2008). More than just letting them play: Parental influence on women's lifetime sport involvement. *Sociology of Sport Journal* 25, 538–559.

Doran, G. T. (1981). There's a S. M. A. R. T. way to write management's goals and objectives. *Management Review* 70 (11), 35–36.

Douge, B. (1999). Coaching adolescents: To develop mutual respect. *Sports Coach*, Summer, 6–7.

Doward, J. (2012). London 2012: Team GB medallists pay tribute to home crowd's support. 5 August. *Guardian/Observer*. Retrieved 01 September 2014, www.theguardian.com.

Downward, P., and Jones, M. (2007). Effects of crowd size on referee decisions: Analysis of the FA Cup. *Journal of Sports Sciences* 25 (14), 1541–1545.

Duck, S. (1994). Two minds together in social context. In S. Duck, *Meaningful Relationships: Talking, Sense and Relating* (97–126). Thousand Oaks, CA: Sage.

Duda, J. L., and Balaguer, I. (2007). The coach-created motivational climate. In S. Jowett and D. Lavallee (eds), *Social Psychology of Sport* (117–130). Champaign, IL: Human Kinetics.

Duda, J. L., Williams, G. C., Ntoumanis, N., Daley, A., Eves, F. F., Mutrie, N., and Jolly, K. (2014). Effects of a standard provision versus an autonomy supportive exercise referral programme on physical activity, quality of life and well-being indicators: A cluster randomised controlled trial. *International Journal of Behavioral Nutrition and Physical Activity* 11 (1), 10.

Dugdill, L., Brettle, A., Hulme, C., McClusky, S., and Long, A. F. (2008). Workplace physical activity interventions: A systematic review. *International Journal of Workplace Health Management* 1 (1), 20–40.

Dunn, J. G. H., and Holt, N. L. (2004). A qualitative investigation of a personal-disclosure mutual-sharing team-building activity. *Sport Psychologist* 18 (4), 363–380.

Dweck, C. (1986). Motivational processes affecting learning. *American Psychologist*, special issue: *Psychological Science and Education* 41, 1040–1048.

Ebbeck, V. (1990). Sources of performance information in the exercise setting. *Journal of Sport and Exercise Psychology* 12, 56–65.

Eccles, J. S. (1993). School and family effects on the ontogeny of children's interests, self-perceptions, and activity choice. In J. Jacobs (ed.), *Nebraska Symposium on Motivation, 1992: Developmental Perspectives on Motivation* (145–208). Lincoln: University of Nebraska Press.

Eccles, J. S., and Harold, R. D. (1991). Gender differences in sport involvement: Applying the Eccles expectancy-value model. *Journal of Applied Sport Psychology* 3, 7–35.

Eccles, J. S., Wigfield, A., and Schiefele, U. (1998). Motivation to succeed. In W. Damon (series ed.), N. Eisenberg (vol. ed.), *Handbook of Child Psychology*, 5th edn, vol. 3 (1017–1095). New York: Wiley.

Ede, S., Kamphoff, C. S., Mackey, T., and Armentrout, S. M. (2012). Youth hockey athletes' perceptions of parental involvement: They want more. *Journal of Sport Behavior* 35 (1), 3–18.

Eden, S., and Barratt, P. (2010). Outdoors versus indoors? Angling ponds, climbing walls and changing expectations of environmental leisure. *Area* 42 (4), 487–493.

Eidelson, R., and Eidelson, J. (2003). Dangerous ideas: Five beliefs that propel groups toward conflict. *American Psychologist*, 58, 182–192.

Eklund, R. C., and Crawford, S. (1994). Active women, social physique anxiety, and exercise. *Journal of Sport and Exercise Psychology* 16 (4), 431–448.

Elley, C. R., Kerse, N., Arroll, B., and Robinson, E. (2003). Effectiveness of counselling patients on physical activity in general practice: Cluster randomised controlled trial. *British Medical Journal* 326, 793–796.

Ellis, A., and Dryden, W. (1987). *The Practice of Rational Emotive Therapy*. New York: Springer.

Emmison, M. (1988). On the interactional management of defeat. *Sociology* 22, 233–251.

Emslie, C., Whyte, F., Campbell, A., Mutrie, N., Lee, L., Ritchie, D., and Kearney, N. (2007). 'I wouldn't have been interested in just sitting round a table talking about cancer'; exploring the experiences of women with breast cancer in a group exercise trial. *Health Education Research* 22 (6), 827–838. doi: 10.1093/her/cyl159.

Ericsson, K. A., and Charness, N. (1994). Expert performance: Its structure and acquisition. *American Psychologist* 49, 725–747.

Estabrooks, P. A., and Carron, A. V. (1999). Group cohesion in older adult exercisers: Prediction and intervention effects. *Journal of Behavioural Medicine* 22 (6), 575–588.

Estabrooks, P. A., and Carron, A. V. (2000). The Physical Activity Group Environment Questionnaire: An instrument for the assessment of cohesion in exercise classes. *Group Dynamics: Theory, Research, and Practice* 4 (3), 230–243.

Estabrooks, P. A., Munroe, K. J., Fox, E. H., Gyurcsik, N. C., Hill, J. L., Lyon, R., and Shannon, V. R. (2004). Leadership in physical activity groups for older adults: A qualitative analysis. *Journal of Aging and Physical Activity* 12, 232–245.

Evans, C. R., and Dion, K. L. (1999). Group cohesion and performance: A meta-analysis. *Small Group Research* 22 (2), 175–186.

Evans, L. J. (2002). *Evaluating the Effectiveness of Corporate Running Events in the North-West Region*. Liverpool: Liverpool John Moores University.

Everett, J. J., Smith, R. E., and Williams, K. D. (1992). Effects of team cohesion and identifiability on social loafing in relay swimming performance. *International Journal of Sport Psychology* 23, 311–324.

Eys, M. A., Hardy, J., Carron, A. V., and Beauchamp, M. R. (2003). The relationship between task cohesion and competitive state anxiety. *Journal of Sport and Exercise Psychology* 25 (1), 66–76.

Eys, M. A., Jewitt, E., Evans, M. B., Wolf, S., Bruner, M. W., and Loughead, T. M. (2013). Coach-initiated motivational climate and cohesion in youth sport. *Research Quarterly for Exercise and Sport* 84, 373–383.

Eysenck, M. W., and Calvo, M. G. (1992). Anxiety and performance: The processing efficiency theory. *Cognition and Emotion* 6, 40–434.

Eysenck, M. W., Derakshan, N., Santos, R., and Calvo, M. G. (2007). Anxiety and cognitive performance: Attentional control theory. *Emotion* 7 (2), 336–353.

Fairburn, C. G., and Beglin, S. J. (2008). Eating Disorders Examination Questionnaire (EDE-Q 6. 0). In C. G. Fairburn (ed.), *Cognitive Behaviour Therapy and Eating Disorders* (309–313). New York: Guilford Press.

Fiske, S., and Neuberg, S. (1990). A continuum of impression formation, from category-based to individuating processes: Influences of information and motivation on attention and interpretation. In M. Zanna (ed.), *Advances in Experimental Social Psychology*. New York: Academic Press.

Fiske, S., and Taylor, S. (1991). *Social Cognition*. Reading, MA: Addison-Wesley.

Focht, B. C. (2009). Brief walks in outdoor and laboratory environments: Effects on affective responses, enjoyment, and intentions to walk for exercise. *Research Quarterly for Exercise and Sport* 80 (3), 611–620.

Forgas, J. P., Brennan, G., Howe, S, Kane, J. F., and Sweet, S. (1980). Audience effects on squash players' performance. *Journal of Social Psychology* 111, 41–47.

Foster, C., and Allender, S. (2012). *Costing the Burden of Ill Health Related to Physical Inactivity for Scotland*. NHS Scotland.

Foster, D., Lineham, C., Kirman, B., Lawson, S., and James, G. (2010). Motivating physical activity at work: Using persuasive social media for competitive step counting. Paper presented at the proceedings of the 14th International Academic MindTrek Conference: Envisioning Future Media Environments, Tampere, Finland.

Fox, K. R., Biddle, S. J., Edmunds, L., Bowler, I., and Killoran, A. (1997). Physical activity promotion through primary health care in England. *British Journal of General Practice* 47, 367–369.

Fox, K. R., Cooper, A., and McKenna, J. (2004). The school and promotion of children's health-enhancing physical activity: Perspectives from the United Kingdom. *Journal of Teaching in Physical Education* 23 (4), 338–358.

Fraser, S. N., and Spink, K. S. (2002). Examining the role of social support and group cohesion in exercise compliance. *Journal of Behavioural Medicine* 25 (3), 233–249.

Fraser-Thomas, J., and Côté, J. (2009). Understanding adolescents' positive and negative developmental experiences in sport. *Sport Psychologist* 23, 3–23.

Fraser-Thomas, J., Côté, J., and Deakin, J. (2008a). Examining adolescent sport dropout and prolonged engagement from a developmental perspective. *Journal of Applied Sport Psychology* 20, 318–333.

Fraser-Thomas, J., Côté, J., and Deakin, J. (2008b). Understanding dropout and prolonged engagement in adolescent competitive sport. *Psychology of Sport and Exercise* 9, 645–66.

Fraser-Thomas, J., Strachan, L., and Jeffery-Tosoni, S. (2013). Family influence on children's involvement in sport. In J. Côté and R. Lidor (eds), *Conditions of Children's Talent Development in Sport* (179–196). Morgantown, WV: Fitness Information Technology.

Fredricks, J. A., and Eccles, J. S. (2002). Children's competence and value beliefs from childhood through adolescence. *Developmental Psychology* 38 (4), 519–533.

Fredricks, J. A., and Eccles, J. S. (2004). Parental influences on youth involvement in sports. In M. R. Weiss (ed.), *Developmental Sport and Exercise Psychology: A Lifespan Perspective* (145–164). Morgantown, WV: Fitness Information Technology.

Freedson, P. S., and Evenson, S. (1991). Familial aggregation in physical activity. *Research Quarterly for Exercise and Sport* 62 (4), 384–389.

Frost, R. O., and Henderson, K. J. (1991). Perfectionism and reactions to athletic competition. *Journal of Sport and Exercise Psychology* 13, 323–335.

Funder, D. (1987). Errors and mistakes: Evaluating the accuracy of social judgment. *Psychological Bulletin* 101, 75–90.

Funder, D. (1995). On the accuracy of personality judgement: A realistic approach. *Psychological Review* 102, 652–670.

Funder, D. (2012). Accurate personality judgement. *Current Directions in Psychological Science* 21, 177–182.

Gammage, K. L., Martin Ginis, K. A., and Hall, C. (2004). Self-presentational efficacy: Its influence on social anxiety in an exercise context. *Journal of Sport and Exercise Psychology* 26, 179–190.

Gayton, W. F., Broida, J., and Elgee, L. (2001). An investigation of coaches' perceptions of the causes of home advantage. *Perceptual and Motor Skills* 92, 933–936.

Gearity, B. T., and Murray, M. (2011). Athletes' experiences of the psychological effects of poor coaching. *Psychology of Sport and Exercise* 12 (3), 212–221.

Genevois, C. (2011). The role of parents in the training of beginner tennis players. *ITF Coaching and Sport Science Review* 55 (19), 26–27.

Gidlow, C., and Murphy, R. (2009). Physical activity promotion in primary care. In L. Dugdill, D. Crone, and R. Murphy (eds), *Physical Activity and Health Promotion: Evidence-Based Approaches to Practice*. Chichester: Wiley-Blackwell.

Giles-Corti, B., Broomhall, M. H., Knuiman, M., Collins, C., Douglas, K., Ng, K., and Donovan, R. J. (2005). Increasing walking: How important is distance to, attractiveness, and size of public open space? *American Journal of Preventive Medicine* 28 (2 Suppl 2), 169–176. doi: 10.1016/j.amepre.2004.10.018.

Gist, M., and Mitchell, T. (1992). Self-efficacy: A theoretical analysis of its determinants and malleability. *Academy of Management Review* 17, 183–211.

Gladwell, V. F., Brown, D. K., Barton, J. L., Tarvainen, M. P., Kuoppa, P., Pretty, J., and Sandercock, G. R. (2012). The effects of views of nature on autonomic control. *European Journal of Applied Physiology* 112 (9), 3379–3386. doi: 10.1007/s00421-012-2318-8.

Glover, E. D. (1978). Modelling – a powerful change agent. *Journal of School Health* 48 (3), 175–176.

Gómez, M., and Pollard, R. (2011). Reduced home advantage for basketball teams from capital cities in Europe. *European Journal of Sports Science* 11, 143–148.

Gould, D., Collins, K. B., Louer, L. A., and Chung, Y. C. (2007). Coaching life skills through football: A study of award-winning high-school coaches. *Journal of Applied Sport Psychology* 19, 16–37.

Gould, D., Lauer, L., Rolo, C., Jannes, C., and Pennisi, N. (2006). Understanding the role parents play in tennis success: A national survey of junior tennis coaches. *British Journal of Sports Medicine* 40, 632–636.

Gould, D., Lauer, L., Rolo, C., Jannes, C., and Pennisi, N. (2008). The role of parents in tennis success: Focus group interviews with junior coaches. *Sport Psychologist* 22, 18–37.

Goumas, C. (2013). Home advantage and crowd size in soccer: A worldwide study. *Journal of Sport Behavior* 36 (4), 387–399.

Grandes, G., Sanchez, A., Sanchez-Pinilla, R. O., Torcal, J., Montoya, I., Lizarraga, K., and Serra, J. (2009). Effectiveness of physical activity advice and prescription by physicians in routine primary care. *Archives of Internal Medicine* 169 (7), 694–701.

Greenless, I. (2007). Person perception and sport performance. In S. Jowett and D. Lavallee (eds), *Social Psychology in Sport*. Champaign, IL: Human Kinetics.

Greenlees, I., Bradley, A., Holder, T., and Thelwell, R. (2005). The impact of two forms of opponents' non-verbal communication on impression formation and comparative self-efficacy judgements. *Psychology of Sport and Exercise* 6, 103–115.

Greer, D. L. (1983). Spectator booing and the home advantage: A study of social influence in the basketball arena. *Social Psychology Quarterly* 46 (3), 252–261.

Gucciardi, D. F., Longbottom, J., Jackson, B., and Dimmock, J. A. (2010). Experienced golfers' perspectives on choking under pressure. *Journal of Sport and Exercise Psychology* 32, 61–83.

Guerin, B. (1983). Social facilitation and social monitoring: A test of three models. *British Journal of Social Psychology* 22, 203–214.

Gustafson, S. L., and Rhodes, R. E. (2006). Parental correlates of physical activity in children and early adolescents. *Sports Medicine* 36 (1), 79–97.

Gutiérrez, M., Caus, N., and Ruiz, L. M. (2011), The influence of parents on achievement orientation and motivation for sport of adolescent athletes with and without disabilities. *Journal of Leisure Research* 43 (3), 355–382.

Haase, A. M., Prapavessis, H., and Glynn Owens, R. (2002). Perfectionism, social physique anxiety and disordered eating: A comparison of male and female elite athletes. *Psychology of Sport and Exercise* 3 (3), 209–222.

Hamstra, K. L., Cherubini, J. M., and Swanik, C. B. (2002). Athletic injury and parental pressure in youth sports. *Athletic Therapy Today* 7 (6), 36–43.

Hanrahan, S., and Grove, R. (1990). Further examination of the psychometric properties of the Sport Attributional Style Scale. *Journal of Sport Behavior* 13, 183–193.

Hardcastle, S., Blake, N., and Hagger, M. S. (2012). The effectiveness of a motivational interviewing primary-care-based intervention on physical activity and predictors of change in a disadvantaged community. *Journal of Behavioural Medicine* 35, 318–333.

Harkins, S. (2001). *Multiple Perspectives on the Effects of Evaluation on Performance: Toward an Integration*. Norwell, MA: Kluwer.

Harrington, J. (2008). *Games, Strategies, and Decision Making*. New York: Worth.

Hart, E. A., Leary, M. R., and Rejeski, W. J. (1989). The measurement of social physique anxiety. *Journal of Sport and Exercise Psychology* 11 (1), 94–104.

Harter, S. (1978). Effectance motivation reconsidered: Toward a developmental model. *Human Development* 21, 34–64.

Harter, S. (1982). The perceived competence scale for children. *Child Development* 53, 87–97.

Hartig, T. (2004). Restorative environments. *Encyclopedia of Applied Psychology* 3, 273–279.

Hartig, T., Evans, G., Jamner, L. D., Davis, D. S., and Garling, T. (2003). Tracking restoration in natural and urban field settings. *Journal of Environmental Psychology* 23, 109–123.

Harwood, C. (2011). Enhancing coach-parent relationships in youth sports: Increasing harmony and minimizing hassle. A commentary. *International Journal of Sports Science and Coaching* 6 (1), 61–63.

Harwood, C. G., Douglas, J. P., and Minniti, A. M. (2012). The role of the family in talent development. In S. Murphy (ed.), *Handbook on Sport and Performance Psychology*. New York: Oxford University Press.

Harwood, C. G., and Knight, C. (2009). Understanding parental stressors: An investigation of British tennis parents. *Journal of Sport Sciences* 27, 339–351.

Hayman, R., Polman, R. C. J., Taylor, J., Hemmings, B., and Borkoles, E. (2011). Development of elite adolescent golfers. *Talent Development and Excellence* 3 (2), 249–261.

Health and Safety Commission. (2006). Health and safety statistics 2005/2006 – national statistics. Retrieved 2 April 2013, www.hse.gov.uk/statistics/overall/hssh0607.pdf.

Hellstedt, J. C. (1987). The coach/parent/athlete relationship. *Sport Psychologist* 1 (2), 151–160.

Henderson, J., Bourgeois, A. E., LeUnes, A., and Meyers, M. C. (1998). Group cohesiveness, mood disturbance, and stress in female basketball players. *Small Group Research* 29 (2), 212–225.

Heuzé, J. P., Bosselut, G., and Thomas, J. P. (2007). Cohesion or collective efficacy: What should be the focus of elite female handball team coaches? *Sport Psychologist* 21, 383–399.

Heuzé, J. P., Raimbault, N., and Fontayne, P. (2006). Relationships between cohesion, collective efficacy, and performance in professional basketball teams: An examination of mediating effects. *Journal of Sports Sciences* 24, 59–68.

Hill, D. M., Hanton, S., Matthews, N., and Fleming, S. (2010). Choking in sport: A review. *International Review of Sport and Exercise Psychology* 3, 24–39.

Hill, D. M., Hanton, S., Matthews, N., and Fleming, S. (2011). Alleviation of choking under pressure in elite golf: An action research study. *Sport Psychologist* 25, 465–488.

Hill, D. M., and Shaw, G. (2013). A qualitative examination of choking under pressure in team sport. *Psychology of Sport and Exercise* 14, 103–110.

Hiroto, D., and Seligman, M. (1975). Generality of learned helplessness in man. *Journal of Personality and Social Psychology* 31, 311–327.

HM Government (2013). *Inspired by 2012: The legacy from the London 2012 Olympic and Paralympic Games. A joint UK Government and Mayor of London report*. London: Crown Copyright.

Høigaard, R., Skjekkeland, V., and Johansen B. T. (2003). The relationship between group cohesion and perceived social loafing among junior football players. In R. Stelter and K. K. Roessler (eds), *New Approaches to Sport and Exercise Psychology* (77–78). Aachen: Meyer and Meyer Sport.

Høigaard, R., Tofteland, I., and Ommundsen, Y. (2006). The effect of team cohesion on social loafing in relay teams. *International Journal on Applied Sports Sciences* 18, 59–73.

Holt, N. L., and Black D. E. (2007). Parenting styles and specific parenting strategies in youth sport. *Journal of Sport and Exercise Psychology* 29, S170.

Holt, N. L., Black, D. E., Tamminen, K. A., Mandigo, J. L., and Fox, K. R. (2008). Levels of social complexity and dimensions of peer experience in youth sport. *Journal of Sport and Exercise Psychology* 30, 411–443.

Holt, N. L., Knight, C. J., and Zukiwski, P. (2012). Female athletes' perceptions of teammate conflict in sport: Implications for sport psychology consultants. *Sport Psychologist* 26 (1), 135–154.

Holt, N. L., Tamminen, K. A., Black, D. E., Mandigo, J. L., and Fox, K. R. (2009). Youth sport parenting styles and practices. *Journal of Sport and Exercise Psychology* 31, 37–59.

Holt, N. L., Tamminen, K. A., Black D. E., Sehn, Z. L., and Wall, M. P. (2008). Parental involvement in competitive youth sport settings. *Psychology of Sport and Exercise* 9, 663–685.

Horn, T. S. (2004). Lifespan development in sport and exercise: Theoretical perspectives. In M. R. Weiss (ed.), *Developmental Sport and Exercise Psychology: A Lifespan Perspective*. Morgantown, WV: Fitness Information Technology.

Horn, T. S., Byrd, M., Martin, E., and Young, C. (2012). Perceived motivational climate and team cohesion in adolescent athletes. *Sport Science Review* 21, 25–49.

Horn, T. S., Glen, S. D., and Wentzell, A. B. (1993). Sources of information underlying personal ability judgments in high school athletes. *Pediatric Exercise Science* 5, 263–274.

Horn, T. S., and Horn, J. L. (2007). Family influences on children's sport and physical activity participation, behavior, and psychosocial responses. In G. Tenenbaum and R. C. Eklund (eds), *Handbook of Sport Psychology*, 3rd edn (685–711). Hoboken, NJ: Wiley.

Howie, L. (2004). *The Official FA Guide for Football Parents*. London: Hodder and Stoughton.

Hughes, A. R., Mutrie, N., and MacIntyre, P. (2006). Effect of an exercise consultation on maintenance of physical activity after completion of phase III exercise-based cardiac rehabilitation. *European Journal of Cardiovascular Prevention and Rehabilitation* 14, 114–121. http://www.ecehh.org/research/#!blue-gym. Retrieved 28 October 2013.

IBIS (2013). Gyms and fitness centres market research report (SIC R93.130, March). Retrieved 25 June 2013, www.ibisworld.co.uk/market-research/gyms-fitness-centres.html.

Jackson, J. (1993). Realistic group conflict theory: A review and evaluation of the theoretical and empirical literature. *Psychological Record* 43, 395–415.

Jackson, R. C., Ashford, K. J., and Norsworthy, G. (2006). Attentional focus, dispositional reinvestment and skilled motor performance under pressure. *Journal of Sport and Exercise Psychology* 28, 49–68.

Jago, R., Brockman, R., Fox, K. R., Cartwright, K., Page, A. S., and Thompson, J. L. (2009). Friendship groups and physical activity: Qualitative findings on how physical activity is initiated and maintained among 10–11 year old children. *International Journal of Behavioural Nutrition and Physical Activity* 6 (4).

Jago, R., Fox, K. R., Page, A. S., Brockman, R., and Thompson, J. L. (2010). Parent and child physical activity and sedentary time: Do active parents foster active children? *BMC Public Health* 10, 194.

Jamieson, J. P. (2010). The home field advantage in athletics: A meta-analysis. *Journal of Applied Social Psychology* 40 (7), 1819–1848.

Jehn, K., and Mannix, E. (2001). The dynamic nature of conflict: A longitudinal study of intragroup conflict and group performance. *Academy of Management Journal* 44, 238–251.

Jõesaar, H., and Hein, V. (2011). Psychosocial determinants of young athletes' continued participation over time. *Perceptual and Motor Skills* 113, 55–66.

Jõesaar, H., Hein, V., and Hagger, M. S. (2011). Peer influence on young athletes' need satisfaction, intrinsic motivation and persistence in sport: A 12-month prospective study. *Psychology of Sport and Exercise* 12, 500–508.

Jõesaar, H., Hein, V., and Hagger, M. (2012). Youth athletes' perception of autonomy support from the coach, peer motivational climate and intrinsic motivation in sport setting: One-year effects. *Psychology of Sport and Exercise* 13, 257–262.

Johansson, M., Hartig, T., and Staats, H. (2011). Psychological benefits of walking: Moderation by company and outdoor environment. *Applied Psychology: Health and Well-being* 3 (3), 261–280.

Jones, M. V., Bray, S. R., and Lavallee, D. (2007). All the world's a stage: Impact of an audience on sport performers. In S. Jowett and D. Lavallee (eds), *Social Psychology in Sport* (103–113). Champaign, IL: Human Kinetics.

Jowett, S. (2002). *The Coach-Athlete Relationship Questionnaire and Dyad Maps Manual.* Research monograph no. 1. Staffordshire: Staffordshire University, School of Health.

Jowett, S. (2003). When the honeymoon is over: A case study of a coach-athlete relationship in crisis. *Sport Psychologist* 17 (4), 444–460.

Jowett, S. (2005). On enhancing and repairing the coach-athlete relationship. In S. Jowett and M. Jones (eds), *The Psychology of Coaching.* Leicester: British Psychological Society. An occasional publication for the Division of Sport and Exercise Psychology of the British Psychological Society.

Jowett, S. (2007). Interdependence analysis and the 3+1Cs in the coach-athlete relationship. In S. Jowett and D. Lavallee (eds), *Social Psychology in Sport.* Champaign, IL: Human Kinetics.

Jowett, S. (2009). Validating coach-athlete relationship measures with the nomological network. *Measurement in Physical Education and Exercise Science* 13, 1–18.

Jowett, S., and Chaundy, V. (2004). An investigation into the impact of coach leadership and coach-athlete relationship on group cohesion. *Group Dynamics: Theory, Research and Practice* 8, 302–311.

Jowett, S., and Cockerill, I. M. (2002). Incompatibility in the coach-athlete relationship. In I. M. Cockerill (eds), *Solutions in Sport Psychology* (16–31). London: Thompson Learning.

Jowett, S., and Cockerill, I. M. (2003). Olympic medallists' perspective of the athlete-coach relationship. *Psychology of Sport and Exercise* 4, 313–331.

Jowett, S., and Cramer, D. (2009). The role of romantic relationships on athletes' performance and well-being. *Journal of Clinical Sports Psychology* 3 (1), 58–72.

Jowett, S., and Cramer, D. (2010). The prediction of young athletes' physical self from perceptions of relationships with coaches and parents. *Psychology of Sport and Exercise* 11 (2), 140–147.

Jowett, S., and Meek, G. A. (2000). A case study of a top-level coach-athlete dyad in crisis. *Journal of Sport Sciences* 18, 51–52.

Jowett, S., and Meek, G. A. (2002). The coach-athlete relationship in married couples: An exploratory content analysis. *Sport Psychologist* 14, 154–175.

Jowett, S., and Ntoumanis, N. (2004). The Coach-Athlete Relationship Questionnaire (CART-Q): Development and initial validation. *Scandinavian Journal of Medicine and Science in Sports*, 14 (4), 245–257.

Jowett, S., and Poczwardowski, A. (2007). Understanding the coach-athlete relationship. In S. Jowett and D. Lavallee (eds), *Social Psychology in Sport* (3–14). Champaign, IL: Human Kinetics.

Jowett, S., Shanmugam, V., and Caccoulis, S. (2012). Collective efficacy as a mediator of the link between interpersonal relationships and athlete satisfaction in team sports. *International Journal of Sport and Exercise Psychology* 10 (1), 66–78.

Juntumaa, B., Keskivaara, P., and Punamäki, R. L. (2005). Parenting, achievement strategies and satisfaction in ice hockey. *Scandinavian Journal of Psychology* 46, 411–420.

Kamphoff, C. S., Gill, D, and Huddleston, S. (2005). Jealousy in sport: Exploring jealousy's relationship to cohesion. *Journal of Applied Sport Psychology* 17 (4), 290–305.

Kanters, M. A., Bocarro, J., and Casper, J. (2008). Supported or pressured: An examination of agreement among parents and children on parents' role in youth sports. *Journal of Sport Behavior* 31 (1), 64–80.

Kaplan, S. (1995). The restorative benefits of nature: Toward an integrative framework. *Journal of Environmental Psychology* 15 (3), 169–182.

Kaplan, S., and Kaplan, R. M. (1989). *The Experience of Nature: A Psychological Perspective.* Cambridge: Cambridge University Press.

Kavussanu, M., and Roberts, G. C. (2001). Moral functioning in sport: An achievement goal perspective. *Journal of Sport and Exercise Psychology* 23, 37–54.

Kavussanu, M., White, S. A., Jowett, S., and England, S. (2011). Elite and non-elite male footballers differ in goal orientation and perceived parental climate. International *Journal of Sport and Exercise Psychology* 9 (3), 284–290.

Kawachi, I., Kennedy, B. P., Lochner, K., and Prothrow-Stith, D. (1997). Social capital, income inequality, and mortality. *American Journal of Public Health* 87 (9), 1491–1498.

Keegan, R. J., Harwood, C. G., Spray, C. M., and Lavallee, D. E. (2009). A qualitative investigation exploring the motivational climate in early-career sports participants: Coach, parent and peer influences on sport motivation. *Psychology of Sport and Exercise* 10, 361–372.

Keegan, R. J., Spray, C. M., Harwood, C. G., and Lavallee, D. E. (2014a). A qualitative synthesis of research into social motivational influences across the athletic career span. *Qualitative Research in Sport, Exercise and Health.* doi: 10.1080/2159676X.2013.857710.

Keegan, R. J., Spray, C. M., Harwood, C. G., and Lavallee, D. E. (2014b). A qualitative investigation of the motivational climate in elite sport participants. *Psychology of Sport and Exercise* 15 (1), 97–107.

Keegan, R. J., Spray, C. M., Harwood, C. G., and Lavallee, D. E. (2010). The 'motivational atmosphere' in youth sport: Coach, parent and peer influences on motivation in specializing sport participants. *Journal of Applied Sport Psychology* 22, 87–104.

Kelley, H. H., Berscheid, E., Christensen, A., Harvey, J. H., Huston, T. L., Levinger, G., McClintock, E., Peplau, L. A., and Peterson, D. R. (1983). *Close Relationships.* New York: Freeman.

Kelly, M., Huntley, J., Carmona, C., Crombie, H., Jagroo, J., and Naidoo, B. (2008). Workplace health promotion: How to encourage employers to be physically active. In National Institute of Clinical Excellence (ed.). London: Department of Health.

Kidman, L., McKenzie, A., and McKenzie, B. (1999). The nature and target of parents' comments during youth sport competitions. *Journal of Sport Behavior* 22, 54–67.

Kiesler, D. J. (1997). *Contemporary Interpersonal Theory: Research and Personality, Psychopathology, and Psychotherapy.* New York: Wiley.

Kimiecik, J. C., and Horn, T. S. (1998). Parental beliefs and children's moderate-to-vigorous physical activity. *Research Quarterly for Exercise and Sport* 69 (2), 163–175.

Kirby, J. (2009). The importance of role models in making adolescent girls more active: A review of the literature. Child Adolescent Health Research Unit, University of Edinburgh.

Kirk, A. F., Higgins, L. A., Hughes, A. R., Fisher, B. M., Mutrie, N., Hillis, S., and MacIntyre, P. D. (2001). A randomized, controlled trial to study the effect of exercise consultation on the promotion of physical activity in people with type 2 diabetes: A pilot study. *Diabetes Medicine* 18 (11), 877–882.

Kirk, A. F., Mutrie, N., Macintyre, P. D., and Fisher, M. B. (2004). Promoting and maintaining physical activity in people with type 2 diabetes. *American Journal of Preventive Medicine* 27 (4), 289–296. doi: 10.1016/j.amepre.2004.07.009.

Knight, C. J., Boden, C. M., and Holt, N. L. (2010). Junior tennis players' preferences for parental behaviors. *Journal of Applied Sport Psychology* 22, 377–391.

Knight, C. J., and Holt, N. L. (2013). Strategies used and assistance required to facilitate children's involvement in tennis: Parents' perspectives. *Sport Psychologist* 27, 281–291.

Knight, C. J., Neely, K. C., and Holt, N. L. (2011). Parental behaviors in team sports: How do female athletes want parents to behave? *Journal of Applied Sport Psychology* 23, 76–92.

Kohn, A. (1992). *No Contest: The Case against Competition*. Boston: Houghton Mifflin.

Koning, R. (2005). Home advantage in speed skating: Evidence from individual data. *Journal of Sports Sciences* 23 (4), 417–427.

Koning, R. H. (2011). Home advantage in professional tennis. *Journal of Sports Sciences* 29 (1), 19–27h.

Krendl, A. C., Gainsburg, I., Ambady, N. (2012). The effects of stereotypes and observer pressure on athletic performance. *Journal of Sports and Exercise Psychology* 34 (1), 3–15.

Krueger, J., and Funder, D. (2004). Towards a balanced social psychology: Causes consequences, and cures for the problem-seeking approach to social behavior and cognition. *Behavioral and Brain Sciences* 27, 313–327.

Kruisselbrink, L. D., Dodge, A. M., Swanburg, S. L., and MacLeod, A. L. (2004). Influence of same-sex and mixed-sex exercise settings on the social physique anxiety and exercise intentions of males and females. *Journal of Sport and Exercise Psychology* 26, 616–622.

Lafferty, M. E., and Dorrell, K. (2006). Coping strategies and the influence of perceived parental support in junior national age swimmers. *Journal of Sports Sciences* 24, 253–259.

Landolfi, E. (2013). Exercise addiction. *Sports Medicine* 43 (2), 111–119.

Lantz, C. D., Hardy, C. J., and Ainsworth, B. E. (1997). Social physique anxiety and perceived exercise behavior. *Journal of Sport Behavior* 20, 83–93.

Lavallee, D., Kremer, J., Moran, A. P., and Williams, M. (2004). *Sport Psychology: Contemporary Themes*. Basingstoke: Palgrave Macmillan.

LaVoi, N. M. (2007). Interpersonal communication and conflict in the coach-athlete relationship. In S. Jowett and D. Lavallee (eds), *Social Psychology in Sport* (29–40). Champaign, IL: Human Kinetics.

LaVoi, N. M., and Babkes Stellino, M. (2008). The influence of perceived parent created sport climate on competitive youth male hockey players' good and poor sport behaviors. *Journal of Psychology: Interdisciplinary and Applied* 142 (5), 471–495.

Leary, M. R. (1992). Self-presentational processes in exercise and sport. *Journal of Sport and Exercise Psychology* 14, 339–351.

Leary, M., and Forsyth, D. (1987). Attributions of responsibility for collective endeavors. *Review of Personality and Social Psychology* 8, 167–188.

Leary, M., and Shepperd, J. (1986). Behavioral self-handicaps versus self-reported handicaps: A conceptual note. *Journal of Personality and Social Psychology* 51, 1265–1268.

Le Bars, H., Gernion, C., and Ninot, G. (2009). Personal and contextual determinants of elite young athletes' persistence or dropping out over time. *Scandinavian Journal of Medicine and Science in Sports* 19, 274–285.

Leo F. M., Sánchez-Miguel, P. A., Sánchez-Oliva, D., and García-Calvo, T. (2010). Interactive effects of team cohesion on perceived efficacy in semi-professional sport. *Journal of Sports Science and Medicine* 9, 320–325.

Lerner, M., and Miller, D. (1977). Just-world research and the attribution process: Looking back and ahead. *Psychological Bulletin* 85, 1030–1051.

Lewin, K. (1934). *A Dynamic Theory of Personality*. New York: McGraw-Hill.

Lewko, J. H., and Ewing, M. E. (1980). Sex differences and parental influence in sport involvement. *Journal of Sport Psychology* 2, 62–68.

Li, F. Z., Fisher, K. J., Brownson, R. C., and Bosworth, M. (2005). Multilevel modelling of built environment characteristics related to neighbourhood walking activity in older adults. *Journal of Epidemiology and Community Health* 59, 558–564.

Locke, E. A., and Latham, G. P. (2002). Building a practically useful theory of goal setting and task motivation. A 35-year odyssey. *American Psychologist* 57 (9), 705–717.

Lorimer, R., and Jowett, S. (2010). The influence of role and gender in the empathic accuracy of coaches and athletes. *Psychology of Sport and Exercise* 11, 206–211.

Loughead, T. M., Colman, M. M., and Carron, A. V. (2001). Investigating the mediational relationship of leadership, class cohesion, and adherence in an exercise setting. *Small Group Research* 32 (5), 558–575.

Lyle, J. (2007). A review of the research evidence for the impact of coach education. *International Journal of Coaching Science* 1, 19–36.

Mackay, G. J., and Neill, J. T. (2010). The effect of 'green exercise' on state anxiety and the role of exercise duration, intensity, and greenness: A quasi-experimental study. *Psychology of Sport and Exercise* 11 (3), 238–245.

Maddux, J. E., Norton, L. W., and Leary, M. R. (1988). Cognitive components of social anxiety: An investigation of the integration of self-presentation theory and self-efficacy theory. *Journal of Social and Clinical Psychology* 6 (2), 180–190.

Malik, S. H., Blake, H., and Suggs, L. S. (2013). A systematic review of workplace health promotion interventions for increasing physical activity. *British Journal of Health Psychology*. doi: 10.1111/bjhp.12052.

Marcelino R., Mesquita, I., Palao, J. M., and Sampaio, J. (2009). Home advantage in high-level volleyball varies according to set number. *Journal of Sports Science and Medicine* 8, 352–356.

Marcus, B., and Forsyth, L. (2009). *Motivating People to Be Physically Active*, 2nd edn. Champaign, IL: Human Kinetics.

Marcus, B., Rossi, J. S., Selby, V. C, Niaura, R. S., and Abrams, D. B. (1992). The stages and processes of exercise adoption and maintenance in a workplace sample. *Health Psychology* 11, 386–395.

Markland, D., Ryan, R. M., Tobin, V. J., and Rollnick, S. (2005). Motivational interviewing and self-determination theory. *Journal of Social and Clinical Psychology* 24 (6), 811–831.

Marsh, H. A. (1987). The big-fish-little-pond effect on academic self-concept. *Journal of Educational Psychology* 79, 280–295.

Martens, D., Gutscher, H., and Bauer, N. (2011). Walking in 'wild' and 'tended' urban forests: The impact on psychological well-being. *Journal of Environmental Psychology* 31 (1), 36–44.

Martin, K. A., and Fox, L. D. (2001). Group and leadership effects on social anxiety experienced during an exercise class. *Journal of Applied Social Psychology* 31 (5), 1000–1016.

Martin, K. A., Leary, M. R., and O'Brien, J. (2001). Role of self-presentation in the health practices of a sample of Irish adolescents. *Journal of Adolescent Health* 28 (4), 259–262.

Martin, L. J., Carron, A. V., and Burke, S. M. (2009). Team building interventions in sport: A meta-analysis. *Sport and Exercise Psychology Review* 5, 3–18.

Martin-Ginis, K. A., Burke, S., and Gauvin, L. (2007). Exercising with others exacerbates the negative effects of mirrored environments on sedentary women's feeling states. *Psychology and Health* 22 (8), 945–962.

Masters, R. S. W. (1992). Knowledge, knerves and know-how. The role of explicit versus implicit knowledge in the breakdown of a complex motor skill under pressure. *British Journal of Psychology* 83, 343–358.

McKenna, J., Naylor, P. J., and McDowell, N. (1998). Barriers to physical activity promotion by general practitioners and practice nurses. *British Journal of Sports Medicine* 32, 242–247.

McKenna, J., and Vernon, M. (2004). How general practitioners promote 'lifestyle' physical activity. *Patient Education and Counselling* 54 (1), 101–106. doi: 10.1016/S0738-3991(03)00192-7.

McKiddie, B., and Maynard, I. (1997). Perceived competence of schoolchildren in physical education. *Journal of Teaching in Physical Education* 16 (3), 324–339.

McLeroy, K. R., Bibeau, D., Steckler, A., and Glanz, K. (1988). An ecological perspective on health promotion programs. *Health Education Quarterly* 15, 351–377.

McMurray, R. G., Berry, M. J., Vann, R. T., Hardy, C. J., and Sheps, D. S. (1988). The effect of running in an outdoor environment on plasma beta endorphins. *Annals of Sports Medicine* 3 (4), 230–233.

McNair, D. M., Lorr, M., and Droppleman, L. F. (1992). *Revised Manual for the Profile of Mood States*. San Diego, CA: Educational and Industrial Testing Service.

McNicholas, J., and Collis, G. M. (2000). Dogs as catalysts for social interactions: Robustness of the effect. *British Journal of Psychology* 91 (1), 61–70. doi: 10.1348/000712600161673.

Mellalieu, S. D., Shearer, D. A., and Shearer, C. R. (2013). A preliminary survey of interpersonal conflict at major games and championships. *Sport Psychologist* 27, 120–129.

Melville, D. S., and Maddalozzo, J. (1988). The effects of a physical educator's appearance of body fatness on communicating exercise concepts to high school students. *Journal of Teaching in Physical Education* 7, 343–352.

Mesagno, C. (2009). Choking under pressure: Toward a self-presentation explanation of why athletes use self-monitoring techniques. Paper presented at the 12th World Congress of Sport Psychology, Marrakesh, Morocco (June).

Mesagno, C., Harvey, J. T., and Janelle, C. M. (2011). Self-presentation origins of choking: Evidence from separate pressure manipulations. *Journal of Sport and Exercise Psychology* 33, 441–459.

Mesagno, C., Harvey, J. T., and Janelle, C. M. (2012). Fear of negative evaluation and choking. *Psychology of Sport and Exercise* 13, 60–68.

Mesagno, C., and Hill, D. M. (2013). Definition of choking in sport: Re-conceptualization and debate. *International Journal of Sport Psychology* 44, 267–277.

Mesagno, C., Marchant, D., and Morris, T. (2008). A pre-performance routine to alleviate choking in 'choking-susceptible' athletes. *Sport Psychologist* 22, 439–457.

Midgley, C., Maehr, M., Hicks, L., Roeser, R., Urdan, T., and Anderman, E. (1996). *Patterns of Adaptive Learning Survey (PALS)*. Ann Arbor, MI: Center for Leadership and Learning.

Midtgaard, J., Rorth, M., Stelter, R., and Adamsen, L. (2006). The group matters: An explorative study of group cohesion and quality of life in cancer patients participating in physical exercise intervention during treatment. *European Journal of Cancer Care* 15, 25–33.

Miller, S. T., and Beech, B. M. (2009). Rural healthcare providers question the practicality of motivational interviewing and report varied physical activity counseling experience. *Patient Education and Counselling* 76, 279–282.

Miller, W. R., and Rollnick, S. (1991). *Motivational Interviewing, Preparing People to Change Addictive Behavior*. New York: Guilford Press.

Miller, W. R., and Rollnick, S. (2009). Ten things that motivational interviewing is not. *Behavioural and Cognitive Psychotherapy* 37, 129–140.

Milton, K. (2008). Final Report of the Evaluation of the Eastern and Coastal Kent Exercise Referral Scheme. BHFNC, SSES, Loughborough University.

Mintel (2010). Boom time for budget exercise? Retrieved 25 June 2013, www.mintel.com/press-centre/financial-services/boom-time-for-budget-exercise.

Mitchell, R., and Popham, F. (2007). Greenspace, urbanity and health: Relationships in England. *Journal of Epidemiology and Community Health* 61 (8), 681–683.

Mitchell, R. (2013). Is physical activity in natural environments better for mental health than physical activity in other environments? *Social Science and Medicine* 91, 130–134.

Montgomery, B. (1988). Overview. In S. Duck (ed.), *Handbook of Personal Relationships: Theory, Research and Interventions*. Chichester: Wiley.

Moore, G. F., Moore, L., and Murphy, S. (2011). Facilitating adherence to physical activity: Exercise professionals' experiences of the National Exercise Referral Scheme in Wales. A qualitative study. *BMC Public Health* 11 (935), 1–12.

Moore, L. L., Lombardi, D. A., White, M. J., Campbell, J. L., Oliveria, S. A., and Ellison, R. C. (1991). Influence of parents' physical activity levels on activity levels of young children. *Journal of Pediatrics* 118 (2), 215–219.

Moran, A. (2003). *Sport and Exercise Psychology: A Critical Introduction*. London: Routledge.

MORI. (2011). *Sports Coaching in the UK*, vol. 3. Leeds: SportsCoachUK.

Motl, R. W., and Conroy, D. E. (2000). Validity and factorial invariance of the Social Physique Anxiety Scale. *Medicine and Science in Sports and Exercise* 32 (5), 1007–1017.

Mullen, B., and Cooper, C. (1994). The relation between group cohesiveness and performance: An integration. *Psychological Bulletin* 115 (2), 210–227.

Mullen, R., Hardy, L., and Tattersall, A. (2005). The effects of anxiety on motor performance: A test of the conscious processing hypothesis. *Journal of Sport and Exercise Psychology* 27, 212–225.

Mulvey, P., and Ribbens, B. (1999). The effects of intergroup competition and assigned group goals on group efficacy and group effectiveness. *Small Group Research* 30, 651–677.

Murray, S. B., Rieger, E., Touyz, S. W., and De la Garza García, L. Y. (2010). Muscle dysmorphia and the DSM-V conundrum: Where does it belong? A review paper. *International Journal of Eating Disorders* 43 (6), 483–491. doi: 10.1002/eat.20828.

Myers, T. D., and Balmer, N. J. (2012). The impact of crowd noise on officiating in Muay Thai: Achieving external validity in an experimental setting. *Frontiers in Psychology* 3.

Myers, T. D., Nevill, A. M., and Al-Nakeeb, Y. (2012). The influence of crowd noise upon judging decisions in Muay Thai. *Advances in Physical Education* 2, 148–152.

Naidoo, J., and Wills, J. (2002). *Health Promotion: Foundations for Practice*, 2nd edn. Edinburgh: Balliere Tindall in association with the RCN.

National Institute for Health and Clinical Excellence. (2006). *Brief Interventions and Referral for Smoking Cessation in Primary Care and Other Settings*.

National Institute for Health and Clinical Excellence. (2013). *Physical Activity: Brief Advice for Adults in Primary Care*.

Navarro, M., Miyamoto, N, Kamp, J. van der, Morya, E., Ranvaud, R., and Savelsbergh, G. J. P. (2012). The effects of high pressure on the point of no return in simulated penalty kicks. *Journal of Sport and Exercise Psychology* 34, 83–101.

Nevill, A. M., Balmer, N. J., and Williams, A. M. (2002). The influence of crowd noise and experience upon refereeing decisions in football. *Psychology of Sport and Exercise* 3, 261–272.

Nevill, A. M., Balmer, N. J., and Winter E. M. (2009). Why Great Britain's success in Beijing could have been anticipated and why it should continue beyond 2012. *British Journal of Sports Medicine* 43, 1108–1110.

Nevill, A. M., and Holder, R. L. (1999). Home advantage in sport: An overview of studies on the advantage of playing at home. *Sports Medicine* 28, 221–236.

Nevill, A., Webb, T., and Watts, A. (2013). Improved training of football referees and the decline in home advantage post-WW2. *Psychology of Sport and Exercise* 14, 220–227.

Nicholls, J. G. (1989). *The Competitive Ethos and Democratic Education*. Cambridge, MA: Harvard University Press.

Nicholson, L. (2008). Physical activity and adolescent girls: Workforce training needs analysis. NHS Health Scotland.

Ntoumanis, N. (2001). A self-determination approach to the understanding of motivation in physical education. *British Journal of Educational Psychology* 71 (2), 225–242.

Ntoumanis, N., Taylor, I., and Thøgerson-Ntoumanis, C. (2012). A longitudinal examination of coach and peer motivational climates in youth sport: Implications for moral attitudes, well-being and behavioural investment. *Developmental Psychology* 48, 213–223.

Ntoumanis, N., and Vazou, S. (2005). Peer motivational climate in youth sport: Measurement development. *Journal of Sport and Exercise Psychology* 27, 432–455.

Ntoumanis, N., Vazou, S., and Duda, J. L. (2007). Peer-created motivational climate. In S. Jowett and D. Lavallee (eds), *Social Psychology in Sport* (145–156). Champaign, IL: Human Kinetics.

Nunomura, M., and Oliveira, M. S. (2012). Parents' support in the career of young gymnasts. *Science of Gymnastics Journal* 5 (1), 5–17.

O'Bryant, C. P., O'Sullivan, M., and Raudensky, J. (2000). Socialization of prospective physical education teachers: The story of new blood. *Sport, Education and Society* 52 (2), 177–193.

Office of National Statistics (2013). Labour market statistics – March 2013. Retrieved 2 April 2013, www.ons.gov.uk/ons/rel/lms/labour-market-statistics/march-2013/index.html.

Olivardia, R. (2001). Mirror, mirror on the wall, who's the largest of them all? The features and phenomenology of muscle dysmorphia. *Harvard Review of Psychiatry* 9 (5), 254–259.

Omli, J., LaVoi, N. M., and Wiese-Bjornstal, D. M. (2008). Towards an understanding of parent spectator behavior at youth sport events. *Journal of Youth Sports* 3, 30–33.

Omli, J., and Wiese-Bjornstal, D. M. (2011). Kids speak: Preferred parent behavior at youth sport events. *Research Quarterly for Exercise and Sport* 82 (4), 702–711.

Ommundsen, Y. (2001). Self-handicapping strategies in physical education classes: The influence of implicit theories of the nature of ability and achievement goal orientations. *Psychology of Sport and Exercise* 2, 139–156.

Ommundsen, Y., Roberts, G. C., Lemyre, P. N., and Miller, B. W. (2005). Peer relationships in adolescent competitive soccer: Associations to perceived motivational climate, achievement goals and perfectionism. *Journal of Sport Sciences* 23 (9), 977–989.

Orlick, T. (1986). *Psyching for Sport Coaches' Training Manual*. Champaign, IL: Human Kinetics.

O'Rourke, D. J., Smith, R. E., Smoll, F. L., and Cumming, S. P. (2011). Trait anxiety in young athletes as a function of parental pressure and motivational climate: Is parental pressure always harmful? *Journal of Applied Sport Psychology* 23 (4), 398–412.

Page, K., and Page, L. (2010). Alone against the crowd: Individual differences in referees' ability to cope under pressure. *Journal of Economic Psychology* 31 (2), 192–199.

Pain, M. A., and Harwood, C. G. (2009). Team building through mutual sharing and open discussion of team functioning. *Sport Psychologist* 23 (4), 523–542.

Paradis, K. F., Carron, A. V., and Martin, L. J. (2014). Athlete perceptions of intragroup conflict in sport teams. *Sport and Exercise Psychology Review* 10 (3), 4–18.

Paradis, K. F., and Martin, L. J. (2012). Team building in sport: Linking theory and research to practical application. *Journal of Sport Psychology in Action* 3 (3), 159–170.

Paradis, K. F., Martin, L. J., and Carron, A. V. (2012). Examining the relationship between passion and perceptions of cohesion in athletes. *Sport and Exercise Psychology Review* 8 (1), 22–31.

Partridge, J. A., Brustad, R. J., and Babkes-Stellino, M. (2008). Social influence in sport. In T. S. Horn (ed.), *Advances in Sport Psychology* (270–291). Champaign IL: Human Kinetics.

Paulus, P. B., and Cornelius, W. L. (1974). An analysis of gymnastic performance under conditions of practice and spectator observation. *Research Quarterly* 45, 56–63.

Pavey, T. G., Taylor, A. H., Fox, K. R., Hillsdon, M., Anokye, N., Campbell, J. L. et al. (2011). Effect of exercise referral schemes in primary care on physical activity and improving health outcomes: Systematic review and meta-analysis. *British Medical Journal* 343, d6462.

Payne, W., Reynolds, M., Brown, S., and Fleming, A. (2003). *Sports Role Models and Their Impact on Participation in Physical Activity: A Literature Review*. Victoria, Australia: VicHealth.

Peacock, J., Hine, R., and Pretty, J. (2007). The mental health benefits of green exercise activities and green care. *Mind Week Report*.

Pellegrini, A. D., and Bohn, C. M. (2005). The role of recess in children's cognitive performance and school adjustment. *Educational Researcher* 34 (1), 13–19.

Pellegrini, A. D., Kato, K., Blatchford, P., and Baines, E. (2002). A short-term longitudinal study of children's playground games across the first year of school: Implications for social competence and adjustment to school. *American Educational Research Journal* 39 (4), 991–1015.

Peterson, C., Maier, S., and Seligman, M. (1995). *Learned Helplessness: A Theory for the Age of Personal Control*. New York: Oxford University Press.

Pettersson-Lidbom, P., and Priks, M. (2007). Behavior under social pressure: Empty Italian stadiums and referee bias. *Economics Letters* 108, 212–214.

Phipps, E., Madison, N., Pomerantz, S. C., and Klein, M. G. (2010). Identifying and assessing interests and concerns of priority populations for work-site programs to promote physical activity. *Health Promotion Practice* 11 (1), 71–78.

Pinter, B., Insko, C., Wildschut, T., Kirchner, J., Montoya, R., and Wolf, S. (2007). Reduction of interindividual-intergroup discontinuity: The role of leader accountability and proneness to guilt. *Journal of Personality and Social Psychology* 93, 250–265.

Plante, T. G., Cage, C., Clements, S., and Stover, A. (2006). Psychological benefits of exercise paired with virtual reality: Outdoor exercise energizes whereas indoor virtual exercise relaxes. *International Journal of Stress Management* 13 (1), 108–117.

Plotnikoff, R. C., McCargar, L. J., Wilson, P. M., and Loucaides, C. A. (2005). Efficacy of an e-mail intervention for the promotion of physical activity and nutrition behavior in the workplace context. *American Journal of Health Promotion* 19 (6), 422–439.

Plotnikoff, R. C., Prodaniuk, T. R., Fein, A. J., and Milton, L. (2005). Development of an ecological assessment tool for a workplace physical activity program standard. *Health Promotion Practice* 6 (4), 453–463.

Poczwardowski, A., Barott, J. E., and Henschen, K. P. (2002). The athlete and coach: Their relationship and its meaning. *International Journal of Sport Psychology* 33, 116–140.

Podlog, L., Kleinert, J., Dimmock, J., Miller, J., and Shipherd, A. M. (2012). A parental perspective on adolescent injury rehabilitation and return to sport experiences. *Journal of Applied Sport Psychology* 24 (2), 175–190.

Pollard, R. (2006). Home advantage in soccer: Variations in its magnitude and a literature review of the associated factors associated with its existence. *Journal of Sport Behavior* 29, 169–189.

Polletta, F., and Jasper, J. (2001). Collective identity and social movements. *Annual Review of Sociology* 27, 283–305.

Poolton, J., Siu, C. M., and Masters, R. (2011). The home team advantage gives football referees something to ruminate about. *International Journal of Sports Science and Coaching* 6 (4), 545–552.

Prapavessis, H., and Carron, A. V. (1996). The effect of group cohesion on competitive state anxiety. *Journal of Sport and Exercise Psychology* 18, 64–74.

Prapavessis, H., and Carron, A. V. (1997). Cohesion and work output. *Small Group Research* 28, 294–301.

Pretty, J. (2004). How nature contributes to mental and physical health. *Spirituality and Health International* 5, 68–78.

Pretty, J., Peacock, J., Hine, R., Sellens, M., South, N., and Griffin, M. (2007). Green exercise in the UK countryside: Effects on health and psychological well-being, and implications for policy and planning. *Journal of Environmental Planning and Management* 50 (2), 211–231.

Pretty, J., Peacock, J., Sellens, M., and Griffin, M. (2003). The mental and physical health outcomes of green exercise. *International Journal of Environmental Health Research* 15 (5), 319–337.

Pretty, J., Peacock, J., Sellens, M., and Griffin, M. (2005). The mental and physical health outcomes of green exercise. *International Journal of Environmental Health Research* 15 (5), 319–337. doi: 10.1080/09603120500155963.

Price, M. S., and Weiss, M. R. (2011). Peer leadership in sport: Relationships among personal characteristics, leader behaviors, and team outcomes. *Journal of Applied Sport Psychology* 23, 49–64.

PricewaterhouseCoopers, LLP (2008). Building the case for wellness report. Retrieved 2 April 2013, www.dwp.gov.uk/docs/hwwb-dwp-wellness-report-public.pdf.

Pridgeon, S., and Grogan, S. (2012). Understanding exercise adherence and dropout: An interpretative phenomenological analysis of men and women's accounts of gym attendance and non-attendance. *Qualitative Research in Sport, Health and Exercise* 4 (3), 382–399.

Prochaska, J. J., and DiClemente, C. C. (1983). The stages and processes of self-change in smoking: Towards an integrative model of change. *Journal of Consulting and Clinical Psychology* 51, 390–395.

Prochaska, J. J., and Velicer, W. F. (1997). The transtheoretical model of health behaviour change. *American Journal of Health Promotion* 12, 38–48.

Prochaska, J. J., Velicer, W. F., DiClemente, C. C., and Fava, J. (1988). Measuring processes of change: Applications to the cessation of smoking. *Journal of Consulting and Clinical Psychology* 56, 520–528.

QRESEARCH and the Health and Social Care Information Centre (2008). Trends in consultation rates in general practice: 1994/1196 to 2007/2008: Analysis of the QRESEARCH database. London: NHS Information Centre for Health and Social Care.

Quick, S., Simon, A., and Thornton, A. (2010). *PE and Sport Survey 2009/10 Research Report*, vol. RR032. London: Department for Education.

Raedeke, T. D., Focht, B. C., and Scales, D. (2007). Social environmental factors and psychological responses to acute exercise for socially physique anxious females. *Psychology of Sport and Exercise* 8, 463–476.

Rahim, M. (2002). Toward a theory of managing organizational conflict. *International Journal of Conflict Management* 13 (3), 206–235.

Ransdell, L. B., Wells, C. L., Manore, M. M., Swan, P. D., and Corbin, C. B. (1998). Social physique anxiety in postmenopausal women. *J Women Aging* 10 (3), 19–39. doi: 10.1300/J074v10n03_03.

Resnicow, K., and McMaster, F. (2012). Motivational interviewing: Moving from why to how with autonomy support. *International Journal of Behavioral Nutrition and Physical Activity* 9 (19).

Rhind, D., and Jowett, S. (2010). Relationship maintenance strategies in the coach-athlete relationship: The development of the COMPASS model. *Journal of Applied Sport Psychology* 22, 106–121.

Rhind, D., and Jowett, S. (2011). Linking maintenance strategies to the quality of coach-athlete relationships. *International Journal of Sport Psychology* 41, 55–68.

Rhind, D., and Jowett, S. (2012). Development of the Coach-Athlete Relationship Maintenance Questionnaire (CARM-Q). *International Journal of Sports Science and Coaching* 7, 121–137.

Richardson, C. R., Faulkner, G., McDevitt, J., Skrinar, G. S., Hutchinson, D. S., and Piette, J. D. (2005). Integrating physical activity into mental health services for persons with serious mental illness. *Psychiatric Services* 56 (3), 324–331. doi: 10.1176/appi.ps.56.3.324.

Riemer, H. A., and Chelladurai, P. (1998). Development of the Athlete Satisfaction Questionnaire (ASQ). *Journal of Sport and Exercise Psychology* 20, 127–156.

Riley, A., and Smith, A. (2011). Perceived coach-athlete and peer relationships of young athletes and self-determined motivation for sport. *International Journal of Sport Psychology* 42 (1), 115–133.

Roberts, G. C., and Ommundsen, Y. (1996). Effects of achievement goal orientations on achievement beliefs, cognitions, and strategies in team sport. *Scandinavian Journal of Medicine and Science in Sport* 6, 46–56.

Rogers, R. W. (1983). Cognitive and physiological processes in fear appeals and attitude change: A revised theory of protection motivation. In J. T. Cacioppo and R. E. Petty (eds), *Social Psychology*. New York: Guilford Press.

Rollnick, S. (1997). Whither motivational interviewing? *Journal of Substance Misuse* 2, 1–2.

Rollnick, S., Butler, C. C., McCambridge, J., Kinnersley, P., Elwyn, G., and Resnicow, K. (2005). Consultations about changing behaviour. *British Medical Journal* 331, 961–963.

Rosenberg, M. (1965). *Society and the Adolescent Self-Image*. Princeton, NJ: Princeton University Press.

Rottensteiner, C., Laakso, L., Pihlaja, T., and Konttinen, N. (2013). Personal reasons for withdrawal from team sports and the influence of significant others among youth athletes. *International Journal of Sports Science and Coaching* 8 (1), 19–32.

Rubin, K. H., Bukowski, W. M., and Parker, J. G. (2006). Peers interactions, relationships and groups. In N. Eisenberg (ed.), *Handbook of Child Psychology: Social, Emotional and Personality Development*, 6th edn, vol. 3. Hoboken, NJ: Wiley.

Rusbult, C. E. (1983). A longitudinal test of the investment model: The development (and deterioration) of satisfaction and commitment in heterosexual involvements. *Journal of Personality and Social Psychology* 43, 101–117.

Rusbult, C. E., Verette, J., Whitney, G. A., Slovik, L. F., and Lipkus, I. (1991). Accommodation processes in close relationships: Theory and preliminary empirical evidence. *Journal of Personality and Social Psychology* 60, 53–78.

Ruscher, J., and Fiske, S. (1990). Interpersonal competition can cause individuating processes. *Journal of Personality and Social Psychology* 58, 832–843.

Sadalla, E. K., Linder, D. E., and Jenkins, B. A. (1988). Sport preference: A self-presentational analysis. *Journal of Sport and Exercise Psychology* 10, 214–222.

Sagar, S., and Jowett, S. (2012). Communicative acts in coach-athlete interactions: When losing competitions and when making mistakes in training. *Western Journal of Communication* 76, 148–174.

Sallis, J., and Owen, N. (1999). *Physical Activity and Behavioral Medicine*. Thousand Oaks, CA: Sage.

Salminen, S. (1993). The effect of the audience on the home advantage. *Perceptual and Motor Skills* 76, 1123–1128.

Sánchez-Miguel, P. A., Leo, F. M., Sánchez-Oliva, D., Amado, D., and García-Calvo, T. (2013). The importance of parents' behaviour in their children's enjoyment and amotivation in sports. *Journal of Human Kinetics* 28, 169–77.

Sanders, G. S., Baron, R. S., and Moore, D. L. (1978). Distraction and social comparison as mediators of social facilitation effects. *Journal of Experimental Social Psychology* 14, 291–303.

Sapieja, K., Dunn, J. G. H., and Holt, N. L. (2011). Relationships between perfectionism and parenting styles in male youth soccer. *Journal of Sport and Exercise Psychology* 33, 20–39.

Schlenker, B. R., and Leary, M. R. (1982). Social anxiety and self-presentation: A conceptualization and model. *Psychology Bulletin* 92 (3), 641–669.

Schulz-Hardt, S., Jochims, M., and Frey, D. (2002). Productive conflict in group decision making: Genuine and contrived dissent as strategies to counteract biased information seeking. *Organizational Behavior and Human Decision Processes* 88, 563–586.

Schwartz, B., and Barsky, S. F. (1977). The home advantage. *Social Forces* 55, 641–661.

Schwenk, C. R. (1990). Effects of devil's advocacy and dialectical inquiry on decision making: A meta-analysis. *Organizational Behavior and Human Decision Processes* 47, 161–176.

Scottish Executive (2008). *The Scottish Health Survey 2008*. Edinburgh: The Stationery House.

Scottish Government (2008). *Equally Well: Report of the Ministerial Task Force on Health Inequalities*. Edinburgh: Crown.

Scottish Government (2013). Family doctors to get Scotland active. Retrieved 22 July 2013, www.scotland.gov.uk/News/Releases/2013/03/getscotlandactive07032013.

Scottish Government (2013). *Scotland's People Annual Report: Results from 2012 Scottish Household Survey*. Crown Publishers: Edinburgh.

Shanmugam, V., Jowett, S., and Meyer, C. (2013). Eating psychopathology amongst athletes: The importance of relationships with parents, coaches and teammates. *International Journal of Sport and Exercise Psychology* 11 (1), 24–38.

Shanmugam, V., Jowett, S., and Meyer, C. (2014). Interpersonal difficulties as a risk factor for athletes' eating psychopathology. *Scandinavian Journal of Medicine and Science in Sport*. doi: 10.1111/sms.12109.

Shaw, D. F., Gorely, P. J., and Corban, R. M. (2005). *Instant Notes in Sport and Exercise Psychology*. London: Bios.

Shields, D. L., LaVoi, N. M., Bredemeier, B. L., and Power, C. F. (2007). Predictors of poor sportspersonship in youth sports: An examination of personal attitudes and social influences. *Journal of Sport and Exercise Psychology* 29, 747–762.

Sindik, J., and Vokosav, J. (2011). The differences between top senior basketball players with different situation efficacy in relation to conative characteristics. *Physical Education and Sport* 9 (1), 99–112.

Sjoling, M., Lundberg, K., Englund, E., Westman, A., and Jong, M. C. (2011). Effectiveness of motivational interviewing and physical activity on prescription on leisure exercise time in subjects suffering from mild to moderate hypertension. *BMC Research Notes* 4 (352).

Skinner, N., and Brewer, N. (2004). Adaptive approaches to competition: Challenge appraisals and positive emotion. *Journal of Sport and Exercise Psychology* 26, 283–305.

Smith, A. L. (2007). Youth peer relationships in sport. In S. Jowett and D. Lavallee (eds), *Social Psychology in Sport*. Champaign, IL: Human Kinetics.

Smith, A. L., Gustafsson, H., and Hassmén, P. (2010). Peer motivational climate and burnout perceptions of intensively sport involved adolescents. *Psychology of Sport and Exercise* 11, 453–460.

Smith, A. L., and McDonough, M. H. (2008). Peers. In A. L. Smith and S. J. Biddle (eds), *Youth Physical Activity and Sedentary Behaviour: Challenges and Solutions*. Champaign, IL: Human Kinetics.

Smith, A. L., Ullrich-French, S., Walker, E. G., and Hurley, K. S. (2006). Peer relationship profiles and motivation in youth sport. *Journal of Sport and Exercise Psychology* 28, 362–382.

Smith, M. J., Calum, A., Hardy, J., Callow, N., and Williams, D. (2012). Transformational leadership and task cohesion in sport: The mediating role of intra-team communication. *Psychology of Sport and Exercise* 14, 249–257.

Smith, R. E., and Smoll, F. L. (1990). Self-esteem and children's reactions to youth sport coaching behaviours: A field study of self-enhancement processes. *Developmental Psychology* 26, 987–993.

Smith, R. E., and Smoll, F. L. (2007). Social-cognitive approach to coaching behaviours. In S. Jowett and D. Lavallee (eds), *Social Psychology in Sport* (75–90). Champaign, IL: Human Kinetics.

Smith, R. E., Smoll, F. L., and Cumming, S. P. (2007). Effects of a motivational climate intervention for coaches on young athletes' sport performance anxiety. *Journal of Sport and Exercise Psychology* 29. 39–59.

Smoll, F. L., Cumming, S. P., and Smith, R. E. (2011). Enhancing coach-parent relationships in youth sports: Increasing harmony and minimizing hassle. *International Journal of Sports Science and Coaching* 6 (1), 13–26.

Sorenson, J. B., Skovgaard, T., and Puggaard, L. (2006). Exercise on prescription in general practice: A systematic review. *Scandinavian Journal of Primary Health Care* 24, 69–74.

Spink, K. S. (1999). Mediational effects of cohesion on the leadership behavior intention to return relationship in exercise settings. *Journal of Sport and Exercise Psychology* 21, S102.

Spink, K. S., Wilson, K. S., and Odnokon, P. (2010). Examining the relationship between cohesion and return to team in ice hockey players. *Psychology of Sport and Exercise* 11, 6–11.

Sport England (2009). Sport England Active People Survey 2007/08: Individual sports participation. Office for National Statistics.

Sport England (2012). Active People Survey (APS) results for cycling period: APS2 (Oct 07 / Oct 08) to APS6 (Oct 11 / Oct 12). Office for National Statistics.

Staats, H., and Hartig, T. A. (2004). Alone or with a friend: A social context for psychological restoration and environmental preferences. *Journal of Environmental Psychology* 24, 199–211.

Stafford, L., and Canary, D. J. (1991). Maintenance strategies and romantic relationship type, gender and relational characteristics. *Journal of Social and Personal Relationships* 8, 217–242.

Stafford, L., Dainton, M., and Hass, S. (2000). Measuring routine and strategic relational maintenance: Scale development, sex versus gender roles, and the prediction of relational characteristics. *Communication Monographs* 67, 306–323.

Stein, G. L, Raedeke, T. D., and Glenn, S. D. (1999). Children's perceptions of parent sport involvement: It's not how much, but to what degree that's important. *Journal of Sport Behavior* 22, 591–601.

Stone, J., Perry, Z. W., and Darley, J. M. (1997). White men can't jump: Evidence for the perceptual confirmation of racial stereotypes following a basketball game. *Basic and Applied Social Psychology* 19, 291–306.

Strachan, L., Côté, J., and Deakin, J. (2009). An evaluation of personal and contextual factors in competitive youth sport. *Journal of Applied Sport and Exercise Psychology* 21, 340–355.

Strauss, B. (2002a). Social facilitation in motor tasks. *Psychology of Sport and Exercise* 3, 237–256.

Strauss, B. (2002b). The impact of supportive spectator behavior on performance in team sports. *International Journal of Sport Psychology* 33, 372–390.

Struch, N., and Schwartz, S. (1989). Intergroup aggression: Its predictors and distinctness from in-group bias. *Journal of Personality and Social Psychology* 56, 364–373.

Sugiyama, T., Leslie, E., Giles-Corti, B., and Owen, N. (2008). Associations of neighbourhood greenness with physical and mental health: Do walking, social coherence and local social interaction explain the relationships? *Journal of Epidemiology and Community Health* 62 (5), e9.

Sullivan, H. S. (1953). *The Interpersonal Theory of Psychiatry*. New York: Norton.

Sullivan, P. J., and Feltz, D. L. (2001). The relationship between intra-team conflict and cohesion within hockey teams. *Small Group Research* 32, 342–355.

Sullivan, P. J., and Feltz, D. L. (2003). The preliminary development of the Scale for Effective Communication in Sports Teams (SECTS). *Journal of Applied Social Psychology* 33, 1693–1715.

Sullivan, P. J., and Gee, C. (2007). The relationship between athletic satisfaction and intra-team communication. *Group Dynamics: Theory, Research, and Practice* 11, 107–116.

Swinburn, B. A., Walter, L. G., Arroll, B., Tilyard, M. W., and Russell, D. G. (1998). The green prescription study: A randomized controlled trial of written exercise advice provided by general practitioners. *American Journal of Public Health* 88 (2), 288–291.

Syer, J., and Connolly, C. (1996). *Sporting Body Sporting Mind: An Athlete's Guide to Mental Training*. London: Cambridge University Press.

Tajfel, H., and Turner, J. (1979). An integrative theory of intergroup conflict. In S. Worchel and W. Austin (eds), *The Social Psychology of Intergroup Relations*. Monterey, CA: Brooks/Cole.

Taylor, D., and Doria, J. (1981). Self-serving and group-serving bias in attribution. *Journal of Social Psychology* 113, 201–211.

Telegraph Sport. (2012). Team GB's gold medal winners at London 2012 Olympics. A salute to Team GB's gold medallists at the London 2012 Olympics. *The Telegraph*. Retrieved 01 September 2014, www.telegraph.co.uk.

Tenenbaum, G., Eklund, R. C., and Kamata, A. (2012). *Measurement in Sport and Exercise Psychology*. Champaign, IL: Human Kinetics.

Terry, P., Carron, A. V., Pink, M. J., Lane, A. M., Jones, G. J. W., and Hall, M. P. (2000). Perceptions of group cohesion and mood in sports teams. *Group Dynamics: Theory, Research and Practice* 4, 244–253.

Thirer, J., and Rampey, M. (1979). Effects of abusive spectator behaviour on the performance of home and visiting intercollegiate basketball teams. *Perceptual and Motor Skills* 48, 1047–1053.

Thompson-Coon, J., Boddy, K., Stein, K., Whear, R., Barton, J., and Depledge, M. H. (2011). Does participating in physical activity in outdoor natural environments have a greater effect on physical and mental well-being than physical activity indoors? A systematic review. *Environmental Science and Technology* 45 (5), 1761–1772. doi: 10.1021/es102947t.

Trautwein, U., Gerlach, E., and Ludtke, O. (2008). Athletic classmates, physical self-concept, and free-time physical activity: A longitudinal study of frame of reference effects. *Journal of Educational Psychology* 100 (4), 988–1001.

Treasure, D. C., Lox, C. L., and Lawton, B. R. (1998). Determinants of physical activity in a sedentary, obese female population. *Journal of Sport and Exercise Psychology* 20 (2), 218–224.

Treasure, D. C., and Roberts, G. C. (1995). Applications of achievement goal theory to physical education: Implications for enhancing motivation. *Quest* 47 (4), 475–489.

Triplett, N. (1898). The dynamogenic factors in pacemaking and competition. *American Journal of Psychology* 9, 507–533.

Trost, S. G., Owen, N., Bauman, A. E., Sallis, J. F., and Brown, W. (2002). Correlates of adults' participation in physical activity: Review and update. *Medicine and Science in Sports and Exercise* 34 (12), 1996–2001. doi: 10.1249/01.MSS. 0000038974.76900.92.

Turner, E. E., Rejeski, W. J., and Brawley, L. R. (1997). Psychological benefits of activity are influenced by the social environment. *Journal of Sport and Exercise Psychology* 19, 119–130.

Ullrich-French, S., and Smith, A. L. (2006). Perceptions of relationships with parents and peer's youth sport: Independent and combined prediction of motivational outcomes. *Psychology of Sport and Exercise* 7 (2), 193–214.

Ulrich, R. S., Simons, R., Losito, B. D., Fiorito, E., Miles, M. A., and Zelson, M. (1991). Stress recovery during exposure to natural and urban environments. *Journal of Environmental Psychology* 11, 201–230.

Unkelbach, C., and Memmert, D. (2010). Crowd noise as a cue in referee decisions contributes to the home advantage. *Journal of Sport and Exercise Psychology* 32, 483–498.

Valentine, G. (2000). Exploring children and young people's narratives of identity. *Geoforum* 31, 257–267.

Van den Berg, A. E., Maas, J., Verheij, R. A., and Groenewegen, P. P. (2010). Green space as a buffer between stressful life events and health. *Social Science and Medicine* 70 (8), 1203–1210.

van de Pol, P. K. C., Kavussanu, M., and Ring, C. (2012). Goal orientations, perceived motivational climate, and motivational outcomes in football: A comparison between training and competition contexts. *Psychology of Sport and Exercise* 13, 491–499.

Van Raalte, J. L., Cornelius, A. E., Linder, D. E., and Brewer, B. W. (2007). The relationship between hazing and team cohesion. *Journal of Sport Behavior* 30 (4), 491–507.

van Rossum, J. H. A., and van der Loo, H. (1997). Gifted athletes and complexity of family structure: A condition for talent development? *High Ability Studies* 8, 19–30.

Vazou, S. (2010). Variations in the perceptions of peer and coach motivational climate. *Research Quarterly for Exercise and Sport* 81 (2), 199–211.

Vazou, S., Ntoumanis, N., and Duda, J. L. (2005). Peer motivational climate in youth sport: A qualitative inquiry. *Psychology of Sport and Exercise* 6, 497–516.

Vazou, S., Ntoumanis, N., and Duda, J. L. (2006). Predicting young athletes' motivational indices as a function of their perceptions of the coach- and peer-created climate. *Psychology of Sport and Exercise* 7, 215–233.

Verma, J. P., Modak, P., Bhukar, J. P., and Kumar, S. (2012). A discriminant analysis of team cohesiveness among high performance and low performance elite Indian volleyball players. *Studies in Physical Culture and Tourism* 19 (4), 191–195.

Vincer, D. J. E., and Loughead, T. M. (2010). The relationship between athlete leadership behaviors and cohesion in team sports. *Sport Psychologist* 24, 448–467.

Walker, I., and Smith, H. (2001). *Relative Deprivation: Specification, Development, and Integration*. Cambridge: Cambridge University Press.

Wallace, H. M., Baumeister, R. F., and Vohs, K. D. (2005). Audience support and choking under pressure: A home disadvantage? *Journal of Sports Sciences* 23, 429–438.

Wanzel, R. S. (1994). Decades of worksite fitness programmes: Progress or rhetoric? *Sports Medicine* 17, 324–337.

Warr, P., and Knapper, C. (1968). *The Perception of People and Events*. London: Wiley.

Weiner, B. (1992). *Human Motivation: Metaphors, Theories and Research*. Newbury Park, CA: Sage.

Weiss, M., and Knoppers, A. (1982). The influence of socializing agents on female collegiate volleyball players. *Journal of Sport Psychology* 4, 267–279.

Weissensteiner, J. R., Abernethy, B., and Farrow, D. (2009). Towards the development of a conceptual model of batting expertise in cricket: A grounded theory approach. *Journal of Applied Psychology* 21 (3), 276–292.

White, M. P., Alcock, I., Wheeler, B. W., and Depledge, M. H. (2013). Would you be happier living in a greener urban area? A fixed-effects analysis of panel data. *Psychological Science* 0956797612464659.

White, M. P., Smith, A., Humphryes, K., Pahl, S., Snelling, D., and Depledge, M. (2010). Blue space: The importance of water for preference, affect, and restorativeness ratings of natural and built scenes. *Journal of Environmental Psychology* 30 (4), 482–493. doi: http://dx.doi.org/10.1016/j.jenvp.2010.04.004.

White, R. (1959). Motivation reconsidered. The concept of competence. *Psychological Review* 66, 297–323.

White, S. A. (2007). Parent created motivational climate. In S. Jowett and D. Lavallee (eds), *Social Psychology of Sport* (131–144). Champaign, IL: Human Kinetics.

Widmeyer, W. N., Brawley, L. R., and Carron, A. V. (1985). *The Measurement of Cohesion in Sport Teams: The Group Environment Questionnaire*. London, ON: Sports Dynamics.

Widmeyer, W. N., Brawley, L. R., and Carron, A. V. (1990). The effects of group size in sport. *Journal of Sport and Exercise Psychology* 12, 177–190.

Wigfield, A., and Eccles, J. S. (2000). Expectancy-value theory of motivation. *Contemporary Educational Psychology* 25, 68–81.

Wildschut, T., Pinter, B., Vevea, J. L., Insko, C. A., and Schopler, J. (2003). Beyond the group mind: A quantitative review of the inter-individual intergroup discontinuity effect. *Psychological Bulletin* 129, 698–722.

Williams, A. M., Vickers, J., and Rodrigues, S. (2002). The effects of anxiety on visual search, movement kinematics, and performance in table tennis: A test of Eysenck and Calvo's processing efficiency theory. *Journal of Sport and Exercise Psychology* 24, 438–455.

Williams, J. M., and Harris, D. V. (2006). Relaxation and energizing techniques for regulation of arousal. In J. M. Williams (ed.), *Applied Sport Psychology: Personal Growth to Peak Performance* (285–305). New York: McGraw Hill.

Wilson, V. E., Peper, E., and Schmid, A. (2006). Strategies for training concentration. In J. M. Williams (ed.), *Applied Sport Psychology: Personal Growth to Peak Performance* (404–424). New York: McGraw Hill.

Wolfenden, L. E., and Holt, N. L. (2005). Talent development in elite junior tennis: Perceptions of players, parents and coaches. *Journal of Applied Sport Psychology* 17, 108–126.

Wolfson, S., Wakelin, D., and Lewis, M. (2005). Football supporters' perceptions of their role in the home advantage. *Journal of Sports Sciences* 23, 365–374.

Woodcock, C., Holland, M. J. G., Duda, J. L., and Cumming, J. (2011). Psychological qualities of elite adolescent rugby players: Parents, coaches, and sport administration staff perceptions and supporting roles. *Sport Psychologist* 25, 411–443.

Wormald, H., and Ingle, L. (2004). GP exercise referral schemes: Improving the patient's experience. *Health Education Journal* 63 (4), 362–373.

Worringham, C. J., and Messick, D. M. (1983). Social facilitation of running: An unobtrusive study. *Journal of Social Psychology* 121, 23–29.

Wright, M., Marsden, S., and Antonelli, A. (2004). *Building an Evidence Base for the HSC Strategy to 2010 and Beyond: A Literature Review of Interventions to Improve Health and Safety Compliance*. Norwich: HMSO.

Wuerth, S., Lee, M. S., and Alferman, D. (2004). Parental involvement and athletes' career in youth sport. *Psychology of Sport and Exercise* 5, 21–33.

Wylleman, P., De Knop, P., Verdet, M. C., and Cecič-Erpič, S. (2007). Parenting and career transitions of elite athletes. In S. Jowett and D. Lavallee (eds), *Social Psychology in Sport* (233–247). Champaign IL: Human Kinetics.

Wylleman, P., and Lavallee, D. (2004). A development perspective on transitions faced by athletes. In M. Weiss (ed.), *Developmental Sport and Exercise Psychology: A Lifespan Perspective* (507–527). Morgantown, WV: Fitness Information Technology.

Yerrell, P. (2008). *National Evaluation of TCV's Green Gym*. Oxford: School of Health and Social Care, Oxford Brookes University.

Yoshida, H. (1972). The determinants of interpersonal attraction. *Memoirs of the Faculty of Education Toyama University* 20, 63–82.

Young, J. A., and Pearce, A. J. (2011). The influence of parents in identifying and developing Australian female tennis talent. *Journal of Medicine and Science in Tennis* 17 (1), 22–27.

Zajonc, R. B. (1965). Social facilitation. *Science* 149, 269–274.

Zajonc, R. B., Heingartner, A., and Herman, E. M. (1969). Social enhancement and impairment of performance in the cockroach. *Journal of Personality and Social Psychology* 13, 83–92.

Zander, A. (1982). *Making Groups Effective*. San Francisco: Jossey-Bass.

Zinsser, N., Bunker, L., and Williams, J. M. (2006). Cognitive techniques for building confidence and enhancing performance. In J. M. Williams (ed.). *Applied Sport Psychology: Personal Growth to Peak Performance* (349–381). New York: McGraw Hill.

Index

Achievement Goal Theory, 23
active commuting, 121, 123–124
adherence, 147–150, 160–161, 184–185
anxiety
  cognitive, 32, 78, 91
  somatic anxiety, 78
athlete satisfaction, 34–35
attention restoration theory, 193
attentional cues, 79
attribution theory, 46–47

big-fish-little-pond effect, 114–116
biopsychosocial model of challenge and
    threat, 67–68
brief advice, 171–174, 180–181

choking, 65, 75–78
  distraction based model, 76
  processing efficiency model, 76
  self-consciousness, 76
  self-presentational model, 77
coach leadership, 29–30
  coaching behaviours, 29, 37, 92
  peer leadership, 30
coach-athlete relationship, 3, 30, 35, 84,
    89, 95
  closeness, 4
  commitment, 6
  complementarity, 5
  co-orientation, 6–7
  Jowett's 3+1Cs Conceptual Model, 3–7
cognitive restructuring, 79–80
collective efficacy, 31
communication, 7–11, 37, 99
  interpersonal, 7–9
  mediated, 10–11
competence motivation theory, 116–118
competition, 44–46
  hypercompetiveness, 60
compliance, 182–185
conflict
  aggression, 58–59
  group identity, 56–57
  intergroup, 56
  interpersonal (relationship), 10–12

intragroup, 22, 34, 36
management strategies, 12–16

developmental model of sport
    participation, 85, 93–94

eating-disorder symptoms, 35
ecological workplace model, 128
exercise consultations, 179–180
exercise leader, 149–154, 163–164
  leadership styles and characteristics,
    150–154
exercise referrals, 181–187
expectancy value theory, 85–86

family, 84–100, 199–121
  fathers, 88, 90
  mothers, 88, 90, 95
  parent-athlete relationship, 35, 84, 89
  parental involvement, 85–88, 90–93,
    95, 96
  siblings, 84, 93–97, 100

gender differences, 23–24, 31
goal setting, 37, 131, 136
  ego orientation, 23
  task orientation, 23
green space effect, 193–194, 196–197,
    199–200, 202–204
group cohesion, 160–164, 166
  attraction to the group, 160, 163
  group integration, 160–161
  social cohesion, 135–136, 163–164, 167
  task cohesion, 135–136, 163–164, 167

hazing, 30
health care professionals, 172–174,
    180–181

informational support, 129–131

jealousy, 28

learned helplessness, 50–51
lifespan model, 85, 94